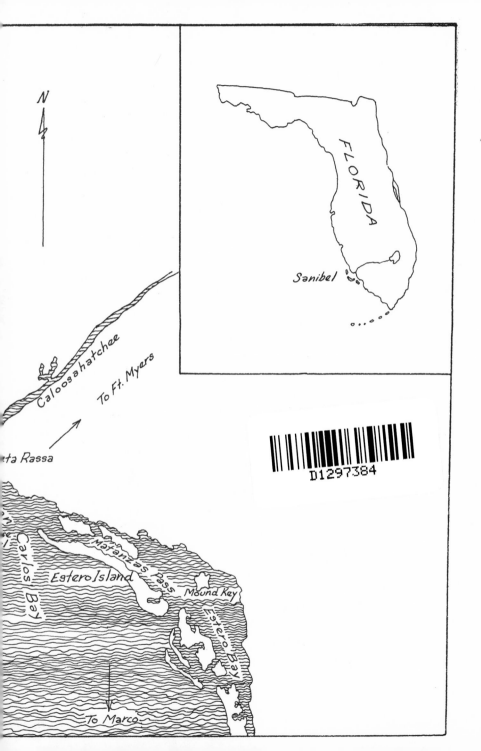

THE SEA SHELL ISLANDS
A History of Sanibel and Captiva
Revised Edition
By Elinore M. Dormer

The first church on Sanibel. From a sketch by Herman von Richtoven. Courtesy of Miss Charlotta Matthews.

The
Sea Shell Islands

A History of
Sanibel and Captiva

ELINORE MAYER DORMER

Illustrated by Ann Winterbotham

Part I—THE KINGDOM OF CARLOS

Chapter

PART II—THE AMERICAN WAY

To all Islanders
Both native and introduced
Who love Sanibel and Captiva
As I do

PREFACE

An island is created by the sea and is its special kingdom. Its very substance is the work of waves, crashing surf and gentle ripples, and there is no shell nor pile of sand that was not water-borne. It is a land that belongs to the ocean; its minerals are in the soil, its mists in the air. No plant grows, nor animal, without its sufferance.

Even more than most, Sanibel and Captiva were blessed with natural assests and it was for that reason that the Indians first came there. They believed themselves part of the earth and although they built settlements, these were kept small lest they overtax the supporting environment.

Today's islanders are lured by a different sort of wealth. It is the aura of the ocean that draws us and our need is to live uncrowded, seeking the joyful expansion of the inner self far from the grinding irritations of urban life. Yet, space is a consumable commodity that cannot be freely given to everyone who reaches for it—for then the sack would be empty. To promise and not deliver is the cruelest of frauds.

The Indians would have looked upon these days with superstitious dread, sure that our abused world would avenge itself—and perhaps it will. We see a frightening similarity to times past, for as conquistadors and traders brought enslavement and disease, so would their modern counterparts, for concrete walls do a prison make and foul air and water, most surely, kill.

We are only tenants on these islands we call ours and after us will come other tenants. For them and for the simple ethic that it is wrong to destroy needlessly, we must become more responsible caretakers.

ACKNOWLEDGEMENTS

My special thanks to Ann Winterbotham, who contributed her pencil sketches to this book; to Betty Lloyd and Lora Sinks Britt, who edited it, and to Magda Freeman and Charles and Julie Keller who translated the Spanish passages. I am most grateful to my sons Bob and Mike, the whole Symroski tribe and Eva Marie DeCourcey, who researched and/or offered helpful advice.

Professor E.A. Hammond made the story of Sanybel possible, Jean Huprich filled some gaps with her family history and Bette and Sterns Williamson's fabulous find, the 1833 Sanybel map, provided an epilogue.

I was greatly helped with the beginning chapters by Dr. William H. Marquardt, Dr. Jerald Milanich, Barbara Schumacher, James Wightman, Lindsay Williams and Dr. Charles Wilson.

Stories of the pioneer families could not have been written without the help of: Francis Bailey, Ferguson Barnes, Anne Bryant, Scotia Bryant, Mr. and Mrs. Hunter Bryant, Jean F. Brock, Dorothy Carman, Robert Carson, James Clifford, Bessie Carter, Mr. and Mrs. Ernest Dickey, J.B. Daniels, Carrie Ebsworth, Adelaide Edgar, Mary and Margaret Fitzhugh, Arthur Gibson, Helen Bowen Hileman, Virginia Jenson, Belton Johnson, Earl Johnson, Marie Kalman, Charlotte Kinzie, Robert Knowles, Mr. and Mrs. Thomas Mitchell, Charotta Matthews, Flora Morris, Genevieve Muir,

Florence Martin, Margaret Mickle, Betty Odom, Mr. and Mrs. Vaughan Pearson, John Peurifoy, Bunny Proctor, Hazel Roberts, Clarence Rutland, Pearl Stokes, George Underhill, Carroll Wadlow, Louise Waldron, Flora Watkins, Charlotte White, Beulah Wiles, Kathryn Williams, Pauline Wilson, Mr. and Mrs. Lee Willis, and Esperanza Woodring.

For more recent history, I depended on Carol Allin, Roy Bazire, Malcolm Beattie, Opal and Willis Combs, Captain Leon Crumpler, Benny Elwell, Bob England, Elsie Fuller, Isiah Gavin, Larry Givens, Sally Cist Glenn, Marian Godown, Harriette Howe, Mildred Howse, Helen Hudson, Susan Karr, Charles LeBuff, Emmy Lu Lewis, Hugo Lindgren, Anne Marsh, Andrew Mellody, Jo Pickens, Edith Stokes, George Tenney, Ed Underhill, Dorothy Wakefield, Karl Wightman, Ann Winterbotham, Lavon Wisher and Dick Workman.

Librarians at the P.K. Yonge Library of Florida History, Sanibel Public Library and Edison Community College Library were most helpful.

Last but not least, sincere thanks to my husband Bob Dormer, who helped in countless ways, and to Arthur Clark who gave encouragement when it was sorely needed.

Elinore Dormer

INTRODUCTION

Sometimes fame bedazzles. As one feature glitters and gleams in the spotlight, the rest of the interesting whole remains in the shadows. This has happened to Sanibel and Captiva Islands for there is much more to them than their famous sea shells. Long before there was a United States, or even a known continent, San Carlos Bay was known, and the very roots of much American history are here on our coastal mainland, our islands and waterways.

In 1500, an unknown mariner explored these places and on the oldest known map of the New World are the contours of our coastline, rough but recognizable, even to the many islands. In 1513, Juan Ponce de Leon dropped anchor somewhere within these waters and in 1521 he received his death wound when he attempted to establish a colony at the mouth of the Caloosahatchee. Narvaez and De Soto, perhaps to avoid the warlike Indians of Carlos, sailed just beyond their domain, but Pedro Menendez, intent on colonizing and Christianizing within Calusa country, almost succeeded in subjugating them.

But men were here long before that. All of these islands lie within an ancient kingdom so vast that archaeologists have but scratched the surface of the mounds that lie on almost every sheltered shore. The sites of the Indian settlements became the productive gardens of the homesteaders who came at the end of the 19th century to grow vegetables and citrus fruit for the northern markets.

However, they were not the first Americans on Sanibel. In 1833, a private investment group established the town of Sanybel at the island's eastern end. It didn't prosper and the colonists, neglected by their government and faced with Indian unrest, returned to New York City a few years later.

As times changed, so did the islands. Today, like most of coastal Florida, they are in the throes of a building boom and face the prospect of overdevelopment and a deteriorating quality of life. Battles have been won and lost but the outcome of the war must be recorded by another historian of another generation.

This, then, is the story of Sanibel and Captiva Islands, once famous for the wealth of their seafood, the excellence of their produce and the beauty of their shells. But for a few flights of fancy, where such are allowable, and assumptions when facts are scanty, it is the truth, which is always more exciting than fiction.

PART I

THE KINGDOM OF CARLOS

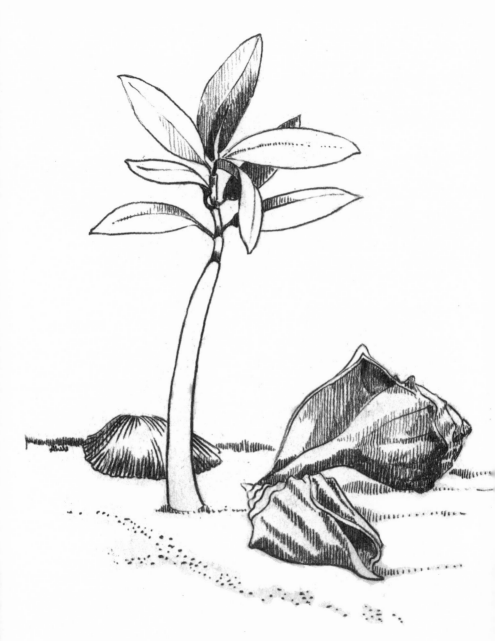

A young red mangrove tree.

Chapter I

"IN THE BEGINNING . . . ."

Perhaps as recently as 10,000 years ago, when Sanibel was part of the coastal mainland, a mammoth or mastodon lived, grazed and died there. In 1970 when a lagoon was dredged in the vicinity of Sanibel City Hall, a piece of its humerus bone, completely petrified, was tossed up with fill to be found by William Compton. Its presence would indicate that other animals, too, roamed this part of Florida. The remains of a giant tortoise, a sloth, a bison and other mammoth or mastodon bones have been discovered within fifty miles of the barrier islands. The climate was much colder then. There were hardwood forests, grassy plains, even cliffs and caverns. Coastal inlets and waterways were lined by red mangrove. Fossil remains of these strange trees with their long, grasping roots that seek the water, have been found in deposits dating back to the beginning of the Cenozoic Era.

Over the centuries, leaf fell upon leaf, twigs, feathers, particles of shell and wood—all sorts of detritus—built the land higher, aided by the littorial drift of sand from northern shores. At the end of the Ice Age, glaciers melting in northern climes caused sea water to rise, gradually flooding the mouths and channels of estuaries and channels of rivers and creeks and spilling over onto low lying land. Thus, Charlotte Harbor was created and

1

San Carlos Bay. About three thousand years ago, when Pine Island Sound was but a ribbon of water, Sanibel-Captiva and Cayo Costa became insular. Although the rise in sea level is not constant, it does continue and one day water will inundate our places of habitation, just as it did those of primitive Indian hundreds of years ago.

Sanibel-Captiva became two islands when a pass opened between them, perhaps one thousand years ago. It has come and gone over the centuries. Sanibel, with an area of about eighteen square miles is larger than Captiva, and, roughly shrimp-shaped, is positioned at 26°25′N.Lat., 82°10′W.Long. Captiva, immediately north of it, is narrower and once was about fifteen miles long.

Sanibel's south-facing beach, with its depth and shallows, provided a favorable environment for the hundreds of species of beautiful sea shells that would one day make it famous. On the sheltered side of both islands, nutrients flowed out of the swamps, nurturing the marine meadows that would be nursery and feeding ground for all kinds of mollusks, crustaceans and fish. Because the islands were located in the southern band of the temperate zone, subject to tropical influences, the flora and fauna of both intermingled, their northerly migrations aided by hurricane winds, the Gulf Stream and the Yucatan Current which flowed twenty-five miles off Sanibel. With a climate temperate in winter and tropical in summer, salt-laden winds and a soil composed mostly of shell in various stages of decomposition, the islands developed a unique natural environment of marine creatures, rare plants and exotic birds.

Into such a paradise stepped primitive men, and their shell mounds, on every sheltered shore of both islands, altered their configurations.

The European explorers, who came to conquer, wrote the first pages of Sanibel and Captiva's tempestuous history.

Fine examples of pre-Columbian Indian art. Ceremonial mask and deer head were carved of wood and painted. From the Cushing Collection. The Florida State Museum.

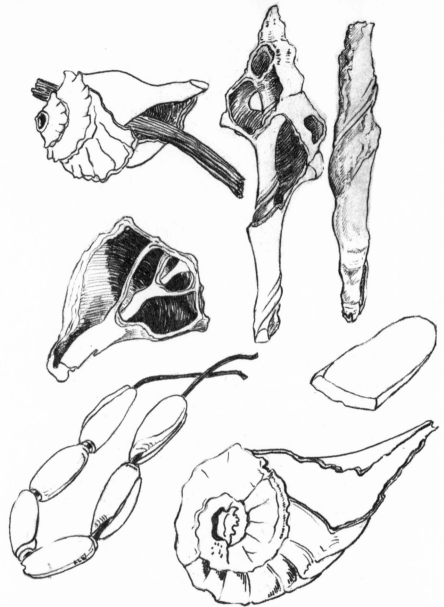

The implements and an ornament of a Shell Age People. Top: pick hammer, pick, awl; middle: half hammer, scraper; bottom: necklace, dipper.

Chapter II

THE FOOT OF MAN

Twelve thousand years or so ago, primitive, nomadic Indians moved into the Florida peninsula. From the Fort Myers area northward, they left evidence of their hunting prowess—projectile tips. Some of these were large, chipped spear points called Suwannee points, because in Florida, they were first found along that river.

Central Florida was a plateau then, much of it covered with hardwood forests, and the coast was fifty to seventy miles farther out into the Gulf of Mexico. Men, clad in hides, hunted in small bands, stalking wooly mammoths, cave bears, brown sloths and sabre-tooth tigers in the bogs and swampy places by springs and streams where they came to drink. Floundering in the mire, the animals became easy victims to the dark, wiry men and their sharply pointed spears and atlatls. If the kill was large, the family or tribal group moved to the site, remaining there until the food supply ran out.

Recent, very valuable finds at a spa thirty miles north of Fort Myers have added much to our knowledge of these Paleo Indians. Skindivers, Col. William Royal and Genie Clark, exploring Warm Mineral Springs, discovered human bones there in 1958 but it was 1971 before the Bureau of Historic Sites and Properties sent diver-archaeologists to study the site.

It was established that the sinkhole contained ledges

seventy to ninety feet below the surface of the water. Here, wooden pegs shaped by men had been driven into the sides, presumably to descend into caverns below, dry at that time. On the ledges and in the orifice thirty-five feet below, deposits were found of human skeletal remains five thousand years old and bones, including those of a mastodon or mammoth, a giant land turtle, a sloth and an extinct bison, all remarkably well preserved because of the low oxygen content of the 86 °F spring water.

The most exciting event, however, occurred in December, 1972, Dr. Wilburn Cockrell, head of the Florida team, spotted a human skull at a depth of forty feet. It has since been scientifically dated to 8,200 B.C., plus or minus 145 years, and was then the oldest human remains ever discovered in the eastern United States and the best verified in North America.

Apparently a burial site, the place yielded a valuable artifact in October, 1973. Cockrell and another archaeologist, Marion Almy, found a hook-shaped piece of shell, with some of the original glue still clinging to it, which had been part of an ancient atlatl. This weapon consisted of a handle into which a spear or long dart was fitted. The early Spaniards, finding the southwest Florida Indians using them, called the weapon a "shooting stick" and noted the tremendous force of the projectile hurled from them.

At about that time, a marine archaeologist, Carl Clausen, was exploring Little Salt Spring, three kilometers away. First believed to be a shallow pond, it proved to be another sinkhole, three hundred feet across and almost 240 feet deep, which contained organic material twelve thousand, possibly fifty thousand years old. The property was owned by General Development Corporation. At Clausen's suggestion, the General Development Foundation, a non-profit organization, was created by them in 1974. The Corporation then deeded

Little Salt Spring and twenty acres surrounding it to the Foundation. The Research Facility, headed by Clausen, was set up there. In 1979, ninety-five percent of the funding still came from the Foundation.

As explorations got underway, it became apparent that the Spring was a natural time capsule with two distinct periods of human occupation, the Paleo Indian, 12,000 to 9,000 years ago, and the Archaic, 6,800 to 5,200 years ago. These primitive people were attracted by the fresh water which the spring then provided. Apparently, they had made a good meal of a giant land tortoise. Divers found the cooked remains with the sharp stake that killed it between the upper and lower shells.

The most important artifact recovered from this earlier period was a nonreturning oak boomerang of a type never before found in the Western Hemisphere. It well could be the oldest ever discovered anywhere. Also recovered was an oak mortor similar in style to some of those Frank Cushing pulled from the mangrove muck of Key Marco in 1896.

The second and later habitation was characterized by a vast cemetery which these Indians left behind. It began in a muck-filled slough and as ground water level dropped, it extended into the basin of the pond. There were believed to be about one thousand burials in each place. Portions of the bodies were wrapped with grass and they were interred with or on boughs of wax myrtle. The muck had preserved them in excellent condition, so much so that a skull was found with a portion of the brain in it, the convolutions still discernible. A human bone nearby was dated to six thousand years ago.

Wooden artifacts, bone, stone and shell tools had been buried with their owners and a small incomplete wooden tablet or plaque was of great significance. It was ridged and seemed to bear the partial profile of a long-necked or long-billed bird. It resembled one of those recovered at Key Marco in 1896. These ceremonial burials in muck with their artifacts suggest a link between these archaic people and those of a much later time, the pre-Columbians of the 13th and 14th centuries.

In 1978 the explorations at Little Salt Spring came to a halt for lack of funds. But surely this would be temporary for the unique site could yield even more fabulous finds in the years to come.

It is still generally accepted that the first real villages and semi-permanent settlements appeared in Florida toward the end of the Preceramic (before pottery) Archaic period, 7000 B.C. to 5000 B.C.. and that these were built on both fresh and salt water shell middens. Vestigal mounds composed of fresh and salt-water mollusks have been found along the St. John's River and Withlacoochee but because the seas have been rising over the centuries, marine shell middens of this very early period are rare. Presently, the only one known to be on Florida's Gulf coast is at Osprey, fifty miles north of Captiva.

The inhabitants of these villages were not so nomadic as their predecessors nor so warmly clad, for the climate had become warm by that time. Of moderate height, dusky-skinned with long, black hair, the men wore deer-skin loincloths, the women short aprons of Spanish moss and the children nothing at all. Their settlements had no more than two or three families or about thirty people who lived in thatched shelters and ate such food as could be hunted or gathered. They cooked over open fires, with their only "pot" a hide bag in which they put foodstuffs and water, then added a burning hot stone from the fire.

The Indians on the coast ate mostly fish and mollusks but they also hunted with weapons of steatite, a non-Florida rock which must have been obtained through barter. From this flint-like substance and large, heavy shells they also made implements, such as axes, scrapers, knives and drills; celts, gouges and hammers.

The earliest known pottery was found in a section of southeast Georgia-northeast Florida. That which dates from 2000 B.C. is flat on the bottom, plain and tempered with shredded palmetto fibers, Spanish moss or grass. Later, distinctive designs incised on the sides of a pot indicated its origin, such as Sanibel Incised, with its row of tick marks forming a simple chevron or running V. Found on Sanibel Island, it dates to 750-900 A.D.

We can reasonably assume that the Indians who produced this pottery were the forebearers of the Calusa, now extinct, who were found on the islands of San Carlos Bay by the early Spanish explorers. Their domain included the islands and coastal areas from Charlotte Harbor to some point south of Marco and their mounds were on every sheltered shore. The first anthropologist to discover and explore them was Frank Hamilton Cushing in 1895. His paper delivered to the American Philosophical Society November 6, 1896, electrified archaeologist and anthropologists of his time and aroused their admiration, envy and criticism. No other report of this kind had dealt so specifically with local prehistory.

"Early in the spring of 1895, Captain W.B. Collier, of Key Marco, southwestern Florida, found, while digging garden-muck from one of the little mangrove swamps that occur, like filled-up coves, among the low-lying shell-banks surrounding his shore-island home, several ancient wooden articles and some pieces of netted cordage." So begins Frank Cushing's account of his most exciting adventure and the most extensive archaeological discovery ever made in Florida or along the east coast of the United States.

Digging dirt for his garden, Collier at first had not recognized the rotting wooden objects his spade un-

9

covered, but the "root-strands" that clung to it looked strangely cord-like. Moments later, turning up a highly polished ladle made from a whelk shell, he realized he had found artifacts of very old origin.

A few days later, Charles Wilkins, a winter visitor tarpon fishing near Marco, heard of the discovery and spent a day digging out other objects which included wooden cups, more ladles, conch tools, and a fairly well-preserved animal figurehead, carved of wood. Excited by his finds, Wilkins hurried to Naples where he showed them to a British friend, Colonel Durnford, who immediately returned with him to Marco.

The two men worked for two days and uncovered more objects in the mangrove muck as sea water continually flooded their excavations. Two weeks later, while passing through Philadelphia, Colonel Durnford showed their finds to the curator at the museum of the University of Pennsylvania and to Cushing, who happened to be there. Cushing instantly recognized their worth and volunteered to investigate the area where they were found.

Less than two weeks later, Cushing was in Punta Gorda where he procured a small fishing sloop and, with two men to man it, sailed forth one glorious evening in May to explore Pine Island Sound, San Carlos Bay and all of the sheltered waters as far south as Marco.

As they headed south, it seemed that there were little islands everywhere, all of them thickly overgrown with mangroves. Deciding to explore the first they came to, Cushing made his way through the mangrove roots to higher ground and there an astonishing sight met his eyes. Somewhat delapidated shell embankments formed a maze of channels and basins, and beyond them a series of platforms rose terrace-like to the foundations of great, level-topped mounds, some nearly thirty feet high! Excitedly, he hacked his way through the thick underbrush—vines, cacti and century plants—and

climbed the sides of the mounds, as little brown rab-
bits scurried away before him and snakes slithered
across his path. Stopping occasionally to pull away
weeds, he could see that the mounds were built entirely of shells, chiefly large ones, blackened by age.
Some of the terraces held shallow depressions
bordered by retaining walls, perhaps used for gardens
or drainage basins, with graded ways leading up to
and through them.

When he'reached the summit, Cushing saw that the
terraces he had climbed were part of a single, huge
elbow-shaped foundation. At its bend was a group of lof-
ty, narrow and elongated mounds which stretched out
fanlike across the summit like a mighty, outstretched
hand. Beyond this were other foundations, like ruined
fortresses, and between them was a deep, open space
more than an acre in extent, now clogged with
mangroves. This, he concluded, had been a sort of
courtyard of water and the troughs between the
"fingers" channels by which Indians in canoes could
come and go. Descending into it, he found tool heads,
pot sherds, bones and charcoal, all looking quite fresh.
He surmised that they had been thrown or dropped
from the dwellings which, probably on pilings, had
once lined this great water court. By all indications,
the whole key was of artificial origin, built up from
submerged land by the hand of man whose only
material was shell.

The sun was setting over an outgoing tide as Cushing
and his companions approached Pine Island and dropped anchor. Two dilapidated and deserted fishing
shacks, perched unsteadily on long pilings, were at the
entrance to a sort of lagoon enclosed by oyster bars that
seemed, by their symmetry, to have been formed on
man-made seawalls. As they watched, a large school of
fish, pursued by sharks and porpoises, rushed into the
shoals where hundred of pelicans, cormorants, gulls and

11

other sea birds waited, lining the sides like so many interested spectators. In the wild melee that ensued as the fish were attacked from below, above, and even on the sides by stalking heron, Cushing thought he saw the reason for it all. In the same way, men once had stood on the sides of the fish pounds and as others drove the fish in, they netted what they needed.

As these enclosures built up with silt, they were allowed to become gardens or basins for rain water and other pounds were built in the sound. The older terraces, gradually built higher, eventually supported mounds and crowning the tops of these were the temples, dwellings of the chiefs and assembly or storage buildings, all quite safe from high water or enemy attack. As the first day ended, the pieces of the puzzle had begun to fall into place and, succeeding beyond his wildest dreams, Frank Cushing stepped back into the kingdom of the Calusas—about 1350 to 1500 A.D.

The next day, exploring Josselyn's Key, more mounds and courts were found but it was Demorey's Key that would prove to be, in some respects, the most remarkable of all. Trimly oval and deeply wooded, it was surrounded by a massive seawall, constructed mainly of whelks, about twelve feet high and level and broad on the top. Crowning the middle elevation on a terrace was a sort of truncated pyramid and, once again, Cushing found it necessary to chop his way to the top.

Hoping to get an overall view of the key, he climbed high into the crooked, red-skinned limbs of a huge gumbo limbo tree which was growing out of the inner edge, but as he craned to see, his foot suddenly slipped and he fell, crashing through a tangle of vines which clung to the lower branches. He was unhurt but the force of his fall had torn away some of the concealing brush and what he saw amazed and excited him. He was beside an altar-like platform which was faced up with large whelk shells, their spiraled, larger ends laid

12

out in an artistic pattern in a mosaic of busycons. Excavation revealed that it was very large with another smaller platform near it. This smaller platform and the graded approaches were closely tiled with very large clam shells laid convex side up. Obviously, there had once been a very imposing temple on Demorey's Key.

The usual fish pounds were there which seemed to have been built up from depths four or five feet below the surface to the water. They were strongly constructed of a kind of shell breccia, the first layer being conchs driven or wedged point end down into the original reef or bar, around which was packed a native clay-like marl which time had hardened into a highly effective cement.

Battey's Landing had once been separate but in 1895, it was part of Pine Island. The old water courts were being used for gardens by two men, Mr. Kirk and Captain Rhoades, who were its total population. Cushing estimated that the mounds were sixty feet high, more than twice the height they are today. The Indian settlement had stretched more than three quarters of a mile along the shore of Pine Island and was one fourth mile wide. Here, too, there was a great canal, thirty feet wide, which led into two lakes within the pinelands, the last of which had a high, oval mound in its center that contained human bones. This colony was the most recent and highly developed and its oval mound was both temple and burial place.

In contrast, the sites on the southern end of Pine Island seemed to date back to much earlier key dwellers and here, too, was an abandoned site. A second mound recently had been partly demolished to build a boulevard around the end of the island. It had cost its builder ten thousand dollars, and Cushing added ruefully, probably was the most beautiful shell road in all of southwest Florida.

Now the expeditioners turned their attention to "Sanybel" Island and from St. James City crossed Pine

Island Sound to Wulfert where the mounds were similar to those on Pine Island but were undisturbed. Although this settlement had progressed a little further, here, too, it seemed that some natural calamity had overwhelmed it. Some portions of the work had been washed away by subsequent storms but what was left enclosed more mangrove swamp than had either of the colonies near St. James. As in other places, well-defined canals led into the shell ridges which were higher at the middle and eastern ends, where there were unfinished foundations.

Digging inward from the shoreline, Cushing found numerous shell implements, and pottery sherds, and, at one point, evidence that some large building had crowned the terrace. He thought he saw evidence of a plastered wall and foundations built up from the shoal or reef into which large shells had been driven, point first. Above the first layer, the work was most painstaking and artistic indicating that it had been a place of importance, a temple, perhaps, or a tribal meeting house. As on Demorey's Key, the outer and inner faces of the whole elevation had been faced with a beautiful mosaic of whelks.

The party now headed for Tarpon Bay where homesteader Samuel Ellis had found human bones beneath some stumps he had been digging out of his garden. The ancient Indian colony that had been there had been covered with sand over the centuries but apparently a shell causeway once had led to a round, enclosed space, now filled with black soil and overgrown. It was in this little hummock that Sam Ellis had been working and excavating nearby; the men discovered that it was full of broken, shattered human bones and a few skulls, still intact but very fragile. Few relics of any sort were there except punctured shell ladles which, like the dismembering and breaking up of skeletons, probably were part of the burial ritual. The place was typical of the Calusa's strange little mortuary lakes or water courts, with their central islets crammed with human bones. Ellis had discovered an island of the dead, established centuries before white men set foot on Sanibel.

Time was growing short and taking some skulls with him, Cushing regretfully left the area, surmising correctly that countless unexplored shell mounds existed on Sanibel, Captiva and islands nearby. His score, however, was impressive. In Charlotte Harbor, Pine Island Sound, San Carlos Bay and Matlacha, he had discovered seventy-five ancient settlement sites, forty of which were gigantic.

The expedition headed for Estero Bay where Mound Key, then occupied by the Johnson family, towered sixty feet over them. Cushing's estimate is hard to reconcile with today's figure of thirty-one feet but perhaps it was even higher when it was the site of Calos, the principal town of the Calusa. The colony of San Anton was established there in 1566 by Pedro Menendez de Aviles and Mrs. Johnson had a collection of old Spanish relics which included Venetian beads, small ornaments, scraps of copper sheeting and a copper-gilt locket lost long ago by someone who must have treasured it. Within was a faded portrait and a still more faded letter written on parchment and sent, some three hundred years ago, to a Spaniard on Mound Key—to whom it must have seemed the end of the world.

It was on Marco, however, that Frank Cushing would assemble the magnificient archaeological collection that would earn him the acclaim he so deserved. Approaching the outer islands, their fringes of mangrove much deeper than those farther north, he judged correctly that they contained older ruins. He began digging near old Marco Village where Captain Collier had made the initial discoveries and within a short time had found the remains of short piles, decayed thatch, slender timbers and some hearth-like material. He called the place "Court of the Pile Dwellers."

After arranging with Collier to return with an expedition, Cushing went back to San Carlos Bay to further explore some of the ruins there. But by now the Florida summer had set in with a vengeance and the mosquitos and sandflies swarmed out of the swamps in such great clouds that the men had to stay within the smoke of smudge fires to be able to work at all. This led to another thoughtful conclusion: the Indians had built out into the open waterways to escape, in some measure, the biting insects. Centuries earlier, explorers viewing the pile dwellers of the Venezuelan coast had reached the same conclusion.

The Pepper-Hearst Archaeological Expedition arrived on Marco in February, 1896. A deal was made with Captain Collier to leave piles of muck in exchange for any artifacts found, and while the arrangement might seem uneven in retrospect, it suited all concerned. The collection was to reach staggering proportions and today is in the careful custody of the Smithsonian Institution, the Museum of the University of Pennsylvania and the Florida State Museum at Gainesville.

The excavation of the "Court of the Pile Dwellers" proved almost incredibly difficult as it lay under water most of the time and was thickly overgrown with mangroves. However, by removing some of the trees, digging trenches, bailing with buckets and throwing up banks of earth, the men could search the area for a few hours each day, sometimes with hands deep in muck and water. It was hot, breathless and buggy but so tremendously rewarding that Frank Cushing wrote, "Never in my life, despite the sufferings this labor involved, was I so fascinated with or interested in anything so much, as in the finds thus daily revealed."

Articles of wood far outnumbered other things and were colorfully painted, some looking so new as to be unbelievable. Yet only half of them survived the exposure to air. In the end, the men were able to secure and bring away in fairly good condition more than one thousand of the precious examples of Indian art in perishable materials and many hundreds of objects of shell, bone and horn. In the years that have ensued, no collection of Calusa artifacts has ever equalled it.

From what he found, Cushing believed that the Indians lived in rectangular huts, thatched with marsh grass and, while modern anthropologists might disagree, he thought that they were walled with a sort of clay plaster applied to latticed saplings. The houses next to the lagoon rested on a platform-piling arrangement ingeniously designed to work with the natural movements of the tides. For furnishing, there were heavily platted mats, probably floor coverings, and some strange, little wooden stools with prong-like legs, hollow on top and up to a foot in length. Some seemed to be headrests and remains were found of what might have been platted, cone-shaped pillow, once filled with moss or deer hair.

The pre-Columbian Indian housewife was well supplied with utensils—a variety of fired pottery, baskets, shell cups, knives made of bone or shark's teeth and spoons of bivalves. Both men and women had personal adornments and a very special find was a beautiful, small brooch carved of hard wood in the shape of an angelfish, its spots inlaid with tortoise shell. Also, there were ear buttons, labrets, lip-pins, carved beads, cord-knobs and pendants. Some of the ear buttons were large and resembled the piercing eyes of some monstrous fish, probably worn by warriors; others, decorated with involuted figures or circles, must have had ceremonial significance. Highly polished plates of shell might have been worn thrust through the earlobe while iridescent ends of pinna shells bore holes for attaching, perhaps to necklaces and bracelets, or dangled from waist or knees.

Transportation was by canoe and the lost or cast-off toys of long ago, worn by the hands of children, were small replicas. All were dugouts but they were different in detail to suit their specific use. There were flat bottom punts for the inland, shallow waterways, swift, high-ended craft for the open Gulf and clumsy cargo carriers, but most interesting were the double canoes which utilized both paddles and sails. These remained relatively unchanged as late as the 18th century and were frequently described by both the biographers of Menendez in 1574, and the writers of the century following.

The amount of paraphernalia concerned with navigation, fishing, tools and implements reached staggering proportions. An anchor was made by the careful arrangement of a cluster of triton shells filled with clay and marl; and there were nets and fish line of tough fibers, hooks shaped from forked twigs, numerous shell sinkers and even some lures for fishing—small plates of pinna shell with fixed double hooks carved from deer horn. Barbed harpoons were conspicuously absent leading to the conclusion that nets were sufficient for taking fish from the pounds.

Picks, hammers, adzes, gouges, chisels and celts made from large, heavy shells have been found by the basketful on all these islands, but on Marco, Cushing unearthed the most elaborately carved object he had ever seen in this country. It was a wooden handle to a shell chisel which had been worked to look like some biting or gnawing animal. There also were many saws, some created from the lower jaws of kingfish but one efficient little tool, made of the socket section of deer horns, held replaceable blades of shell or the large teeth of a shark or an alligator.

It was to this very clever invention of fish teeth tools that Cushing, and more recently, Florida anthropologist John Goggin, gave credit for the preeminence of these people in the art of woodcarving. Both believed that the highest expression of this art is found in the highly skilled craftmanship of ceremonial masks which were found in pairs. A figurehead resembling a wolf, an exquisitely carved pelican, a leather-back turtle and a bear each had its counterpart in an elaborately carved and painted human mask. Today, these magnificient pieces are considered among the finest examples of Indian woodcarving in eastern North America.

However, of all ceremonial art objects discovered at Marco, probably the one most significant to the Indian culture of this coast was a thin board bearing a very well-rendered painting of a crested bird, perhaps a jay, or a kingfisher or a combination of both. It would seem to represent the bird-god of these ancient people and bore a paddle under its dextral wing to signify dominance over the water, while four "sign circles" issuing from the mouth were intended to indicate its dominance over the four corners of their sea and island world.

While digging close to the seawall, the men discovered what seemed to be a witch doctor's "bag of tricks," strewn within a small radius as if the owner, himself, had dropped it. His accoutrements included a rattle of crab claws, the carapace of a gopher turtle, and the skull of an oppossum and that of a weasel painted black and white to look vital. There also were some brilliantly colored scallops which had been on a hoop and some natural but strangely-shaped pearls, possibly used for soothsaying. That this prophet and shaman was also a medical practitioner was apparent from his "instruments"—a little sucking tube made from the wing bone of a pelican or crane and a sharp lancet of fish bone set in a wooden handle of the kind used by other southern Indians in blood-letting and ceremonial skin-scratching. Perhaps even more exciting was the discovery of a complete set of appurtenances for serv-

19

ing the sacred Casine, or "Black Drink," a solemn ceremony described three hundred years ago by the French explorer, Rene de Laudonnier and one hundred years later by the shipwrecked sailor, Jonathan Dickinson.

As was bound to happen, some artifacts were lost because they were not recognized in time. Such was the case of the "double" sunray clams, *Macrocallista nimbosa Solander*, of which the party found so many, they thought they had dug into a natural bed and tossed them away. When they pulled from the muck a whole shell neatly bound with still-green palmetto leaf, they found inside a painting of an outstretched hand, while other shells contained drawings or sometimes, seaweed, symbol of potency. How many of these symbolic and sacred objects they had thrown away, they could only guess.

As he reviewed the work of the expeditions and assessed what had been found, Frank Cushing concluded that at the time of their discovery by white men, the key dwellers were chiefly Maskokian (or of the stock to which not only the Muskogee, but also the Choctaw, the Hitchiti an other tribes of the Creek Confederacy belonged) and were by no means a new people. However, he also believed that before these later tribes invaded or infiltrated the island colonies, another group from the south already had established themselves, probably Arawak or Carib, whose origins were in South America. As evidence, he presented certain of his finds, such as pointed paddles and the atlatls of which he had found many, while bows were entirely lacking. Aided by ocean currents, or blown by hurricane winds, as some of the Spaniards were, these Indians arrived from the south in sea-going canoes and finding our shores prolific in food supplies, had never penetrated the interior but built, through many generations, artificial islands on natural reefs or shoals. The Calusa were known to have had a colony of Cuban Indians of very ancient origin. Cushing saw many similarities in the art forms and mound building of the Maya and thought that the early inhabitants of the islands of Carlos shared a common heritage with them, their roots somewhere off the coast of northern South America.

The theory that raised the most eyebrows, however, then and now, was the suggestion that some of the more northerly Indians, of the Mississippi Valley, Tennessee and southern Ohio had a common origin with the Indians of Florida's southwest coast; that this culture spread northward, not through barter alone but also through the landward movement of the people themselves.

Doctors, they say, bury their mistakes and architects cover them with ivy. An anthropologist can only equivocate but Cushing had no opportunity to do this. On April 10, 1949, he was dining with his wife when he choked on a fish bone. He died before help could reach him.

Gordon R. Willey, in his *Archaeology of the Florida Gulf Coast*, 1949, called his speculations the "most extreme" of Gulf coast anthropologists and John M. Goggin, anthropologist expert on Florida Indians, believed the Calusa colonies had been on coastal mainland and they became insular with the rising of the sea. He allowed only that certain Calusa methods spread north through Florida. Yet, as long as men dig to learn, there will be surprises. The Pepper-Hearst Expedition members assembled their impressive collection through back-breaking work and were blessed with a very necessary ingredient—luck. As yet, no other group has been so successful.

Actually, few have tried. Southwest Florida's formidable mosquito-infested mangrove swamps have trapped the treasures of the water-courts and held them for centuries, defying mere men who splash and stumble through the tortuous roots. For that reason, and despite heavy development, this area contains the only large mound complexes in all of Eastern United States which have not been investigated. Although anthropologist Clarence B. Moore visited some of the Cushing sites (but not Sanibel or Captiva) in 1900 and 1904, he found little of value and tended to downgrade Cushing's achievement.

During the winter of 1927 and 1928, Henry B. Collins, archaeologist emeritis of the National Museum of Natural History, investigated shell heaps and sand mounds in Lee, Collier and Hendry Counties for the Smithsonian Institution. On Captiva, he excavated a small burial mound located in a mangrove swamp on the property of Clarence Chadwick who lived in the Manor House, now part of South Seas Plantation Resort. It was associated with a large shell midden and consisted of two distinct strata of dissimilar burials. At the top, in several feet of fine beach sand, were piles of loose, disjointed bones which previously had been buried or kept for a time elsewhere. Below this, in broken shell and sand from the Gulf beach, was an older burial of skeletons laid out in a prone position with limbs flexed. Water seepage had turned this material into a rock-like substance and although the bones were in good condition, they had to be extracted with hammer and chisel. Fragments of earthenware cooking pots had been carefully placed around some of the skulls.

Dr. Collins recovered some potsherds and bones which included seventy skulls but the most unusual discovery was the base of the mound itself. Along the edge of the mound was a border of large whelk shells, sixteen inches to three feet wide, arranged in two and three rows with the large ends facing the mound and curving around it. On the opposite side, sloping upward from the base, was a pavement of potsherds among which were four pieces of human occipital bone. Three of them belonged to different skulls. The bones of these Indians of unknown origin were believed to be more than one thousand years old.

Until recently, the digging on Sanibel was of the leisurely Sunday afternoon variety—people exploring for the fun of it. There have been some exciting finds. Two intact plain clay pots, one containing rabbit bones, were pulled from the muck at Ladyfinger Lake at Woodring's point. Projectile points made of flint and the sharp end of a whelk also were found there. At Wulfert, Kesson's Bayou yielded old Spanish bottles and three crucifixes. One of these was set with blue stones, three on the left and four on the right, where Christ's hands would have been.

In 1971, a newly dug lagoon at Ross Mayer Hummock on San Carlos Bay revealed evidence of a prehistoric camp site when a large clod of clay, believed to have lined a firepit, rolled out of a cut bank. It proved such a potpourri of ancient trash as to put a glint in any archaeological eye. Along with the expected charcoal, broken clam shells and splintered bones were pieces of bog iron, chips and chunks of a low grade flint (native to south Georgia) and some fine artifacts. Some of these obviously had been traded. A cup was fashioned from an unusually large Shark's Eye shell, a hammer and celt, of excellent workmanship, from a whelk and a scraper and an ax head was made from the lip of a Queen Conch, a species not found in Sanibel waters. Stone items included a half-finished ax head of chert, a crude hammer of limestone and small round stones of indeterminate use. Cut from deer antler were sockets or adze handles, needles and a hammer. The cache was radiocardon dated to 430 A.D., ± 100 years.

Several years later, the almost complete skeleton of an Indian woman was found at the edge of the same lagoon. It was stretched out with one leg flexed and well preserved in mangrove muck. Her "medical record," as compliled by an anthropologist, a chiropractor and the author's dentist, had quite a lot to tell about such an ancient lady. About five foot four inches tall, she was between forty and fifty years old at the time of her death and bore no signs of foul play. Her bones were straight as were her teeth which showed no decay. They were worn down to the pulp, however, by a gritty diet. This and arthritis in her spine must have caused her some pain. She died from causes unknown about four hundred years ago.

Islanders took great pride in the first scientific exploration of a mound on Sanibel which was begun in 1974 and completed two years later. It was initiated and organized by Sanibel resident and anthropologist Charles J. Wilson. Dr. Wilson happened to be driving by the Karl Wightman property in Wulfert when he noticed several Indian mounds, apparently undisturbed, with large gumbo limbo trees growing on top of them. They were most intriguing and he conceived the idea of excavating them. Mr. Wightman generously gave his consent and soon Wilson had organized a team of volunteers. Shortly thereafter, he was appointed Assistant Research Professor by the University of Florida.

It was decided to excavate one of the two most visible mounds and the rather flat courtyard between them. Directed by Dr. Wilson, and in his absence by his "straw bosses" Barbara Schumacher, Marie Kalman and Elinore Dormer, Sanibel-Captiva residents and visitors got to work at the site. They were helped by students from Lee County's Edison Community College, Oberlin College of Ohio and the University of Florida. Throughout two winters, the team moved and sifted heaps of mound material. When summer came, they were driven away by rain and biting insects—as Cushing had been.

Sanibel-Captiva Conservation Foundation sponsored the project and would provide most of the money to see it through. The Florida State Museum analyzed the mound material while Dr. Jerald T. Milanich, assistant Curator of Anthropology, served as advisor. His help proved invaluable. Dr. Lee High, who led the group from Oberlin, defined the geological strata at the site. At the University of Miami, a husband and wife team, Dr. Holly Caldwell and Ray H. Caldwell, worked on the carbon dating under the direction of Dr. Jerry Stipp.

The final report, finished in March, 1976, was entitled "The Wightman Site: A Study of Prehistoric Culture and Environment on Sanibel Island, Lee County, Florida." It was the master's thesis of Arlene Fradkin of the University of Florida. Her work had been funded on a cost sharing basis by the Conservation Foundation which paid $1,050, and the Florida State Museum which provided matching funds in the form of a graduate assistantship.

The results of the dig were surprising. The periods of habitation did not run chronologically from historic times at the top of the mound or earth to prehistoric times at the bottom. The most recent occupancy was believed to be about 700 A.D. while the storm-driven material, *i.e.* debris disturbed by natural elements, was about two thousand five hundred years old, suggesting the presence of people on Sanibel shortly after it emerged as an island. By all indications, they were very primitive for their tools, implements and ornaments were crude.

Specifically, there seemed to have been two main periods in the mound; a submound at ground level and slightly below and a constructed mound over that. The submound extended into the courtyard with a lens of beach sand through it, suggesting that the Indians had been driven away by a terrible storm and stayed away long enough for an oyster bar to form. Then people returned, built a second mound where the first had been and lived there without further construction for hundreds of years.

The courtyard contained two clay floors, one older than the other. There were many firepits for warmth and cooking and in one was an eleven-inch block of limestone, a rock not native to Sanibel. The floors were littered with bone fragments, mostly those of deer and fish, but there were big bones also which might have been bear, manatee or seal. There was much charcoal and laminated and unlaminated pottery sherds of the common sand tempered variety, some of which had ticked rims. Crude shell tools, including an ax head of sandy limestone, were unearthed as were stone and shell pendants, an incised tooth and sharks' teeth with drilled holes. Projectile points were found and bone pins but there was nothing to indicate that these Indians cultivated crops or carved wooden objects. They were a Shell Age people who unaccountably left the site long ago; a spectre tribe, barely preceived in what they left behind.

It is believed that the Wightman Site is part of the unexcavated complex of canals and mounds visited by Cushing in 1895 and John Goggin in 1940. It was Goggin who originated the designation "Sanibel Incised" for a type of decorated pottery, sherds of which were shown him at that time. He did not collect these himself nor did the Wilson team ever find any.

Goggin and his friend, Charles Brookfield, Director of Florida Audubon Society, had been invited to Wulfert by G.J. Kesson, farmer and entrepreneur of sorts. The mounds were located across a shallow creek from Sanibel proper and he operated the place, which he called "Mysterious Island", as a tourist attraction. As he poled his customers to it, he lectured them on the strange ways and dark doings of his Indians. Afterward, they were conducted along a palm-lined trail to his "Kitty Museum" laid out beneath his dilapidated stilt house on Kesson's Bayou. There they could browse through his artifacts, buy produce or shells and finally "feed the kitty", *i.e.* put money in a big jar placed there for that purpose.

Goggin described what he could see of Mysterious Island as mainly shell with a little soil and other refuse. He went on to say:

> "This shell has been used to build an elaborate series of embankments, platforms, mounds and other features. There are a number of circular basins, some with muck bottoms and others dry. This would be a good place to duplicate Cushing's finds of wooden objects at Key Marco. One large circular basin with a dry interior has steep sides rising to over 10 feet. The creek which separates this site from Sanibel Island has a branch slough which runs along one side of the shell site and would have afforded easy access by means of canoe."*

Goggin then looked over the several hundred potsherds in Kesson's collection finding most of them plain but some with ticked rims and just three which he named "Sanibel Incised". He assigned the site to Glades I Period (*ca.* 400 B.C. to 1 A.D.). Although Sanibel is within the Calusa subarea, as Goggin defined it, the occupants of this particular place predated the coming of white men by perhaps two thousand years.

Non-native rocks, such as vesicular flint and smooth river pebbles of quartzite or chalcedony, had been found and Kesson had over four hundred Busycon (whelk) hammers and about one hundred picks. There was a long flint projectile point but three stone pendants had been sold or given away before the Goggin visit. Of very great interest, but since lost, burned or stolen, were three crucifixes which Kesson had found washed up in

* Archaeological Site File, University of Florida, Site #L54.

front of his house. These were wood framed with brass with a brass figure of Christ, typical of those worn by Catholic clergy. They ranged in size from one and a half inches to five inches and were not jeweled.

Kesson's death, some years later, was as bizarre as his life had been. He had an unusual arrangement with the men who had come and gone from his employ, mostly drifters, who received no wages. Instead, it was bed, board and a piece of paper, Kesson's will, in which the current hired hand was named heir to all his worldly goods. This included the ramshackle house and the land on which it stood. Neighbors shook their heads and pointed out possible dangerous consequences but the old man shrugged them off. Since his health was poor, a series of hopefuls came and went—disgruntled by the hard work with no pay—as the wheel of fortune spun and spun. Where it would stop, nobody knew.

But finally, stop it did in the early 1940s when a man named Bill Duffey was working there. The old man, feeling ill that morning, had remained in bed. Duffey left coffee on the stove for him and went off to shell on the beach. A little before 9 A.M., fishermen in their boats saw flames shoot up but by the time they reached the house, it had burned to the ground. In the glowing embers lay the charred remains of G.J. Kesson, still on his iron bedstead.

It was not the first time a Kesson home had burned to the ground but the unusual conditions of the will prompted an investigation. There was no evidence of foul play and Duffey soon sold the property and left the island.

In recent years, that section of Wulfert has been altered by fill and development but Kesson's island still exists, largely intact, within the confines of J.N. "Ding" Darling Sanctuary. The miasma of mystery still hangs over it.

In 1985 the University of Florida formed the Institute

of Archaeological and Paleoenvironmental Studies to bring together archaeologists, biologists, geologists, historians, photogrammeters and other scholars who would work together in the study of past environments and cultures. The Southwest Florida Project, under the direction of Dr. William H. Marquardt, became its first major project. Supported by the National Science Foundation, the University of Florida and private contributions, it would explore the very hub of the Calusa kingdom, an area extremely important to American history, yet never before studied on such a grand scale.

Time was of the essence. The vast shell mounds on these shores and islands were threatened not only by the natural attrition of wind and water but increasingly by people. The impact of the few hundred who farmed and fished in the early 1900s was minimal but by the 1980s there were hundreds of thousands of residents in southwest Florida. With them came builders with heavy equipment who, overnight, could transform our coastal mounds into business and home sites. Nothing could stop development in unprotected areas but Indian culture at least could be examined before it disappeared under slabs of concrete.

Marquardt, other scientists and volunteers, began with archaeological testing at Josslyn Island, Buck Key, Useppa Island and Cash Mound in Lee and Charlotte counties. A time range of approximately 3500 B.C. to A.D. 1350 was established with the oldest finds on Useppa Island. Buck Key, at Captiva's back door, yielded artifacts dating to approximately 1050 to 1350 A.D. Bone and shell tools were found as well as pottery sherds which when reconstructed became a bowl with the rim bearing human fingerprints where its maker had pinched a design. Before it became part of the rubble of centuries the last hands to touch it were those of Calusa Indians. A section of the island which had been

29

Skeleton of an Indian woman buried on Buck Key about 700 years ago. Photo by the Institute of Archaeolgy and Paleoenvironmental Studies, Florida State Museum, University of Florida.

a burial ground contained the skeleton of a woman buried in a fetal position with the skulls and a few bones of four other individuals placed carefully around her.

Meanwhile, fish and quahog clams were collected for comparative study and core samples were taken under the water and islands of Charlotte Harbor—Pine Island Sound. Geologists could determine from the sediments the nature of the environments at the time Calusa inhabited the area. Preliminary studies in the fluctuations of sea level seemed to indicate that this was coastal mainland three thousand years ago.

Exploring these sites was like turning the pages of a book that the Calusa themselves had written. Revitalizing a people, their culture and their environment is a lengthy and difficult process but well worth the effort not just for the knowledge it sheds on our past but also for its practical application in the management of present day archaeological and natural resources. Much remains to be done. The work will continue as long as there is financial support.

A Florida Panther

Chapter III

DISCOVERY, MAPS, AND PLACE NAMES

Juan Ponce de Leon, on his first voyage of discovery in 1513, sailed north along the Gulf Coast of Florida and at some point beyond Captiva, turned landward. Going south "as far as some islands that make out to the sea,"* he brought his expedition through an entrance and landed to take on wood and water and careen the *San Cristoval*. Historians generally agree that the projecting islands were Captiva and Sanibel and that Ponce's first west coast landing was within the Pine Island Sound-San Carlos Bay area, for this was the northern limit of Calusa territory.

The intention had been to explore, take possession and seize Indians for slaves, but met by hostile forces, the men did not penetrate far into the interior and stayed close to their ships. On three occasions, the Calusa Indians attacked them and in these David *vs.* Goliath-like encounters one Spaniard and more than eighty Indians died.

After remaining in the area for several weeks, Ponce's force departed southward to return to San Carlos Bay in 1521 with colonists. There are reliable accounts of these expeditions, but Juan Ponce was not the first

---

* Edward W. Lawson, *The Discovery of Florida and Its Discoverer, Juan Ponce de Leon*, St. Augustine, 1946, p. 16.

white man to find the islands of Carlos. Nor did he, or anyone else, name Sanibel in honor of Queen Isabella.

When the French seemed to threaten Spanish dominance in Florida in 1565, the Council of the Indies addressed a note to King Phillip II which indicated that Spanish ships had been in Florida since 1510. Probably, Spaniards and others were prowling the coastal waters before that. The Caribbean colonies functioned on a system of serfdom and it is assumed that there were clandestine slaving operations years before the explorations of Ponce. Slavers were supposed to be licensed and pay fees to the crown but Cuban authorities seldom, if ever, cracked down on their illegal activities.

It is possible that Amerigo Vespucci, Italian-born pilot in the service of Spain, was the actual discoverer of Florida. He is credited with four voyages to the New World during which he explored the east coast of South America. He could have gone on, as he claimed, to Mexico, circumnavigated the Gulf of Mexico, and rounding the tip of Florida, sailed north to 35° N. Lat. He returned to Seville in 1500 with Indian slaves but never was able to prove that he had done all this. A letter he said he had written to Piero Soderini of Florence describing this voyage was published in 1504 but the original was never produced and Vespucci's claim to the discovery of Florida was ruled invalid in a court case at that time.

Nevertheless, some historians believe that he supplied the information for the oldest known map of Florida, the Cantino Map of 1502, made for Albert Cantino in behalf of the Portugese Duke of Ferrera. If this is the map referred to by the 16th century historian Peter Martyr as "one drawn by the Portugales, where unto Americus Vespucci is said to have put his hande," it would appear to end the argument.

Although rudimentary, this remarkable map generally follows the contours of the Florida peninsula with

34

place names that accurately describe it. The wide, sandy beaches of the eastern shore do, indeed, form a "white coast" (*Costa Alva*), and such words as *gato, largatos* and *nilcor* could refer to the panthers and alligators indigenous to Florida and the all too adundant insects. Even more significant is the distinctive indentation of the west coast where two inlets near each other are shown in the approximate position of Charlotte Harbor and San Carlos Bay. We believe they are just that, with the Peace River and the Caloosahatchee draining into them. Offshore, somewhat wrongly placed but not really at random, are some small dots which would represent Sanibel, Captiva, Estero and Pine Island along with the many little keys near them. Someone must have explored the coast of Florida to have even roughly charted it and, although we have no proof, we think it was Amerigo Vespucci in 1500.

In 1527, six years after the death of Juan Ponce de Leon, Alonso de Chaves, Cosmographer to the King of Spain, issued a guide for mariners, *Quatri Partitu en Cosmografia Practica, y por Otro Nombre Espejo de Navegantes,* which included a section on southwest Florida. In it, Cayo Costa, Captiva and Sanibel combined are called *Costa de Carocoles,* Coast of Seashells. It is located between Bahia Honda, today's Charlotte Harbor, and *Bahia de Juan Ponce* where the coast is crescent-shaped with a shallow inlet; an apt description of Sanibel and Tarpon Bay. Since the guide mentions many places known to have been named by Ponce, it is not unlikely that he also named these three islands Coast of Seashells. Only Cayo Costa, also called La Costa, retains part of the original designation.

Although historians of Ponce de Leon and explorer Antonio de Cordova make oblique references to an island that probably was Sanibel, it is first described in detail by Bernard Romans, Holland-born navigator in the service of England who surveyed the west coast

35

of Florida in 1769. In his instructions to mariners, he says:

> "This nook in the land forms what the Spaniards call *Ensenada de Carlos*, i.e. Charles' Bay: the piece of coast that trends E. and W. is the beach of an island called Sanybel. This place is further remarkable for a great number of pine-trees without tops standing at the bottom of the Bay like which there is no spot in the whole extent of this coast. The northernmost entrance* is likewise remarkable for a singular hammock, or grove of pine-trees standing very near the beach and the only one of its form and kind in all these parts."

It was not Romans who gave Sanibel its Spanish name, however, or, more correctly, the garbled version of a Spanish name, for such it is. This was the end product of a mistake several times repeated—the misinterpretation of the abbreviation S. which in Spanish can mean "south" or "saint (masculine)."

Early so-called maps actually were charts with information and notations for mariners sailing along a largely unknown coast. Land masses, large or small, were not named unless they had some special significance, and Sanibel did not—except for a very fine harbor at its southeast tip, known and used since the first voyage of Ponce de Leon. This was referred to in sailing instructions of 1757 but the first map we have showing it is dated 1765. It appears as *Puerto de S. Nivel,* and on an official Spanish Army map of 1768 (#53), *Puerto de S. Nibel.* B and v being interchangeable,

---

* Wulfert, at Sanibel's northern end, still has the only real pine trees on the island.

both names mean the same thing: South Plane Harbor. It was a good, descriptive label for ships at sea to whom the island would appear to be quite level, its surface parallel to the horizon.

Why, then, Sanibel? Because S can also mean saint, although this is usually written *Sn.* and in 1757, an illustrious pilot, Don Francisco Maria Celi, so interpreted it, perhaps from a chart splashed with sea water, for there is no St. Nivel nor any proper name remotely like it. Pilot of the Spanish Royal Fleet, he reported in his Journal of Surveys that en route to the port of (today's) Tampa, he passed *Punto de Sanivel*, Sanivel Point.

Others, too, would err. While map #53 of the Spanish Geographic Service was correct, #54, published the same year, read *Puerto de Sn. Nibel*, giving official credence to a saintly nonentity. Bernard Romans added to the confusion by calling it Sanybel one time and San Ybell another and his map of 1774 was widely distributed. The following year, the Spaniards published #55, the Thomas Jefferys Map, which said, simply, Sanibel, and variously misspelled, so it would remain. It is sheer fiction that the island itself, small and unimportant, was named in memory of Queen Isabella by Juan Ponce de Leon—for what kind of compliment would that be?

The origin of the name of Captiva is more obscure but it would seem that the island was named for the pass and not *vice versa*. In 1757, Celi refers to a *boca* "which they call *Del Cautivo*," Captive's Entrance (or Mouth) north of today's Upper Captiva Island. This very short pass between Captiva Island as it once was, and La Costa extends from the open Gulf to Pine Island Sound, at the north end of which is Charlotte Harbor. Most old maps showing *Puerto de S. Nivel* also show *Boca* or *Voca del Cautivo* but not until much later was the island named. In 1833, the colonists of "Sanybel" called it Captive Island and in 1837, John Lee Williams called today's Captiva "Capativa" and Upper Captiva "Muspa," which was an Indian village of Chief Carlos, the last to survive, the name of which became synonymous with Calusa. Probably, Williams erred for old Spanish maps designated Cape Romano as Punta Muspa, the coast between there and the Caloosahatchee as their land and their town at or near Punta Rassa. He also shows a very narrow passage between Captiva and Upper Captiva which he called "Bocca Secca," although on older maps, *Boca Seca*, Dry Mouth, was between Sanibel and Captiva, and Captiva was one long island.

After the Williams map, the name reverted to "Captive" and was corrupted into Captiva during the latter half of the nineteenth century. The name conjures up romantic fantasies and it is no wonder that a pirate story was invented to go with it. We see in our mind's eye the captured high-born maidens languishing in the shade of the palmettos and gazing wistfully seaward. Will good men and true come to deliver them out of the clutches of the dastardly buccaneers? Sadly, probably not, for in all likelihood, the ladies were not held in such an accessible place.

Apparently, then, it was Captiva Pass which was historically significant and we search the pages of our past for the reason it was so named. The Spanish word "cautivo," masculine singular, would refer to one man or boy and since the name appears while the Indians still held sway over the islands, we assume that he was their prisoner sometime before this opening was so designated and mapmakers made note of it and began publishing.

The Calusa and Timacua, whose kingdoms bordered each other at about that place, held hundred of Christian prisoners over the years, most of whom met untimely deaths as human sacrifices, but few of these attained any degree of fame and fewer still were

38

connected with any great historical occasion. Still, although it was very long ago, there was one such captive of the Timacua and a highly dramatic series of events which some historians believe happened near Charlotte Harbor. With no proof whatsoever, we believe that the story of Captiva is the story of Juan Ortiz.

In the early spring of 1528, Panfilo de Narvaez, adventurer and conquistador, sailed from Cuba in command of a large exhibition with which he expected to explore Florida and take for himself and his king the great wealth he felt confident was there. Driven by storms up the west coast of the peninsula, he landed in the Carlos Bay-Charlotte Harbor area and, arranging for a rendezvous with his ships, he set out on foot with a large force of men into the interior. But the ships were unable to make contact with the marchers and after almost a year of searching, they returned to Cuba to report that these men were lost.

But Doña Narvaez, who had been anxiously awaiting the return of her husband, was unwilling to accept the presumption that he was dead and, since she was a wealthy woman, she equipped a pinnace at her own expense and sent it forth to search for him. She ordered the captain to seek out and reconnoiter every inlet and waterway, scrutinize every beach and shore and virtually scour the coast from the Florida Keys northward. This the captain was doing when he reached Captiva Pass and decided to examine further the general area where he believed the men had last been seen.

As they turned into the mouth of an inlet, they saw ahead some Indians on the shore, waving in a friendly manner, and nearby, what appeared to be a piece of paper stuck into the slitted end of a stick thrust into the beach. Here might be the message from Narvaez—or was it? Warily, the Spaniards dropped anchor to discuss the situation, but in the end, two young men volun-

39

teered to retrieve the "letter" and as the others watched, they rowed ashore—and stepped into an ambush! Unable or unwilling to go to their aid, the captain shouted an order to hoist anchor and the small vessel made its escape into the open Gulf. Predictably, the men on shore could not long defend themselves and one soon was dead and the other, Juan Ortiz, barely eighteen years old, was taken prisoner.

Unfortunately, Narvaez had passed that way before, stopping at a Timacua town called Ucita, after its chief, called a *cacique*, and there had perpetrated a violent and grisly atrocity. At first, all had gone well as he and his men rested, but when they prepared to push on, their demands for food, goods, slaves, and bearers seemed excessive to the *cacique* and he refused to meet them. Infuriated, Narvaez pulled forth his sword, and as the horrified villages looked on, he slashed the nose from the face of their leader. Then, to further intimidate them, he ordered the chief's aged mother be dragged forth and in the sight of her bleeding and agonized son, she was thrown to the Spanish dogs which killed and devoured her.

Less than a year later, by a bitter stroke of fate, Juan Ortiz, of a noble Spanish family and hardly yet a man, became the innocent victim of these same Indians who carried him off in triumph to their chief.

Ucita had had many months to brood and plot revenge and his reaction to the appearance of Juan could only be described as fiendish glee. The youth was trussed to a lattice of saplings, like a piece of barbecue meat, and a fire was laid under him. It was an occasion of great excitement and the villagers thronged to see the show— but not all took pleasure in it. Among the spectators were the daughters and wife of Ucita and as the fire was lit and the flames shot upward, they no longer could endure such cruelty. Running forward, they threw themselves at the *cacique's* feet, pleading that the young man be spared. Reluctantly, he gave in to them and the seared and suffering Ortiz was removed from the scene.

With great compassion, the women dressed his burns with the juice of herbs, brought food and found him a place to rest, but his troubles were just beginning. Years later, when he joined De Soto, he told the bizarre story of his wretched servitude in the town near Charlotte Harbor.

Historians differ, somewhat, in their accounts of Juan Ortiz's serfdom among the Timacua, but all agree that it was hard, that he was worked to exhaustion, cruelly treated and frequently harassed because the disfigured *cacique* so ordered it. Yet, on these days, more than ever, his gentle friends fed and cared for him.

Ucita knew of this division in his household but his bitterness did not extend to the women he loved and for a time, he chose to ignore it. Still, the presence of the young Spaniard was a festering wound and to further remove him from his sight, he ordered that he stand watch, night and day, at the town mortuary

It was the custom of Gulf Coast Indians to place their dead in boxes and keep them above ground until the flesh fell from the bones, then, with due ceremony, the skeleton was broken or cut up and the bones buried. These coffins were not tightly sealed and it fell to Juan Ortiz to guard the corpses from marauding animals, his only weapon a handful of short, spear-like darts. Although sickened by the stench of decaying flesh, he managed to be an effective guardian until, one fateful night, he fell asleep to be awakened in the early hours of the morning by the sound of falling boards. Fearfully, he confirmed his worst suspicions—some predatory animal had made off with the body of a child, dead just two days, and he, Juan Ortiz, was good as dead if he could not recover it.

Frantically, he ran through the forest and finally came out on a broad trail. As he slowed to a cautious walk, he heard a most weird sound—as if the dog were gnawing bones in the woods beside the road. Parting the bushes quietly, Juan saw, dimly in the moonlight, a large animal feeding on the stolen corpse. Silently uttering a prayer, he drew forth a dart and threw it with all his might at the crouching beast. Although he heard no further sound, the night sky clouded and it was not until dawn that he saw, greatly elated, that he had killed the animal—a huge panther—with an exceedingly lucky shot. Returning the small corpse to its coffin, Ortiz then seized the dead cat by the foot, and dragging it into town, he threw it at the feet of the chief, dart still in place. The Indians viewed this feat with almost superstitious wonder and for a time, the young man was a hero.

Ucita, however, resented more than ever this foreigner in their midst and decided that Ortiz would be sacrificed on the next feast day. He sternly instructed his wife and daughters that he no longer would permit their interference and this they sorrowfully accepted.

Nevertheless, the eldest daughter approached Juan and told him secretly that she had arranged his escape. He was to go to a certain place that night where a man would be waiting to guide him beyond the bridge to the town of another chief, Mucozo. This *cacique*, she told him, loved her very much and had asked for her hand in marriage. She knew, for her sake, he would give the slave asylum.

Flabbergasted at both the news of his sentence and the chance of reprieve, Juan Ortiz humbly thanked her for all her charities and those of her mother and sisters. When the time came to do so, he fled the town of Ucita, never to return.

As the princess so confidently expected, Mucozo received the runaway kindly and eventually installed him as his chamberlain. All this brought a hornet's nest down on his head for Ucita soon learned of the where-

42

bouts of his captive and demanded his return. When Mucozo suggested that one badly-used slave was not worth all the ruckus, his irate neighbor used his influence with another chief, Mucozo's brother-in-law, Urribarracuxi, who tried every inducement and threat to force the return of the Spaniard to his tormenter.

But Mucozo stood firm and so incurred the lasting enmity of Ucita who now, of course, would not permit him to marry his daughter. Thus, the Timicuan princess and her noble suitor were forever lost to each other, perhaps the cruelest sacrifice of all.

Mucozo was twenty-six years old at that time, and very handsome. The Inca, Garcilaso de la Vega, a historian of the De Soto expedition, would place him a little lower than the angels and maintained that he did not deserve to be born into the barbarous paganism of Florida. Considering the bloodbaths of the con-quistadors and the retaliation of their victims, we cannot but agree.

Mucozo reigned, we believe, somewhere west of the Myakka River, and when his path crossed that of Hernando De Soto, Juan Ortiz was returned to his own people. Ortiz joined the ill-fated expedition, becoming interpreter for the brutal conquerer, who sometimes called himself Son of the Sun. Exhausted, half-starving and ill, he died during the winter of 1541 in an Indian town called Autiamque on the south bank of the Arkansas River.

The various names of San Carlos Bay reflect a succession of men whose presence there made it important. It was the first bay on Florida's west coast to be known geographically and historically and first appears on the Conti de Ottoman Freducci Map of 1514-1515. It seems to be labeled "Stababa," one of several versions of the name of the Calusa chief at the time of Juan Ponce's first visit in 1513. Other sources call this *cacique* "Stapana" and "Escampaba." The second Borgian Map of 1529, while calling the Caloosahatchee *Rio de Stapana*, refers to San Carlos as the Bay of Juan Ponce, as do most maps published after the conquistador was mortally wounded there in 1521.

Pedro Menendez de Aviles referred to it as the Bay of Juan Ponce when he wrote his king in 1565 that he would build a fort there. Later, he named it *San Anton* after St. Anthony of Padua to whom he prayed before embarking for Florida. He called today's Estero Bay *Bahia de Carlos* because it was within the immediate domain of Carlos, king of the Calusa at that time. In 1769, a bay south of San Carlos was designated by Romans and others as Juan Ponce Bay, giving rise to much misinformation as to where Ponce de Leon fought his last battle. The real Juan Ponce Bay became Carlos Bay and remained unchanged, until 1835, when for reasons unknown, the Bradford Map of Florida called it Bay St. Charles and from that time until the end of the 19th century, it was sometimes Carlos, sometimes San Carlos. Today, it is San Carlos Bay, generally believed to have been named by the Spaniards after the saint, but quite the contrary. The great *Cacique* Carlos remained defiantly pagan to the day of his beheading.

Charlotte Harbor, the southern half of which was controlled by the Calusa, has often been confused with Carlos Bay and has undergone many name changes. It was discovered at the same time and on a map of 1527, it is *Bahia Honda*, Deep Bay, believed named by Ponce de Leon. It might have been *Bahia d'Espiritu Sancto* (Bay of the Holy Spirit) of De Soto but the Indians called it Tampa. It was still Tampa in 1694, according to a letter of Bishop Calderon of Cuba, who wrote that it was four leagues beyond "the inlet called Carlos." In 1757, Celi put the Port of Tampa at the Bay of Tocobaga, its present site, and in 1769, Romans, another notorious misplacer of names, did also, thus leaving today's Charlotte Harbor nameless. Then, acting as if

44

he had discovered it, Romans named this large estuary for Queen Charlotte, wife of George III of England, thus stripping it of its historic designation.

The first town of Tampa was Calusa Indian, located on today's Useppa Island, where in the early 1800s a man named José Caldez had a fish camp. Then, it was called Caldez Island or Josefa, the feminine of José which also was the name of his boat. It became Guiseppe in 1870 when an Italian fisherman, then living there, gave the census taker the Italian version of Jose and the whole thing became more confusing and amusing with the arrival of American homesteaders and fishermen who called it Useppa and spelled it accordingly.

Estero is a Spanish word meaning estuary or inlet and was a descriptive term often found on old maps. Apparently, this was picked up as a proper name by English speaking people and applied to both bay and island. Estero Bay was once the Bay or Harbor of Carlos because that chief had his principal town on Mound Key, in the middle of it.

Matanzas Pass, between Estero Island and the mainland, took its name from the Spanish word *matanza* (massacre) so named by Ponce de Leon in 1513, because eighty Indians were slain or wounded there. Although today it seems too narrow to be the safe port the Spaniards sought, they successfully defended their ships.

Matlacha (pronounced mat-la'-shay), the pass between Pine Island and the mainland, means shallow water in the Seminole language.

Shallow Blind Pass, between Sanibel and Captiva, appears on Roman's map as "Boca Seco," an obvious misspelling of *Boca Seca*, Dry Mouth. In 1848 it appears as Ciago Bay (Blind Bay), misplaced from the Tampa area. It makes an easy transition to Blind Pass.

On the John Lee Williams map of 1837, there is a

"Bocca Secca" between Captiva Island and Upper Captiva which is very narrow and did not appear on earlier maps. Apparently, this has filled in and washed out many times.

Before 1921, there was a neck of land called The Narrows on Captiva. But in October of that year, a hurricane swept through there creating Redfish Pass.

Caloosahatchee is an anglicized Seminole word meaning Calusa River, but it was once *Rio de Stapana*, named after a Calusa chief, and on a Spanish map of 1597, it is *Rio de Perlas* (or *Perlas*), River of Perlas. It appears on a Spanish map dated "17 ," as Rio Sanibel. In 1833, Sanybel colonists called it the Sanybel River.

Punta Rassa, at the mouth of the Caloosahatchee, has continuous occupancy for many centuries. Its present name, without the extra "s," is Spanish for Flat Point, and the old Calusa town of Muspa probably was located there. The village of Calusa-hatchee of the late 1700s, is believed to have been the same place, but by 1832, it was gone and a Spanish fishery was operating at the site. With the outbreak of the Seminole Wars, the fishing industry was temporarily defunct and in 1837, Ft. Dulany was built at Punta Rassa.

It was occupied and enlarged by Federal troops in 1864, but after the Civil War, it was abandoned and by 1867, George Shultz had set up his telegraph station in the somewhat ramshackle barracks. Eventually, he rebuilt it and Shultz House became a well-known hotel and Punta Rassa, an export point for shipping cattle to Key West and Cuba.

Mound Key, in Estero Bay, inhabited by Indians as early as 500 A.D., is mostly shell mound, and while probably it was once twice as high, today it rises thirty-one feet above the surrounding waters, with one other place, the highest point in Lee County. In 1969, state archaeological studies established it as the one-time site of the principal Calusa town of Calos or Carlos, and probably it was the same as Guchi or Juchi, as the name appears on the Freducci Map, or the 'Tuchi' of Fontaneda. The palace of the chief was located there on one of the high mounds and on the other was the Spanish garrison of San Anton, established by Menendez in 1566. It was abandoned and burned in 1569 and both Spaniards and Indians left the island, but apparently the Calusa returned to it and rebuilt their capital. In 1697, five Franciscan monks landed on "Key Carlos" in an unsuccessful attempt to establish a mission there, but by the early part of the 19th century, the once-mighty tribe was non-existent, except perhaps, for a few individuals who might have joined the Spanish Indians at local fisheries. After Florida was opened up to the homesteaders, Americans moved into the Carlos Bay area and John Butterfield followed by the Johnson family lived on Mound Key which, by then, sometimes was called Johnson Island. After them, the land was acquired by the Koreshan Unity, a communal religious group, which in 1961, bequeathed its part of the island to the State of Florida. Now, again known as Mound Key, it is part of Koreshan State Park. In 1970, it was included in the National Register of Historic Places.

In his *Memoir* of 1545, Hernando d'Escalante Fontaneda lists twenty-seven villages and towns of Carlos but does not locate them. Since then, map makers have misplaced names, historians have incompletely or incorrectly reported events and the history of Florida's southwest coast has become a tangled ball of yarn. Otherwise responsible historians have lumped Charlotte Harbor, San Carlos Bay and connecting waterways into an all inclusive "Charlotte Harbor" with or without the qualifying word "area." This is inexcusably misleading for the two are geographically and ethnically different and such a generality confuses the locations of important historic events. We would put a plague on the English queen—and give the islands of Carlos back to the Indians.

A Spanish brigantine.

Chapter IV

EXPLORATION AND CONQUEST

Juan Ponce de Leon, officially the discoverer of Florida, was born in San Servas, Province of Campos in Spain and was of a noble house of the Kingdom of Leon. He was a soldier, a veteran of the last war against the Moors where he had earned a ruthless reputation. He first viewed the New World in 1493 when he accompanied Christopher Columbus on his second voyage of discovery, and when Columbus returned to Spain, Ponce stayed on in Hispanola, now Santo Domingo. Here he subdued an Indian revolt, captured its leader and eventually became Administrator. Two years later, he moved to Puerto Rico where he had learned there was gold, and enslaving the very Indians who had showed him the first ore, he maneuvered to have himself appointed governor.

Ponce's great plantation was run most profitably with a seemingly inexhaustable supply of Carib Indian slaves who died like flies of disease, starvation and overwork and often were buried where they dropped. Escapes were rare, mostly because of the governor's dog, Bezerillo, whom the Indians believed to be a demon in animal form. The giant greyhound, trained to run down a fleeing man and rip him to pieces, became as notorious as Ponce himself. More companion than pet, he shared in his master's prizes and became rich in his own right.

Juan Ponce lived his life of ease until 1512 when a change of power in the factions which controlled the royal court resulted in his ouster as governor. He still had his plantation and great wealth but he craved action and his imagination was fired by stories he had heard of an island to the north. Bimini, the Indians said, had a miraculous spring which restored a man's youth and vigor, and to Ponce, now fifty-two, the idea was most pleasing. If he seemed credulous, so were others. The Caribbean Indians had traveled in search of it many times, and even the Calusà believed that such a fountain of youth existed. Spanish historians of that day, Oviedo, who knew Ponce, and Gomara, both state that he went in search of "the fountain which rejuvenated or restored youth to old men" although he also expected to find gold and take slaves.

Traveling to Spain, Juan Ponce found King Ferdinand receptive and a bargain soon was struck wherein he would bear all the expenses of his own expedition while the king would get the treasure and some of the slaves. He was given a patent on February 23, 1512, with it the title of Adelantado, with powers of jurisdiction over the island of Bimini and for twelve years, one tenth of all the revenue and profits.

It took Ponce more than a year to settle his affairs and equip the expedition but, finally, on March 3, 1513, he set forth with two caravels and a brigantine to find Bimini.

As the head of an officially sanctioned expedition, Juan Ponce de Leon was required to submit his report in triplicate but no such document has been found in Spanish Archives, nor have the ship's log survived. Historians of the day wrote only briefly of his discoveries and it was not until 1601 that a detailed, day by day account of the voyages was published. It was contained in a ponderous volume, *Historia de los Hechos de los Castillanos*, by Antonio de Herrera, an official Spanish historian who had access to all the material in government files at that time. Although it is believed that some of the passages were interpolated by the author, it is considered the most authentic account known of the expedition to Florida.

Although their set course took them through the Bahamas, the ships somehow missed the small island of Bimini. Instead, on March 27, 1513, they sighted the Florida peninsula and, believing it to be their destination, sailed north along its east coast. It was April 2 when Ponce, searching for a harbor, decided upon a landing place and ordered the vessels to drop anchor not far from the mouth of today's St. Johns River. Sometime within the following six days, the company went ashore and claimed the land for the king of Spain, naming it *Pascua Florida* because it had been discovered during the Easter season.

The ships again set sail on April 8, skirting the shore in a northerly direction, but finding no end to it, they turned and sailed south, hugging the coast. It was April 20 when they sighted Indians on shore, and anxious to communicate with them and take on wood and water, the two caravels came in close while the brigantine, unable to anchor in the deeper, swiftly flowing water, drifted out of sight. The Indians called to them in a friendly manner but as the men stepped ashore, they were attacked with arrows and armed staves tipped with sharpened bone and fish spines. After one seaman was knocked unconscious by a clout on the head and two others were wounded, a retreat was ordered. Under cover of darkness, the caravels sailed off to the mouth of a river, there to await the brigantine.

Here again they were harassed, this time by sixty warriors, but the Spaniards managed to beat off the attackers and take a prisoner, an Ais Indian who would serve as their pilot. Ponce named the river *La Cruz* and left in it an inscribed rock, which has never been found.

On May 8, the small fleet rounded a point of land, now non-existent, which they called *Cape Corrientes* because of the swiftness of the currents which almost swept them past it. They anchored on the sheltered side near a village called *Abaioa* , leaving there to sail as far as two islands to the south, the larger one of which they named *Santa Marta*. Friday, May 13, they sailed on reaching an island they called *Pola* and two days later, they were passing the Florida Keys. The Indian told them that these islets were a place of suffering and because the rocks on them loomed like agonized men, Ponce named them *Los Martires*, the martyrs.

Proceeding up the Gulf Coast, the vessels already were within the territory of the Calusa, but because they were well out to sea, they were not observed. On May 23, they turned landward and the following day they coasted without landing to the south, as far as some islands which jutted out into the sea, and because it appeared that there was an entrance between them and the coast for ships, they came in to gather firewood and to careen the *San Cristoval.*

Since they were entering Calusa country, the projecting islands would be Captiva and Sanibel, but it is not known, exactly, where the men landed or by what route they reached San Carlos Bay. However, because inscribed rocks have been found (and lost again), which might, or might not have been genuine, we would speculate.

It is possible that the ships came in from the sea at Captiva Island and landed there, placing a small inscribed rock at its mid-section, or in a *boca* if The Narrows was then under water. Then, by means of some entrance, they came into Pine Island Sound and noting a sheltering hook of land on Pine Island's western shore, they dropped anchor. Here, they careened the *San Cristoval* and perhaps, as was his custom, Juan Ponce instructed that a rock (or rocks) be carved indicating

52

his presence.

Regardless of who carved them and when, the discovery of these mysterious rocks presents an interesting sidelight to island history. Shortly after 1900, Jesse Carter, exploring The Narrows on Captiva, found a slab of shell breccia about six inches long on which was carved, with a flourish, "Ponce de Leon—1513." Jesse took it home to show the family and it was around the house for many years. A visitor saw it and offered to take it north with him to find out if it was genuine. Many weeks passed and finally the slab was returned, broken in two as if by a hammer, with a brief note stating that it had no value. The family lost interest in it after that and when they moved from Captiva in 1921, the pieces were thrown out with the trash.

The Pine Island rocks were discovered about 1926. Fisherman Lee Willis and a group of friends were coon hunting on the sandflats behind a wide band of coastal mangroves when they came upon an enormous rock on the top of which was carved, "Ponce de Leon—1513." It was done in flowing style, the letters very worn and overgrown with moss. On other rocks nearby were a rough rendering of a sailing ship and an arrow pointing into the woods.

Many years later, Willis's son Robert met an anthropologist who was examining Gault Key and offered to show him the ship carving. Deeply engrossed in Calusa culture, the man declined. One year later, Hurricane Donna, roaring in with sand and silt, completely obliterated the Ponce rocks.

The *San Cristoval*, its hull cleaned of the barnacles and accretions of long weeks at sea, was back in the water ten days later and the men aboard the ships when the first Indians appeared and called to them. This time, in their new found wisdom, the Spaniards refused to be enticed ashore. When they raised their anchor to repair it, several warriors in canoes approached the vessel and tried to seize the anchor chain. Alarmed and angry, some of the sailors launched a boat and beating off the attackers, pursued them to the beach where they broke up some old canoes and took four women captive. For some reason, this seemed to "break the ice" and for a time, peace prevailed with a little bartering on the side.

On June 4, as Juan Ponce awaited a wind to go in search of the Calusa chief, * a Spanish-speaking native approached and told him that the *cacique* was sending gold for trade. As attention aboard the ships was thus diverted, war canoes put out from shore and once again, an attempt was made to raise the anchor chain of Ponce's ship, the Indians apparently hoping that a stiff breeze would cause it to drift ashore. Instead, another caravel bore down on them and several Indians were killed. In the wild melee that ensued, one Spaniard was mortally wounded by an arrow which pierced his armor, becoming the first casualty of the expedition. When the fracas ended, Ponce returned two prisoners as a peace overture, hoping, in vain, that their chief would confer with him.

The following day, the ships were moved to a pass in order to better defend them. There a battle erupted which lasted an entire day and at the end of it eighty Indians, who were the entire attacking force, were dead or had been carried away severely wounded. Because of the carnage, the Spaniards called the place *Matanza,* Massacre.

For the few days they remained, the Spaniards met no further resistance and Ponce led a small party on a superficial exploration of the mainland. But they found neither treasure nor mystic spring and after twenty-one days among the islands of Carlos, they pulled up anchor and sailed southward.

* Herrara calls this chief Carlos but probably his name was Stapana or Escampaba.

54

Before leaving the Gulf of Mexico, the ships dropped anchor off some tiny islets which Ponce named *Tortugas* because huge marine turtles were nesting there in great numbers. Here, they restocked their larder with turtle meat and eggs, sea birds and seafood then searched the Florida Keys and southeast coast for treasure. They found nothing there nor in the Bahamas, so the ship commanded by Juan Perez de Ortibia (with Anton de Aliminos as pilot) was sent to find the real Bimini, for now Ponce knew he had discovered a new land. On September 23, he returned to Puerto Rico. Older by some months, he had found no gold and few slaves.

Shortly after his return to Puerto Rico, Juan Ponce sailed for Spain where King Ferdinand warmly received him. Because he had added considerably to Spanish holdings in the New World, he was knighted, his coat of arms showing the three islands of Puerto Rico, Bimini and Florida. Ponce was made governor of the last two and with these rewards, he returned home. Organizing a force of men, he went in search of a band of Carib who had been harassing the colonials, but once again, all did not go as planned. He led his men into an ambush and was lucky to escape with his life. Leaving subordinantes to pursue the fleet-footed foe, he went into semi-retirement at his plantation.

Four years later, Francisco de Cordova set sail from Cuba with a single ship and 110 men. He had intended to explore Central America and trade there but when he arrived in Yucatan, he found the natives hostile. In the fight that erupted, several Spaniards were badly wounded and there seemed no alternative but to scrap the expedition and return home. They were en route to Cuba when a hurricane struck, severely damaging the vessel, and it became necessary to find some place to land. As it happened, Anton de Aliminos, pilot to

Juan Ponce de Leon, also was pilot to Cordova and he knew the Florida coastline as far as Sanibel and Captiva islands. Since the ship had been blown off course in that direction, he suggested that they continue that way and find a safe harbor, perhaps having in mind *Puerto de S. Nivel* at Sanibel's eastern end which he would have known as the best along that part of the coast.

There was a historian with the expedition, Bernal Diaz, who later wrote in his *Verdadera Historia* that they landed near an estuary which opened into the sea, a description which fits San Carlos Bay. Aliminos remarked that he had visited those parts before with Juan Ponce and the Indians had attacked them.

Mindful of the warnings of the pilot, lookouts were posted and those men able to work were sent ashore to dig a well. They had just finished it when the attack came, so silently that the sentry was overcome before he could warn the others. Warriors seized a landing craft but at the first cry of alarm, men from the ship swarmed ashore. There was a fierce battle and twenty-five Indians were killed before the rest of them withdrew. The Spaniards, mauled and weary, loaded their wounded aboard the ship and sailed for Cuba. En route, four more men died, among them Cordova, himself.

In 1519, other seafarers sailed into San Carlos Bay but they were only passersby. Four caravels under the command of Alonzo de Piñeda, seeking a passageway to Asia, cruised the Gulf as far as Vera Cruz in Mexico. He found that Florida was not, after all, an island but a continent, and in the process, delineated the coastline for mapmakers.

Other adverturers were exploring Florida's east coast and perhaps their exploits stirred Juan Ponce to organize his second expedition to establish a colony there and once again at his own expense, he equipped two vessels. Loaded with 250 soldiers, settlers, priests and Dominican friars; implements, seed, livestock, and about fifty horses, the two caravels were, in every sense of the word, tight little ships.

Armed with a patent given him by the new Spanish monarch, Charles I (who would become Charles V of the Holy Roman Empire) Juan Ponce set forth February 20, 1521. Foolishly returning to the very center of the Calusa kingdom, he brought the expedition into the deep channel of San Carlos Bay. Still rankling from their last encounter with him, which the Spaniards themselves had described as a massacre, the Indians watched as the white men disembarked onto a promontory at the mouth of the Caloosahatchee, but a few miles from their principal town. It would appear that this was Punta Rassa, the same landing place Menendez chose forty-six years later because currents and depths made it possible to get very close to shore.

The weary voyagers rested and refreshed themselves and within a few days began to build a settlement from which they planned to explore the interior by way of the broad and beautiful Caloosahatchee. For the Calusa, this was the signal to attack and they did so in force, apparently taking the colonists by surprise. Eighty Spaniards were killed and Ponce received an Indian arrow in his thigh, a wound that would prove mortal. By the time the battle was over, about twice as many Calusa had died but still they had won a victory for the decimated and demoralized settlers wanted only to escape. Loading their leaders and the rest of the injured onto the ships, they sailed for Puerto Principe, Cuba, and here the battle-scarred Ponce died.

Ponce de Leon's body was carried to Puerto Rico where his tomb is inscribed in Latin:

> "Beneath this tomb a strong Lion's bones repose and he surpassed in deeds the deeds of heroes."

57

But the lion was no match for the Florida wildcats and even after him, no single force or single disaster would conquer the ferocious Calusa. Juan Ponce opened the door, but it took many people, many things and many centuries to destroy the kingdom of Carlos.

Num. 53. Plano de las Provincias de la Florida. Por D. Juan Joseph Elix-
io de la Puente. Ano 1768. 1: Puerto de S. Nibel; 2: Voca de el Cautivo;
3: Puerto de Voca Grande.

By permission of Servicio Geografico y Historico del Ejercito. Madrid.

The Calusa Indians were a handsome people.

Chapter V

THE CALUSA KINGDOM

In the fall of 1545, two years after the ruinous end of the De Soto expedition, a small fleet of three ships put forth from Cartagena bound for Spain, loaded to the gunwales with passengers, silver bars and jeweled ceremonial objects taken from the temples of the Incas. Aboard a caravel were two sons of a well-to-do government official of the country now known as Colombia. Hernando d'Escalante Fontaneda, age thirteen, and his brother were to be educated in Spain and had with them twenty-five thousand dollars in gold.

A few days out of port, the fleet ran into heavy weather which developed into one of those roaring hurricanes for which the region is notorious. The vessels pitched and tossed in the wildly turbulent sea as a shrieking wind tore away rigging and superstructure and the crews tried in vain to keep control. Inevitably, they were blown toward the shipwreck coast, and there, like so many matchsticks, they broke up on the rocks of *Los Martires*.

Hernando d'Escalante and most of the other passengers were cast ashore more dead than alive amidst the scattered wreckage. By break of dawn, the storm had passed beyond them and in the serenity of the day that followed, they buried their dead and settled down uneasily to take stock of their situation. It was not long before the Tequesta Indians, vassals to the Calusa, had discovered them.

The castaways were taken prisoner and transported by canoe to the Bay of Carlos, the hub of the Calusa nation, and here, as was his custom, the *cacique* viewed the goods and people and decided which of it would be his and which he would bestow on lesser chiefs.

It was well known that the Florida Indians made human sacrifices to their gods and probably most of the men eventually died this way. But many of the women were spared to become wives to the warriors, and although no mention is made of his brother, the child, Escalante, was taken in tow by the royal household and became a favored slave of King Carlos I.

Hernando d'Escalante Fontaneda was a prisoner of the Indians of Florida for seventeen years, the first nine of which he spent in the service of Carlos. Presumably, he lived at the principal city of Calos on Mound Key although he frequently accompanied that great chief as he traveled afar to attend to the business of his vast territory.

When he was twenty-two, Fontaneda was given to a vassal chief, Oathxacua, whose east coast kingdom was in the vicinity of Cape Canaveral. Here, in 1562, or perhaps a year or two later, he was liberated along with another survivor of the same shipwreck by Rene Laudonniere, the French explorer who helped Jean Ribault establish the French Protestant colony of Ft. Caroline near present day St. Augustine. He effected the release of the Spaniards by offering beads, mirrors and trinkets to any Indian who would bring in bearded prisoners, and within a few days, the hirsute Hernando and his equally hairy companion arrived at the camp. One of the men had secreted almost a half pound of gold in his knee-length hair and this, in gratitude, he presented to Laudonniere. Since they had lived as Indians, the food and clothing seemed strange at first, but they were ecstatic at their delivery. When they cut their hair, they saved it to show back in Spain.

The Spaniards told Laudonniere all they knew of Florida and its Indians and he was much impressed. Anxious for them to relate this to those planning a New World colony, he left at once for France, taking the men with him. One of them was taken directly to Paris where Queen Catherine de Medici and the Cardinal of Bourbon questioned him closely. After the French court had left the city, the Spanish ambassador, Frances de Alava, spirited him away to Spain.

Pedro Menendez de Aviles was organizing his expedition to Florida at that time and Fontaneda joined it as interpreter. He eventually returned to Carlos Bay but his relationship with the great colonizer was not friendly. In his *Memoir* which he published in Spain in 1574, he claimed Menendez never paid him, even though he had once saved the life of the Adelantado by revealing a plot against him.

Fontaneda's account of his life among the Indians, addressed to King Phillip II, deals with shipwrecks, conquistadors, Florida geography, Indians and the personal complaints of the author. Considering his opportunity to observe the Calusa at short range, information on them is disappointingly sparse, perhaps because he held them in very low regard. Nevertheless, some very pertinent facts emerge and the *Memoir* is a very valuable document.

The name, variously spelled Carlos, Calos, Calusa and Caloosa, meant fierce, brave and skillful which they were. Their territory extended south from Charlotte Harbor to the outer islands of the Florida Keys and inland to Lake Okeechobee, which the Indians called Mayaimi. At the height of their power, they were more than four thousand strong and controlled the southern end of the Florida peninsula.

The Calusa chief ruled fifty towns and the east coast

tribes of Ais, Jeaga and Tequesta were vassals who paid him tribute. As each accepted him as "king," the presiding chief presented him with a wife, often a daughter or sister. In this way, they honored him and showed their subservience, at the same time, creating a ruling class which was interrelated. These relationships were further complicated by sibling marriages for the ruling chief, *e.g.* Carlos, was required by tribal custom to marry one of his sisters. This created rival factions but the chiefship usually was passed down from father to son.

Before the coming of the white men, the Calusa lived much as their ancestors had, their diet leaning heavily to fish and seafood with some game, roots and wild fruits. They used earthenware pots, baskets and a great variety of utensils fashioned from shells, bone and wood. As befitted the climate, they were scantily clad, the men wearing breechcloths of plaited palm or dressed deer hide and the women, short aprons woven of Spanish moss which still grows at the sites of old settlements.

While their essential clothing was simple, their ornamentation was not, judging from the large amount of personal paraphernalia found by the Pepper-Hearst Expedition of 1896. When they chose, they could lavishly bedeck themselves and after shipwrecks brought such things to their shores, they hung strips of silver and gold from neck, waist and knees as they went through their often frenzied dances. Sometimes quite overdoing it, the celebrants could hardly move for the weight of these precious metals.

For no apparent reason other than cosmetic, they painted their bodies red, and let their hair grow very long, wearing it tied up or back. Warriors had long sharp fingernails probably to use as weapons, but neither men nor women disfigured themselves and the Spaniards considered them handsome people, the men big with fine physiques and the women well-proportioned with "good countenances." This description was expanded to "beautiful" in the case of *Cacique* Carlos' principal wife, whose grace and gentle charm was not lost on them. Her appearance at a banquet honoring Menendez, February 1566, quite impressed the historian of that expedition:

> "She was twenty years old, very comely and beautiful with very good features, she had very fine hands and eyes, and looked from one side to another with much gravity and all modesty; she had a very good figure, for even among the many Indian women who were there seen to be handsome, not one was as handsome as that one; her eyebrows were very well marked, and she wore at her throat a very beautiful collar of pearls and stones and a necklace of gold beads; she was naked like the other, the *cacique's* sister, with only a covering in front."*

The warlike Calusa were artistically gifted, their woodcarving unsurpassed by any tribe on America's east coast and rivaling that of the Indians of the Pacific Northwest. Their tools were ingenious as well as beautiful and with them they turned out everything from dugout canoes to sacred ceremonial objects. Architecturally, the terraced settlements on shell mounds served by canals were well suited to their marine-oriented environment. Probably for reasons of protection, the most important towns were on islands and the largest of them had perhaps thirty-six houses with a population of two hundred people. Each large settlement was crowned with a temple and a tribal meeting house or palace which was sometimes very large. At the

---

* Jeannette T. Conner, *Pedro Menendez de Aviles Memorial* by Solis de Meras. P. 147.

reception in honor of Menedez, Spanish historians on the scene estimated that there were one thousand people within the palace of the *Cacique* Carlos and half as many directly outside it. The building had windows and contained interior platforms on which the chief and his sister were seated. Assuming it was as other south Florida Indian structures, it was built of timber, thatched and open at one end as are present day Seminole chickees.

But it was not artistry that kept the Calusa free. They were great warriors with a variety of weapons which included spears, "saber clubs" which were both club and atlatl, war clubs, stilettos made of bone, and a sort of tomahawk made with a large whelk shell with drilled holes through which was thrust a wooden handle. Anthropologist Frank Cushing found no bows and believed that arrows were shot from a curved shooting stick or atlatl.

While the Spaniards held sway over them, guns, metal swords and knives are withheld from the Calusa and Menendez would have gone much further. He recommended to his king that they be taken into slavery to protect shipwreck victims, but added, in fairness:

> "They are so bloodthirsty in this because they consider it a great glory and victory for them, and that other caciques of the interior may hold a high opinion of them and they may triumph, saying that they live on the seashore and are the masters of the Christians and hold them as slaves. They follow this custom because they consider it the pious and natural order of things . . . "*

Fontaneda also believed that the Calusa had to be ensalved and he claimed to have saved many Christians

* Jeanette T. Conner. *Colonial Records of Spanish Florida*, Vol. I P. 35.

with his intervention. Nevertheless, he tells of the *cacique* asking him why the captives were so disobedient and after being told that they did not understand the commands, no more of them were killed for that reason.

The Calusa worshipped three main gods, the most powerful of which ruled over such things as celestial movements and the weather. Under him were two other gods, one concerned with the affairs of the kingdom and the other with war. There were certain set holidays and religious festivals to honor each but it seems the celebration of the harvest was the most dreaded by the Christian captives. Each year, one of them would be sacrificed, his head lopped off, and with much dancing about, presented to the idol of the fruits of the earth which was believed to feed on the eyes. When Menendez finally came to rescue them, there were but twelve prisoners left alive of the more than two hundred who had fallen into Calusa hands over a twenty-year period. However, before white men were deposited on their shore, Calusa and other Florida Indians made human sacrifices of prisoners of war or even their own people. When the son of a great chief died, he was accompanied into the spirit world by some of the children of his subjects and when a *cacique* or his wife died, servants were put to death to serve them.

The tribe had what anthropologists call an intricate death complex which included burial mounds, secondary interments and these human sacrifices. On Sanibel there was a "colony of the dead" within a mortuary lake or lagoon (in which all of the bones were broken or dismembered) on Tarpon Bay and others on all three islands, Sanibel, Captiva and Buck Key. They suggest that, like the Timacua, there was a sort of mortuary removed from the town where corpses were left to decompose, then the skeletons broken or dismembered and buried in mounds reserved for that purpose, some exclusively for children.

The shamans were all powerful, and were sorcerers, priests and medicine men. The temples, the sacred objects and the celebration of the holidays were all their responsiblity. At the beginning of summer, which probably was harvest time as it is for the Seminole, these witch-doctors donned grotesque horned masks and ran through the villages day and night shrieking and howling like wild beasts. On quieter occasions, they wore masks emblematic of the deities and paraded, led by women singing.

The ruling chief was a semi-religious figure believed to have supernatural powers, his sorcery insuring the tribe of the continuing bounty of earth and sea. He retired at fixed intervals to a house away from the town and there, with two or three friends, practiced his magic. Taboos were such that no one came near for fear of being put to death.

Ceremonials surrounded the Florida Indians, not the least of which was the brewing and serving of the sacred *cassine* which white men called "the black drink." The Timacua, Jaega and Ais tribes were known to have used it and we assume the Calusa did also since stained utensils for that purpose were found on Marco. A noxious liquid, difficult to keep down, it was believed, erroneously, to be made from the leaves of a shrub common to the sandy shores of Florida, yaupon, which consequently was named *Ilex vomitoria.* Wild foods expert Euell Gibbons insists that the name maligns this plant, pointing out that tea made from it is mildly stimulating, wholesome and delicious. The emetic concocted by the Indians, probably in secret, must have contained other ingredients.

The purpose of the *cassine* drinking ceremony, used at council meetings by the Timacua, seems to have been to separate the stronger stomachs from the weaker ones and so prove—what? Indian lore is full of mysteries.

When a Spanish garrison was established on Mound

Key in 1566, the Calusa, for the first time in their history, were open to the scrutiny of the civilized world. At that time, their chief was Carlos II, twenty-five years old, a big man, handsome, intelligent, crafty and imperious. As his father before him, he was rich and powerful, ruling over fifty towns which included a colony of Cuban Indians who had come in very ancient times in search of the miraculous spring and youth-giving stream which Fontaneda called the River Jordan.*

It was the custom of the tribe to be known by the name of its chief and Carlos I was thought by the Spaniards to have taken the name of their king, Charles V, because he was a powerful monarch and the *cacique* wished to identify with him. It is more likely, however, that the name that sounded like Carlos to them already had been used in its various forms some time before their coming.

Pedro Menendez sought to convert the Calusa rather than conquer them and the man on whom this burden fell was an erudite, conscientious Jesuit priest, Father Juan Rogel, whose letters to his superior give much insight into the character of the Calusa and the events which led up to the abandonment of Fort San Anton.

We learn with no surprise that the Calusa were "energetic, turbulent and intractable" but the good padre also believed that they were more sinned against than sinning. "For wherever we Spaniards go," he wrote, "we are so proud and haughty that we crush all before us. Thus the soldiers at the fort have begun to treat the natives as if they had been conquered in war. They so abuse and oppress them that the Indians refuse to tolerate it." He complained that while he had his hands full with the Calusa who were "so untamed, restless and evil beyond belief," these problems were

---

* According to his *Memoir* (p. 29), so did Juan Ponce. "It is cause for merriment, that (he) went to Florida to find the River Jordan."

nothing compared to his trials in trying to keep the soldiers from harming them.*

The Calusa, perhaps even more than other Florida Indians, were free spirits, proud, intelligent and emotional. Family ties and loyalties ran deep and hoping to Christianize them, Menendez sent young people to Cuba to be educated. Still, labor in the vineyard of the Lord proved very unproductive. While Father Rogel made small gains in the beginning, it soon became apparent that the faltering faith of his little flock waxed and waned in direct proportion to the available cornmeal.

Nor could Carlos be molded or manipulated. He tried one abortive plot after another to rid himself of the Spanish occupiers until finally his machinations became intolerable to Menendez. Captain Reynoso, the fort's commander, was ordered to dispose of him. As Father Rogel pleaded in vain to save them, Carlos and twenty of his principal chiefs were lured into the fort on the pretense of a conference and there set upon and beheaded.

The execution of Carlos sent shock waves the whole length and breadth of south Florida and undoubtedly marked the beginning of the end of Spanish influence there. The Spaniards chose Don Felipe, nephew of Senquene and adopted son of the chief before him, to succeed Carlos but he proved as obstinate as his relative and refused to become a Christian unless he was permitted to marry his sister, as tribal law decreed. Hated and feared, only Spanish support kept him in power. In spring, 1568, Don Felipe put fifteen rebellious chiefs to death and when Rogel and his party returned from Cuba a few weeks later, they found the Indians dancing about with the heads of four more.

---

* Ruben Vargas Ugarte, "First Jesuit Mission in Florida," U.S. Catholic Historical Studies, XXV. P. 82.

Don Felipe had a very short reign. When he got out of hand, the Spaniards executed him and it seems that a cousin of Carlos, Don Pedro, became chief. By that time, however, it didn't matter, for the Calusa, completely demoralized, burned their town on Mound Key and fled into the forest. Since the soldiers could not subsist without the labor and help of the Indians, Menendez ordered them to St. Augustine and the fort of San Anton was abandoned. When the Spaniards sailed from Carlos Bay, about three years from the day of their arrival, the curtain fell between the Calusa and the outside world. For Menendez, beset by monumental problems with his east coast colonies, had neither the resources nor inclination to concern himself further with southwest Florida.

With the departure of their overlords, tribal wounds were healed, Calos was rebuilt and for more than a hundred years, the Calusa thrived, prospered and forged ahead, reaching the climax of their culture around the middle of the 17th century. With metal tools and skills learned from the Spaniards, who had intermarried with them, their highly developed art improved and expanded to include cast silver, glass blowing, cult objects of gold, silver and copper and incised, cutout and embossed sheet metal ornaments.

Eventually, they began a working relationship with Cuban fishermen, which would explain the survival of the very old Spanish place names, and ocasionally there was some contact with Spanish officialdom. In 1612, Governor Juan de Olivera sent Lieutenant Juan Rodrigues de Cartaya and twenty soldiers to scout out their activites. The launch dropped anchor near the palace of the chief and they were greeted by more than sixty canoes filled with Indians bearing gifts. The chief himself, riding in splendor in a canoe paddled by forty braves, warmly welcomed them and presented the lieutenant with two gold *chaguales*, an ornament worn on the forehead, weighing about two ounces each. A Negro who had been a shipwreck victim was turned over to the Spaniards along with the promise to free any other castaways who might fall into their hands. Exalting in his reception, Lieutenant de Cartaya recommended in his report that missionaries be sent to Calos but such a day was not yet at hand.

The son of the *cacique*, three ranking chiefs and fifteen warriors came to St. Augustine in 1688 to confer with the governor and during their amicable meeting were given gifts. Pressed to receive missionaries, however, they continued to demur and so matters remained until November 1697, when five Franciscan friars decided to take matters into their own hands.

They arrived at night and hoping to impress the idolaters, they proceeded to march with cross and candles in solemn procession through the town of Calos. Taking one horrified look at the hooded, shrouded figures, the Indians, in panic, took to the woods. The next night, however, they were better prepared for the spooky invasion. As the monks once again entered the village, braves sprang from the shadows brandishing hatchets and, with wild yells, they tore the clothing from the terrified men, who raced, naked and unnerved, back to their boats. Badly shaken but unharmed, the would-be missionaries finally reached Matacumbe Key where Christian Indians took pity on them and helped them return to their own people. This was the first and last Franciscan attempt to Christianize the untamed Calusa.

Trade with Cuba continued to increase and the Calusa freely came and went from Havana, a twenty-four hour trip from Key West. They were permitted this privilege in exchange for their promise to allow fourteen missionaries to work among them, but there is no indication that these men ever arrived.

Meanwhile, the Indians traded fish, pelts, tree bark, fruits and cardinal birds in cages, a favorite pet of

72

Spanish sailors who paid from six dollars to ten dollars a piece for them. Indian commerce for the month of March, 1698, amounted to more than eighteen thousand pesos or $17,000, a figure that would include all of the tribes. The Calusa were held in very low esteem and a historian of that time, Barcia, remarked that while they had been exposed to Spaniards for some time, they still went nearly naked, wearing their long hair tied back, and, if anything, were more barbarous than ever, "drawn by their own instincts toward all the abominable vices."*

The Cuban traders were not permitted to sell firearms and heavy weapons to the Calusa but far more deadly were the terrible diseases which they transmitted to the previously isolated natives. As the islands were opened to commerce, so was a whole Pandora's Box of deadly illnesses and the Indians died by the hundreds of smallpox, chicken pox, measles, tuberculosis and yellow fever. In a vain attempt to quarantine, the sick were taken to some isolated area to die apart, one such place being Fisherman's Key off Punta Rassa where workmen digging shell for a road in 1913 unearthed hundreds of whole skeletons lying in positions that would indicate that they had been overcome by some terrible calamity. Another such find was made in Tampa during the Florida boom and these bones, too, were dated to the late 17th century suggesting that epidemics swept through this coast at that time.

Disease began the deterioration of the Calusa nation as diminished in numbers and power they became the victims, once again, of slave hunters, this time invading Yamassee Indians led by the English. In 1704, there were perhaps twenty-five thousand Florida Indians; by 1840 they were virtually extinct, the semi-civilized

* Anthony Kerrigan, "Chronological History of the Continent of Florida," by Andres de Barcia, P. 52.

Apalachee the first to go. Gov. James Moore of South Carolina led these raids into Spanish-Indian territory and in the succeeding years Lower Creek Indians, who were promised land, and renegades and adventurers attracted by the lucrative slave trade, combined forces.

It was inevitable that the broad Caloosahatchee would become a target for the slave hunters who moved up the stream quietly paddling their canoes. Then, as one would capture wild animals, they seized the unwary Indians—men, women and children—as they fished or collected firewood. Some of the Calusa escaped to hide in the Big Cypress, some fled to the Florida Keys but many hundreds were taken into slavery. In 1709, Lt. Nairne, notorious for his forays along the St. Johns River, informed the Earl of Sunderland that the Indians under his control had to go as far as "the point of Florida" in quest of booty. In 1712, the Calusa and others made their last stand on the island now known as Key West. Some escaped to Cuba in seventeen canoes but most died defending themselves. Spaniards of a later date, finding there a vast area strewn with human bones, named the place *Cayo Hueso*, Island of Bones.

Today's Mikasuki Indians, of the Seminole tribe, have in their oral tradition the story of the last years of the real Florida Indians. According to this, their predecessors were called by the general name of yathampa:Li:, "bad people," because they killed Seminole, and of these, vaguely remembered, are kalasa:Li:, Calusa, whose river was kalashahci, Caloosahatchee. The kalasa:Li: were believed to be Spanish and their name often was used as a synonym for Spaniard.

The Bad People spoke a language different from the Seminole dialects and they were "wild," moving silently and easily through the swamps of their country. They were first seen coming out of the water at Pine Island in the form of fiddler crabs, and later on, were found by the Spaniards with whom they became closely allied. The Bad People girls were pretty and many married Spanish men and went to live at a hammock called Hanging Skirt which was ten miles southwest of Ocala. In time, all or most of the (Pine Island) Bad People came to live at that settlement and there they were given guns and supplies and taught how to plant corn.

To the north and just two days walking distance from this Spanish-Indian settlement was a Seminole town called in Muskogee Two Hickory Trees Stand Up and for many years the people of the two places traded peacefully and even intermarried, the Seminole husband, as was the custom, then joining his wife's family in Hanging Skirt. But eventually the Spaniards turned the Bad People against their neighbors and after a series of incidents, the Seminole attacked Hanging Skirt and in a fierce, hard-fought battle which lasted four days, they were victorious. However, they were unaware that gunpowder was stored there and after they had set fire to the village a terrified Negro emerged to warn them that the whole place was about to blow up. Explode it did and after that, what was left of Hanging Skirt became known as Broken Big Explosion!

Most of the people of the town were killed but the Bad People who survived the raid fled south pursued by Seminole who took prisoners and sold them to white people for knives, lead and powder. In one instance, they overtook a family and after killing the father, they sold his wife for five dollars and his small daughters for two dollars and fifty cents each.

A few Bad People who escaped their enemies crossed the Peace River and settled in a place about fifteen miles south of Clewiston where they built canoes and used the old mounds as a dancing place. The site of this settlement is now known in English as Tony's Mound because after the Calusa had gone, a Seminole nicknamed "Sells Tony" (because he did once) cultivated a garden there.

Opinions differ as to when the Calusa ceased to be. Bernard Romans observed an old Indian field on Key Largo in 1769 and refers to the Florida Keys as "the last retreats, and skulking places, of the Calusa savages, when their more potent neighbors, the Creeks, drove them off the continent." He says that the last remnants of them, about eighty families, emigrated to Havana in 1763. William Barton wrote in 1774, however, that he was told by an old Creek of northern Florida that there was a Calusa town called Calusa-hatchee near Carlos Bay, but in 1799, Benjamin Hawkins lists "Cull-oo-sau-hat-che" with the towns of the "Simenolies." Probably, this was the town once called Muspa which by 1832 had become the site of a Spanish fishery employing "Spanish Indians."

In 1932, Frances Densmore, who lived and worked among the Mikasuki Indians, recorded seventeen Calusa songs sung by the so-called Medicine Man of Cow Creek. The old man said that the songs came from captive Bad People, the Spanish-speaking "mountain (mound?) men" whom the white people called Calusa. Anthropologist John Goggin believed that the last of these captives were absorbed into the tribe about 1840 and their influence can be seen in the Seminole Chickees which are remarkably similar to the Calusa dwellings and very different from the wooden-sided, bark-shingled houses once used by the Seminoles of northern Florida. Also, the change in settlement pattern from large towns to small camps could have been on the advice of the Calusa who had found them better for reasons of defense as well as the practical aspect of supplying food for fewer people.

The Mikasuki-Seminole claim not to know what was the ultimate end of the Calusa but they have their legends. They say that some went down the Shark River to Cuba where they settled, others up north to intermarry with whites and a fair number were captured and sold. However, there are those who believe that there are still Bad People around somewhere in the Everglades, but that they are invisible. Others say they are there, all right, wild and free, but not invisible. It's just that they look like deer.

Menendez is greeted by Chief Carlos.

Chapter VI

PEDRO MENENDEZ AND THE FORT OF SAN ANTON

On the 14th of February, 1566, as a brigantine of the fleet of Pedro Menendez neared Sanibel Island, the men aboard observed a canoe with a lone occupant put out from shore. As it drew near, a man dressed as an Indian hailed them in Spanish and drawing alongside, he told the astonished sailors that he was a Christian, one of many captives held by the *cacique*, Carlos. He had been waiting for them for eight days, for one of their number had been told in a dream that rescue was near.

When he boarded the ship he showed them a cross, which he called his letter, and eloquently pleaded for the ships to enter the harbor and liberate the other prisoners. The Adelantado, arriving at that moment on another brigantine, heard this story and, deeply moved, he fell to his knees before a cross, as did his men. He believed that his prayers had been answered for part of his mission was to emancipate all Christian captives held by the Calusa and seek word of his son Don Juan who had been shipwrecked some years before.

Pedro Menendez de Aviles, seafarer, colonizer and administrator, was born in the mountainous seacoast area of northern Spain where, at the tender age of fourteen, he ran off to sea and participated in fighting against the corsairs who then ranged the coast. It was the beginning of a lifetime of distinguished service to Spain and an illustrious career from which he would reap great honors, but few solid rewards, monetary or otherwise. He was a brilliant man who had invented and received a ten-year patent on a device to measure longitude, a compelling leader, and an educated aristocrat who delighted equally in good music and the rough and rousing life of seafarer turned soldier-explorer. He was ethical, honest and deeply religious, yet all his life he nursed a great hatred for Protestants and unmercifully waged war on them.

Menendez was thirty-five years old when King Phillip appointed him to the post of Captain General of the Armada of the Indies, over the protests of the *Casa de la Contratacion* which governed the American trade and traditionally chose its own man. Because of this, he incurred its enmity and was severely hampered in his efforts to colonize Florida.

In 1565, concerned by the threat posed by the French colonists on Florida's east coast to his country's dominance, the Spanish monarch sent his Captain-General to clear out the interlopers, but since the two countries were officially friendly, his instructions were private and precise. Menendez was to search the coast as far north as Newfoundland for settlers and corsairs of any nation not subject to Spain and destroy them in any way he saw fit. Also, under a patent of March 20, 1565, he was to colonize this new land and was given the titles of Adelantado, Governor, and Captain General of Florida. Accordingly, mostly at his own expense, he equipped six sloops, four smaller vessels and a large ship on which to carry five hundred colonists, one hundred of whom would be soldiers, one hundred sailors, one hundred artesans and one hundred married couples. Also included were monks and Jesuit priests.

In spite of heavy storms, the armada reached a point north of Cape Canaveral on August 25, 1565, and three days later on the feast of St. Augustine, they entered a harbor and deposited some of the colonists on shore to establish the first permanent settlement in the continental United States. This thye named San Augustin and after resting there for several days, the Adelantado set out on foot with men and artillery for Fort Caroline, some fifty miles away.

Pedro Menendez was a man of great talent, even genius, and was resourceful, efficient and completely incorruptible but with one great flaw: he was a pious and vicious bigot. To him, the Lutherans were an evil and detestable sect and destroying them was as wiping out a pestilence. As he intended, the garrison was taken by surprise. The Spanish forces met virtually no opposition as they went about the coldblooded massacre of 142 settlers, sparing only women and girls, boys under fifteen years of age, and those men who professed to be Catholic. Then, ordering that the fort be repaired and a chapel constructed of the timbers of a French galley, Menendez named it San Mateo, and spending no more time there, he set out to find Jean Ribault, Fort Caroline's commander, whose ill-timed departure in search of the Spaniards had spelled the doom of French colonial hopes in Florida.

Ribault and his men had put to sea but, as fate would have it, they ran into a storm and were shipwrecked. The Spaniards, happily assured that God was, indeed, on their side, rounded up the castaways in two separate forays and executed them. However, there were special courtesies for the captain and eight of his top men, who, for a day or more, were wined and dined as they tried in vain to ransom their lives. Then, bound and led to a remote spot among the sand dunes, they were given one last chance to confess their sins and embrace the Catholic faith. But this the Frenchmen would not do. With his last breath, Jean Ribault spoke quiet words of courage and faith in his God. Then, as he and his

81

comrades sang a Protestant hymn, they were "put to the knife."

Sailing southward to Cape Canaveral, the Spanish forces then wiped out the last remnants of French colonists on peninsular Florida, all of which Pedro Menendez reported to his king, who was most pleased. While it was a time in history when Catholic and Protestants looked for reasons to destroy each other, the whole bloody affair undoubtedly blurs the picture of the great missionary-colonizer. Nothing could restore his tarnished image, nor that of King Phillip II, who would tell Catherine de Medici, Queen of France, that he knew nothing of it. As might be expected, Fort Caroline would be avenged.

Finding the Ais Indians on Florida's southeast coast friendly to them, the Spaniards established a third garrison there, Santa Lucia, then returned to Havana where Pedro Menendez Marquez, nephew of the Adelantado, awaited with reinforcements. The Cuban governor, Garcia Osorio, was sourly uncooperative as usual, but Menendez chose not to feud with him. Writing his king of all that had transpired, he notified him of his intention to build another fort in the Bay of Juan Ponce.

In this letter of December 25, 1565, he asked that the monarch send supplies by his nephew, who would personally bear the letter to court, sailing for Spain as soon as it was penned. He would need, he said, ". . . a thousand leather wine bags holding from three quarters to one gallon, two thousand sandals for the people who travel discovering, certain trade goods for the Indians, some tools to cultivate the land, saddles and bridles for horses, and some farmers with their wives." On February 10, he was ready to sail with five vessels and five hundred men for Florida's west coast.

The appearance of Spanish ships in the bay would come as no surprise to Carlos for the Ais were a kindred tribe and Indian intelligence worked well. Nor could any ship approach with stealth along the southern coast of his territory, much less pass Point Ybel and enter the harbor. Eyes watched as the brigantines approached Punta Rassa where deep water and favorable currents permitted them to anchor so close to shore that men disembarked by leaping—and no one wet a shoe.

Menendez had been well-briefed on the war-like character of the Calusa and his men were armed and ready. But he had come not as a conquerer but a colonizer and it was his burning desire to Christianize the Florida Indians. Therefore, he sent the captive to inform Carlos that he had arrived with gifts and wished to be received by him.

The *Cacique* appeared the following day with an entourage of three hundred armed warriors and was conducted to a place of honor on a platform erected for the occasion. Menendez, resplendent in uniform, disembarked and after the formal greetings, seated himself beside this stalwart young king who ruled all of the tribes of south Florida. Thirty arquebusiers stood by with fuses lighted and the ships, cannons were trained on the assemblage, but Carlos did not intend a confrontation at that time. Instead, he knelt before the Adelantado and turned the palms of his hands upward. On his upturned hands and those of each of the chiefs who followed, Menendez placed his. This was the traditional act of reverence and subjection paid by the Calusa to their superiors.

When this ceremony was over, the Spanish leader presented gifts to all of the Indians and Carlos, handsome in elegant, new clothes, reciprocated with bars of silver salvaged from shipwrecks. It was the honey and biscuits the young chief particularly liked, however, and he suggested that more of the same would be most welcome. Menendez, of course, immediately offered it, but explaining that he had not enough for the whole company, he hustled Carlos and twenty of his principal men aboard a brigantine—and the trap was sprung.

The Indians reacted uneasily as the ship moved out from shore and as an armed Spaniard moved behind each one of them, they recognized their predicament. Feast there was, and more gifts, but afterward, the bad news. Menendez announced that they were hostages for the Christians held by the Calusa and told Carlos that he must deliver them or die. As always, he offered concessions. He promised to be friend and "Elder Brother" to them—a sobriquet that would be broadly interpreted.

Outnumbered and out-foxed, Carlos had no alternative but to send some of his men to fetch the shipwreck victims and within an hour, five women and three men came aboard. Amidst tears of joy, they were welcomed, fed and clothed.

For reasons not explained, the children born of Indian marriages were not included, nor did there seem to be any prospect that they would be. In the end, two of the Spanish women returned to their Indian homes and their children rather than abandon them. The infusion of Spanish blood and Spanish ways apparently began with the first shipwreck.

The next day, Carlos sent word that he wished to receive the Adelantado at his palace at Mound Key. The reception planned, however, was not entirely friendly. There would be a big welcome, a former captive warned, with singing and waving of palms. Then, as a mark of respect, each man would be carried on the back of an Indian toward the village—but not all the way. Warriors, already ambushed where the trail passed through a thicket of trees, waited to kill every one of them.

So forewarned, Menendez declined to enter the canoe sent for him and, instead, boarded his ship and sailed the short distance to the entrance of Estero Bay. When he signalled that he wished to come ashore, no one appeared. Carlos, aware that his plot had gone awry, skulked in his palace.

It was past time for the other ships to arrive and since they had not, the adelantado decided to search for them in a harbor farther north, today's Tampa Bay, where more captives were thought to be held.

He found no Christian captives and, returning to Carlos Harbor, he saw the missing ships at anchor. The men were bartering with the Indians and business was brisk as the soldiers and sailors made small fortunes trading scissors, knives and even playing cards for silver and gold salvaged from shipwrecks.

The captains now realized what a fabulous fortune Carlos must have and when he came aboard to confer with the adelantado, they urged that he be held for ransom. Menendez refused to do this, even though he was deeply in debt. According to his code, it would be "an act of knavery" and doom his chances to Christianize the Calusa.

Nevertheless, the game of cat and mouse continued between them and it would seem that Carlos was next to score. He informed his "elder brother" that since they were now friends, he would present him with a bride—his own sister and one of his wives. She would go to Cuba with others and learn to be a Christian and upon her return, he and all his people would embrace the same faith. In order that the Adelantado might meet the lady and the other royal wives, he invited him to a banquet in his honor the following day and departed.

Menendez arrived at the palace with an impressive entourage. The two hundred arquebusiers, with fuses lighted, were stationed outside while the adelantado and twenty of his gentlemen entered the great hall. Food and wine, even a table with cloth and napkins, were carried up the hill, and because he was seldom without them, Menendez brought his musicians. One man carried his psalter, another a harp and there were

85

drummers, a violinist, three trumpeters, two fifers and, at the end of the procession, a very small dwarf who sang and danced very well.

The expedition's historian tells us that the palace of Carlos was enormous, accommodating perhaps two thousand people, and that there were large windows in the throne room from which one could see a great assemblage outside. Carlos received his guests seated on a dais and nearby, on a slightly lower platform was an ordinary looking young woman of about thirty-five whom Menendez took to be the chief's wife. This, however, was not the case for the quietly dignified lady, wearing only a single necklace and dressed only in a brief apron woven of Spanish moss, was Carlos's sister, and unbeknownst to the Governor, Captain-General and Adelantado of Florida—his prospective bride.

Rising, Carlos put the guest of honor in his place and after the ceremonial show of obeisance, he seated himself next to him. Below them seated on the floor were about one thousand people, half of them women, while outside five hundred girls between the ages of ten and fifteen now began to dance. Everyone seemed extremely happy and eventually, they all danced but the favorite wife of Carlos had not appeared. Menendez had heard that she was young, about twenty, and very beautiful and he had armed himself with a piece of paper on which were written the Indian words for the compliments he would pay her. He asked Carlos to bring the girl to the hall and she soon was seated beside him. Perhaps overly so, he directed his attention to her, his carefully coached remarks bringing such smiles and blushes that her jealous husband soon had had enough, and ordered her to leave. At the Adelantado's insistence, she was permitted to stay to receive her gifts but it is doubtful that she ever appeared again. Besides the risk of losing her, Carlos wanted his sister to receive the full attention of Menendez.

When the meal was served, Indian servants brought several kinds of fish, roasted and boiled, and oysters, both raw and cooked, while the Spaniards added wine, honey and biscuits, quince preserves and sweetmeats. As they dined, the musicians played , the dwarf danced and several Spanish gentlemen sang the songs of their native land. Carlos hushed his company and they listened, rapt, to the sound of the strange and beautiful music.

It had been a festive and enjoyable day when Menendez finally rose to make his farewells, but Carlos was not yet ready to speed the parting guest. The intent of the occasion had been to celebrate the bethrothal of the Adelantado and his sister, hence the joy of the Indians, and the chief now wished the union to be finalized. It was time, he told the thunderstruck Spaniard, to take his new "wife" to the bridal chamber, for to fail to do so would insult his sister, himself and the four thousand people of his kingdom, who surely would interpret his reluctance as scorn and ridicule of the Calusa nation.

Carlos, obviously, was immovable and the Spaniards outnumbered and helpless. The tables had been turned and Pedro Menendez, family man and good Catholic, could do nothing at all about it. Nevertheless, he tried. Nervously, through an interpreter, he told the young *cacique* that Christian men could not sleep with non-Christian women, but this Carlos brushed aside. Pointing out that since the Adelantado was his elder brother, it followed that he, his sister and all his people were then, through this relationship, Christians.

Menendez then delivered a sermon of Christian beliefs, God and the devil, heaven and hell, to which Carlos listened intently. Then, with characteristic candor, he remarked that since he had observed that the Spaniards' customs, their music and their food were all superior to his, then their religion must be also and he wished to adopt it.

Out-maneuvered, the reluctant bridegroom had no choice but to take the compliant young woman, with her retinue of Indians, to his ship lying at anchor outside Estero Bay. Here he consulted at great length with his captains and the consensus was that to antagonize the Calusa at this point would seriously jeopardize the whole undertaking and Christianizing them would become impossible. Although Menendez would have much preferred to search further for an alternative, at the urging of his men, he faced up to the situation with Christian fortitude and with the great efficiency characteristic of him, he planned his Indian wedding.

Bathed and suitably gowned by the Christian women aboard the ship, the Indian princess now seemed more acceptable and with due ceremony she was baptized and named Doña Antonia in honor of San Anton to whom Menendez had prayed for success of his mission. The Adelantado had tents set up on shore and here the wedding supper took place with music and merriment which lasted until two o'clock in the morning. Dona Antonia was wooed with words of flattery, while everybody danced, then Don Pedro requested that she be conducted to her bed and he followed her. In the morning, the bride "arose very joyful" and told her ladies-in-waiting that she was very much pleased. Then she sent for her brother and told him that the marriage had been consummated.

Since he had fulfilled his part of the bargain, Menendez now expected Carlos to do the same, and receiving him on board, he informed him that a large cross would be erected near his palace and in the morning, men, women and children should kiss it and worship there, taking it for their greatest idol and foresaking their pagan ones. But the *cacique* was still cautious. He decided that until his sister returned from Cuba, he would, indeed, worship the cross but not yet abandon the old tribal deities and with this, Menendez had to be content. A cross was set up on the deck, and with music and great devotion, the Adelantado worshipped there as did his company, Doña Antonia, most of her attendants and finally, Carlos and his men. Then giving the cross into the care of the brother-in-law of the *cacique*, Menendez prepared to get underway.

Doña Antonia, three Indian men and four Indian women, as well as seven Christians, were put aboard one of the five ships, which, under the command of Estebano de las Alas, were to go to Havana where Treasurer Juan de Ynistrosa would meet them. Promising to come for her in three or four months, Menendez sailed with two brigantines for St. Augustine.

Conditions had gone from bad to worse at the three colonies which Menendez had established on Florida's east coast. There had been an Indian uprising at Santa Lucia and the colonists, unable to forage for food, were starving. When a caravel finally arrived with supplies, the soldiers seized it and they were sailing off when intercepted by the Adelantado who took them with him to St. Augustine. Here and at San Mateo, mutinies, desertions and hostile Indians had put the forts in desperate straits and, although Menendez did what he could before sailing for Guale, the suffering of the colonists was intense. After establishing the fort of San Felipe on an island off the coast of today's Georgia, he returned to find St. Augustine a heap of smoking ruins, and an Indian war still in progress. Nevertheless, the fort was rebuilt in a new site and in July of 1566, he returned to Cuba.

A lesser man would have given up on what awaited Menendez in Havana. King Phillip had sent an investigator, Licentiate Valderrama, who proved to be coldly uncooperative. The governor, hostile as always, used his office to throw every obstacle in his path, and there were delays and debts. Also, Antonia's Indian companions had sickened and died until only two remained to serve her. Nevertheless, a day or so after his arrival, Menendez met with Valderrama, who showed little interest in his plans and even less concern for his problems. Agreeing only to recommend to the governor that he provide soldiers, he refused to forward Menendez's complaints about Osorio nor would he promise the expedition any money. Depressed and demoralized, the Adelantado returned to his inn to confer with Ynistrosa.

Juan de Ynistrosa, Treasurer of Cuba and a staunch friend and ally of Menendez, was worried lest the deaths of the five Calusa seem suspicious to *Cacique* Carlos, and should his sister also die, surely his wrath would be down on all their heads. He urged Menendez to sail the following day for the Bay of Juan Ponce taking Doña Antonia with him and promised, meanwhile, to intercede for him with the licentiate and send on what food he could obtain.

He spoke warmly of Antonia, telling Menendez that she had astonished the residents of the town with her composure and bearing and that she and a maid servant dear to her learned so quickly that within a few days they knew the required prayers and doctrine. Once again, the perceptive Ynistrosa reminded his friend that he must treat the Indian lady with tact and "make much of her" as he and the townspeople had done. Menendez assured the treasurer that he already had notified Doña Antonia of his intention to call and would do so immediately after dining.

Antonia was the charge of Alonzo de Rojas, an official of the town, whose wife, a lady of considerable social standing, had become her godmother. Doña de Rojas was very fond of the Calusa princess and in teaching her, had noted the quick, sharp mind, an observation she passed on to the Adelantado.

Menendez, arriving with gifts and musicians, found

his Calusa wife quite downcast and it was some time before he could find out what had so depressed and displeased her. Finally, in an outpouring of love, she said she wished that God would kill her, for her husband upon his arrival, had not sent for her—all of which the aristocratic Spaniard heard with inner dismay. Antonia's good will was very important to his plans, but to him, no marriage existed.

Seating himself beside the sad woman, he drew forth his cross, for he was a Knight of the Order of Santiago, and solemnly he explained that men who wore this were not permitted to sleep with their wives for eight days after an expedition against their enemies. He assured her that he was most impatient for the time to pass, for he loved her very much. Antonia, longing to believe him, counted off the remaining six days on her fingers and, happily embracing him, asked to hear the musicians he had brought to entertain her.

The Adelantado remained for more than an hour, then returned to his lodging where, exhausted, he fell into his bed. He believed his little subterfuge had worked— but he had not allowed for the naturally suspicious nature of women.

Shortly after midnight, a drowsy boy opened the door of the inn to admit three womem. One of them, a Spanish lady he recognized, told him that the Adelantado had sent for his wife so Antonia, her maid and her friend, who had been a Calusa captive, were conducted to the room where Menendez lay sleeping. Once inside, the demure princess became the jealous wife and as her companion looked on with alarm and dismay, Antonia seized a lighted candle and began searching for her husband's mistress—in his bed, beside it and even underneath!

Now, of course, thoroughly aroused, the Adelantado watched in complete astonishment and turning to the flustered Spaniard, demanded:

"What is this, sister?"

Then, as Antonia sat at the head of his bed and watched his face, the unhappy woman explained what she had been told and believed to be true. Unable to contain himself, Menendez exploded with laughter.

When he could speak, he turned to his Calusa wife and again told her that he wished the days would speed by but Antonia was unconvinced. Pleading to remain, she pointed out that Carlos would think her scorned and in anger, he would refuse to become a Christian or further befriend the Spaniards. But, once again, Menendez extricated himself from the horns of a dilemma.

She was, indeed, his wife he said, and if she wished, she could lie down with him. But, he added, sadly, if she did so, God would surely strike him dead. Faced with such a predictable calamity, Antonia had no choice but to agree that his life meant more to her than a night together. Embracing him, she reluctantly departed, once more bought off with presents and promises.

The following day, the Adelantado set sail in the patache, *San Cristobal*, accompanied by the shallop, *Sevilla*, with thirty soldiers and seamen, and as passengers, Doña Antonia with her Indian servant and two Spanish women, formerly prisoners. Three days later, they dropped anchor outside Estero Bay and as Indians approached, they were sent to tell Carlos that his sister had arrived. To her great disappointment, Antonia discovered that Menendez did not intend to go ashore but would return to Cuba to get missionaries to teach the Calusa.

Within two hours, Carlos appeared with a flotilla of twelve boats, one of them a ceremonial barge formed by putting a platform on two canoes lashed together, the deck shaded by awnings made with hoops and matting.

With his brother-in-law, Carlos boarded the patache

for a tearful reunion with his sister. During the celebration banquet which followed, he was reminded of his promise to cut his hair, go to Cuba and become a Christian, but after conferring with his chiefs, Carlos declined, giving as an excuse the rebelliousness that then gripped his kingdom.

He departed with Antonia, promising to return more Christian captives the following day but none appeared. Instead, six chiefs arrived with an invitation for the Adelantado to join the royal family at Calos, a bidding coldly rejected. Menendez's message to Carlos was that he believed him a wicked man and a liar, whom he knew to be plotting some treachery. If the Christian captives were not returned, he told the chiefs, the Spanish soldiers would burn the town and behead Carlos and his principal men. In addition to that, he would befriend the enemies of the Calusas.

The Christians were returned shortly thereafter and Carlos himself soon followed, calmly informing the Spaniard that he might kill him, if he wished, or carry him off. But Menendez, who was learning to respect Calusa boldness and perhaps enjoy it, received him graciously.

When Menendez sailed, he had with him the twenty-year-old heir and cousin of Carlos, Don Pedro. Later, he would attempt to marry Don Pedro to Doña Antonia. The intent was to establish a Christian ruling family sympathetic to the Spaniards but there is no indication that such matchmaking ever succeeded.

Menendez's own Indian marriage, however, had immediate, good results. Because they loved Antonia, who was close kin of their chief, the Tequesta Indians of the Florida Keys decided to spare the lives of survivors shipwrecked on their shores.

Jesuit Missionaries.

94

Ann L. Winterbotham

Chapter VII

THE SPANISH OCCUPATION

While Pedro Menendez grappled with the problems of his east coast settlements, matched wits with Cuban officialdom, traveled to Spain and back, fought corsairs and otherwise occupied himself, a trusted lieutenant, Captain Francisco de Reynoso, established the first Spanish colony on Florida's Gulf Coast. He had been ordered to build a blockhouse at Calos, erect a large cross and venerate it twice daily, reciting Christian doctrine, and along with other Christians, try to convert the natives.

San Anton, as the garrison was named, was built on a "small hill," actually, the lower of the two high-shell middens on Mound Key across a valley from the Calusa temple and town. Eventually, the settlement consisted of thirty-five buildings, among them a blockhouse, a chapel and a house for Doña Antonia. It was the only foreign colony ever imposed upon the obstreperous Calusa, and a mere toehold, but the Spaniards managed to hang on there almost three years.

Reynoso, man-at-arms to his majesty, arrived at Calos Harbor in the fall of 1566 with thirty soldiers and the Indian converts, Don Pedro and his servant. Carlos made a great ceremony of welcoming them, professed his friendship for his "elder brother" and had a large house built for the Spaniards, but Reynoso had been warned not to trust him. When the supplies were unloaded from the brigantine, he put several seaman in charge of it and hastened Doña Antonia and six ranking Indians aboard. As Menendez had instructed, they were to be taken to Cuba as hostages for the men left at Calos.

When the ship arrived at Havana six days later, Councilman Alonso de Rojas, Antonia's guardian, was at dockside and the Indians were taken to his home where Señora Rojas warmly welcomed them. But this did not alter the fact that, quite high-handedly, they had been spirited away from Florida. Carlos demanded their return but his ire only intensified the fears of the soldier-colonists and the rift between them widened.

The brigantine which had transported Doña Antonia to Havana returned with a patache, both vessels loaded with supplies which included wine, foodstuffs and cattle. Despite this last item, there was little if any farming on the small island, now called Mound Key which measures but 1.75 miles around its perimeter.

In March, 1567, Reynosa wrote the Adelantado that three times Carlos had tried to kill them and, almost with letter in hand, Menendez sailed for Calos. Within a week, a flotilla of six brigantines lay at anchor in the harbor. To beef up the garrison, Menendez had brought 150 men, and, as a peace overture to her brother, Antonia was returned with her retinue. Also aboard were two Jesuits, Father Juan Rogel and Brother Francisco Villareal, and a peace mission of seven Tequesta Indians who had angered Carlos by sparing Christian castaways. The Adelantado wished to restore friendly relations between the tribes for he was determined to make the Florida Keys safe for shipwreck victims.

He ordered a house be built for Doña Antonia, as he had promised, and a chapel where Juan Rogel might say mass, for the thirty-seven-year-old priest was to remain at San Anton. He began at once to study the

Calusa language while Brother Villareal, who was to be stationed among the Tequesta, became the apt pupil of the Indians brought from there.

Both men were well-trained, dedicated missionaries. While little is known of Brother Francisco's background, Rogel was a native of Pamplona, Spain. He was Licentiate of Arts, Bachelor of Medicine and a student of theology. He entered the Jesuit order in April 1554 and would spend fifty-five years in the Society of Jesus.

Although Menendez was highly disturbed by the conspiracies of Carlos, he still hoped to pacify him and promote his Christian colony within the kingdom of the Calusa. Several times he entertained the young king and as before, he tried to learn the location of the Grand Canal described by Fontaneda. This waterway was used by the Calusa chiefs to travel to Lake Okeechobee and thence to the lands of their vassal tribes. Centuries later, the surveyors of General Zachary Taylor, exploring the source of the Caloosahatchee in 1839, discovered the remains of an ancient Indian canal between Lakes Hicpochee and Okeechobee and it is possible that this was the missing link. But Carlos never would reveal its exact location and Menendez and his captains tried in vain to find it.

Quite unexpectedly, however, Carlos announced that the passage was entered from the bay of Tocobaga, although, of course, it was not. Captain Reynosa had refused to help him but given the right inducement, he believed the Adelantado would sail into the enemy territory, avenge the raid upon the Calusa and liberate a sister who had been taken prisoner.

Menendez was quite obsessed with his dream of a cross-Florida water route by which the Spanish ships could travel quickly from coast to coast. Consequently, within three days of arriving at Calos, the fleet was en route to Tocobaga, fifty leagues north of Sanibel. Their intent, however, was negotiation and impressing this on Carlos, Menendez permitted him and twenty of his men to come along as a peace mission.

They reached today's Tampa Bay the night of the second day and from there the principal town and palace of the *cacique* was some twenty leagues down a salt water canal. It was a dark, moonless night but the Calusa pilot had no trouble finding the way and with a fair wind, the ships sailed swiftly and silently, arriving at their destination, undetected, about an hour before dawn.

Carlos, seething for vengeance, would have attacked at once, burning the town and killing the sleeping populace, but tribal warfare was the last thing the Spaniards wanted. With a raging Carlos closely guarded, a former captive of the Tocobaga was sent ashore in a small shallop to shout the news of the peaceful invasion. Nonetheless, the sight of six Spanish brigantines in the harbor was an alarming sight and most of the townspeople fled in panic. Chief Tocobaga, however, remained calm and when dawn broke, he sent his thanks to the Adelantado for sparing them.

Tocobaga's kingdom was but one small part of the vast Timacua Territory and before he could commit himself to any sort of pact with Menendez, he was obliged to consult the other principal chiefs. At the end of three days, 1,500 warriors had gathered, fine-appearing men, well-equipped with bows and arrows—and an unsettling sight to the outnumbered Spaniards. Menendez, however, remarked that his men were "very joyful" that these Indians seemed to want to do battle and suggested, that to keep the peace, perhaps only the top men need remain. Tocobaga immediately agreed.

At the historic conference the following day, the Tocobagas agreed to terms laid down for peace and occupation and would accept Christian instruction, but since there was no mutual trust between them, a proviso was included: if either Carlos or Tocobaga broke the peace, the Spaniards would support an attack against the aggressor.

Thirty soldiers were left under the command of Captain Garcia Martinez de Cos, who, quite emphatically, did not want the job, but his assignment was in the nature of a punishment for some act of disobedience, and he had no choice. It proved to an unfortunate selection, for the soldiers were badly disciplined and by July, 1568, their abuse and persecution of the Indians had culminated in a massacre at the principal town in which only the chief and his captain-general were spared. In retaliation, the blockhouse was attacked and all the Spaniards there were killed.

But in March of 1567, Menendez did not foresee any of this and after four days at Tocobaga, he set sail, well-pleased with the results of his negotiations. Not so *Cacique* Carlos. Angry and humiliated, he sat on the deck of the ship returning him to Calos. When a passing sailor accidentally dropped the end of a rope on his head, he leaped up in a rage and would have thrown the man overboard had not the Adelantado intervened.

Nor was Doña Antonia happy over the turn of events. She found it inconceivable that Menendez would not war against the enemies of the Calusa nor, as a Christian, destroy their heathen idols. She accused him of having two hearts—one for himself and one for the Tocobaga but none for herself or her brother. Menendez was unable to placate her and they parted with bitterness.

Leaving Father Rogel and fifty additional men at San Anton, Menendez took Brother Francisco to Tequesta then sailed for Havana where his political enemies conspired against him.

Father Rogel ardently pursued his quest to convert the Calusa but it proved uphill work. He was beset at every turn by tribal customs and superstitions and made no gains at all among the adult Indians, the children coming to be instucted only when cornmeal and trinkets

99

were offered as inducements. Carlos jeered at his efforts and the shaman waited for an opportunity to destroy him. Yet the fair-minded, erudite Jesuit continued his thankless job of bringing the word of God and, hopefully, a better life to his Indians. He defended them, agonized over them, and, when he could, taught them Christian morality in an atmosphere that would deny it. The threat against his life, when it came, began as a ceremonial procession and in a letter, Rogel described it:

> "The Indians had conceived a great hatred for me as I had discovered their secrets and profaned their religion; so much so that they tried to coax me outside the fort and carry me to their temple and sacrifice me there, showing their people that no matter what trouble we were, we would adore their idols, and they were intent upon climbing up to our fort with their face masks, coming from a little hill where their houses were to the hill where our fort was, between which there was a small valley through which the procession passed with the women singing praises. Thus they proceeded to the fort where I came out and reprehended them. As they attempted to rush the fort, I went inside, warning Capt. Francisco de Reynoso who came out with a half-lance and knocking one of the leaders in the head, unmasking him. Seeing their idol treated so, the Indians rushed to their huts for arms, but upon returning to the fort, found the Spanish garrison ready."*

So the shamans were turned back but Calusa unrest continued to mount. Carlos had returned from Tocobaga

---

* Rolf, Schell, *1000 years on Mound Key.* P. 39.

determined to rid himself of the Spanish occupiers and Capt. Reynosa found him more conniving and troublesome than ever. The young chief had been taken to Havana and wined and dined there, yet upon returning to his kingdom, he again began harassing the colonists. The breaking point came four months later when Carlos and his men tried to seize a supply ship sent from Cuba to succor San Anton. Menendez ordered his execution along with twenty of his top men and this was done, probably late summer or fall of 1567.

Don Felipe replaced Carlos as chief, but conditions became successively worse and by December, 1567, San Anton was suffering the same privations as the east coast forts. Rogel left for Havana where he hoped to obtain supplies but such help was long in coming and as he waited, he gathered together the servants of the colonials and instructed them in the faith.

Menendez had been in Spain since June of that year, displaying his Indian charges in their tribal dress to the curious townspeople near his home in Aviles. He spent eighteen days with his wife and daughters, then went to Madrid to present himself and his Indians (none of whom were Calusa) at court. Deserters reaching Spain before him had accused him of selling supplies for his own profit but the charges were absurd and before he again left the country, he was awarded high appointments and given some sums of money.

Additional Jesuit missionaries with some Indian converts arrived at St. Augustine at the end of June, 1568. They discovered, to their great shock and dismay, that the people there were destitute and the fort at San Mateo was a heap of ruins. Dominique de Gourgues, a French seafarer and adventurer, had avenged Fort Caroline in a surprise maneuver that caught even his own men unaware for they thought they had signed on for a slaving venture.

Nor was this the only bad news. The fort at Tocobaga had been abandoned and on Florida's southeast coast, Indians of Tequesta had been provoked into an uprising. They had torn down the missionary's crosses and fled into the woods and there hiding near a path that led to a spring, killed unwary passersby. The colonists crowded into the garrison of Santa Lucia and the sudden influx so diminished the food supplies that they were soon starving. They had resorted to cannibalism before help finally came. Probably, it was at that time Brother Villareal returned to Calos.

When Juan Rogel returned to Carlos for an eight-day visit in September, 1568, Don Felipe assured him that he would be baptized when the Adelantado arrived and that all his subjects would follow suit; but this never happened. Father Gonzalo del Alamo was to go to Calos in January, 1569, but his tour must have been short, for Don Felipe, deceitful and cruel, was found out in a plot against the Spaniards and was executed along with fourteen of his men. For the Calusa, this was the last straw. They rose up, burned their houses and fled the island and by June 19 San Anton was abandoned.

Menendez had returned from Spain as Cuba's governor and arrived in Havana sometime after the raid of Gourgues. He didn't return to Spain until September of 1569 but there is no indication that he visited San Anton before it was abandoned, although he intended to do so.

Meanwhile, Father Rogel had been in Gaule, St. Helen and Orista in present day Georgia where he seemed to be making some progress until there, too, a Spanish commander's unreasonable demands on their food supply triggered an Indian uprising. The priest was ordered to take refuge in the fort at Santa Elena and later went with Menendez to investigate the progress of a missionary group at Axacon near Chesapeake Bay. They found the Jesuits had been murdered by a band of Indians led by a turncoat convert, Don Luis. After rescuing a young Spanish boy, Alonzo, who had been protected and sheltered by the brother of San Luis, the Spaniards took the murderers to the ship and after Father Rogel had received their confessions and baptized them, they were hanged.

Juan Rogel outlived all the other Jesuit missionaries sent to Florida at the same time as he had been. He was sent to Mexico in 1571 and lived out his life in Vera Cruz, instructing and ministering to the sick, the poor and the outcasts. His exemplary life and the unusual circumstances of his death led some to believe him a saint. He was ninety years old when he died January 19, 1619 in the home of a friend, who had taken him in when the church and buildings of San Juan de Ulua burned to the ground. They were all at dinner when the frail old man rose to his feet and clasping his hands, gazed raptuously upward. Then, turning smiling eyes on his host, as if to thank him, he died.

As he lay in his coffin, the priest looked asleep, his face beautiful, his body soft and supple. Mourners of high and low estate crowded around the bier to take locks of hair, a piece of garment or touch their rosaries to his body believing these things sacred relics. He was interred beneath the altar in the Mother Church and years later, when the grave was opened, the body of Juan Rogel was found incorrupt.

Menendez returned to Spain but in 1572, he was back in Florida for a short time. In February, 1574, he was appointed Captain General of the great armada which the Spanish king was sending to Flanders, ostensibly to clear the area of pirates, but some believed it was to have been a campaign against the British. Impatient to return to Florida, he wrote his nephew, Pedro Menendez Marques, September 8, 1574, that he expected to end the expedition by spring "...and when that is accomplished, I shall be at liberty to go at once to Florida, not to leave it as long as I live; for that is all my longing and happiness."*

But he never saw Florida again. Nine days later he died at Santander of an illness his doctors diagnosed as indigestion, although there has been a lingering suspicion that he was poisoned. His body lies in a niche in the Church of St. Nicholas in his native city of Aviles, above the tomb his coat of arms and an inscription listing his ranks and honors. Even all of these understate the character of this remarkable man. Pedro Menendez de Aviles, dead at fifty-five, was, we believe, the most heroic figure in all of Florida's history.

---

* Gonzalo Solis de Meras, *Pedro Menendez de Aviles, Memorial.* trans. Jeanette Conner. App. "C"

PART II

THE AMERICAN WAY

Pirates of the mangrove coast.

Chapter VIII

PIRATES—AND THE EARLY SPANISH FISHERIES

After the French and Indian Wars ended in 1763, Florida was ceded to England in exchange for the city of Havana, Cuba, and in 1769, Bernard Romans was sent to explore its coastline. He noted an opening just north of Boca Grande and on his map of 1774, he designated it as Boca Gasparilla. Apparently, the name came from a Spanish source, perhaps a 1765 map which placed *Boca de Gasparilla* north of Tampa Bay. If so, Romans erred in locating it at Charlotte Harbor and bequeathed his mistake to the mapmakers who came after him, all of which would be neither here nor there, were it not for the Gasparilla legend.

The story originated with an old fisherman named John Gomez who lived out his last days on Panther Key in the Ten Thousand Islands. To Reverend Gatewood, who was census taker in 1900, Gomez said he was 125 years old and a native of Madeira. He emigrated to Cuba but getting into trouble there, he escaped by rowboat to the Florida Keys. When Mr. Gatewood first met him, Gomez was living with his wife on a tiny island named after them at the mouth of Fakahatchee Pass.

But to other people, John Gomez confessed to a lurid past of piracy and told hair-raising tales of sinister men, captive maidens and treasure ships. He claimed to have been a member of the crew and brother-in-law of a notorious buccaneer, José Gaspar, called Gasparilla, and said that the island north of Captiva had been named after him.

Up until that time, no one had heard of Gasparilla, but the idea was intriguing and area residents went to see old John, never empty-handed, and stayed to hear him spin his yarns. He died in 1900 in a bizarre accident. He was fishing alone in his boat when he threw his net over while his foot was caught in it. The weight of it dragged him overboard and unable to free himself, he drowned. That same year, he told people he was 120 years old—perhaps because the figure he had given the census taker, 125, seemed unbelievable.

Twenty years later, Pat LeMoyne, who was public relations counsel for the Charlotte Harbor and Northern Railroad in 1920, heard the stories and thought them good advertising material for the railroad and the Boca Grande Hotel which was at its terminus. The pamphlet which subsequently was circulated, proved so popular it was soon out of print but the Gasparilla story continued to be told and retold, each time more fictionalized. Fortunately, the original account was reproduced in its entirety in *Piracy in the West Indies and Its Suppression*, by Francis B.C. Bradlee, published in 1923. While there are many inaccuracies, the few grains of truth are well-worth close examination.

According to the writer, information on Gasparilla came from two sources, Panther Key John and the records of a man named John Gomez, Jr., relationship unknown, who had been kidnapped as a child by Gasparilla and served as his cabin boy. This other John Gomez apparently witnessed the pirate's fatal encounter with the U.S. Navy and was himself captured at that time. He spent ten years in jail in New Orleans then went to Palmetto, Florida, where he lived to the age of seventy. He died and was buried there in 1875.

As the tale is told, José Gasper was an admiral of the Spanish Fleet and an aristocrat in good standing at court until he stole the crown jewels in 1782. Leaving wife and children behind, he took off for the seacoast where he managed to elude his pursuers long enough to collect a band of outlaws and sail off in the Navy's proudest ship.

When he learned that a price had been put on his head, Gaspar swore eternal vengeance and turned to piracy, taking the name Gasparilla, which meant Gaspar the outlaw.* He set up his complex on several islands in Charlotte Harbor, taking the largest and most beautiful for himself, calling it Gasparilla. His house was luxuriously appointed with the finest of plunder and because of his regal life style, fashionable clothes and elegant manners, he sometimes was called King of the Pirates. He was known to be fearless in battle, ruthless and cruel. A fickle lover, he kept a harem of his most beautiful prisoners but the faces were always changing, those out of favor summarily put to death.

The rest of the female captives, wealthy or important enough to bring a good price, were held for ransom, their closely-guarded quarters being twelve rough palmetto log houses arranged in a semi-circle on the shore of Turtle Bay. One hundred yards inland was a pirate cemetery. On nearby Cayopelean (Cayo Pelau?), an observation tower had been built atop a fifty foot high Indian mound and this was constantly manned by a lookout who scanned the waters of the Gulf for ships.

In 1801, a vessel was sighted about forty miles from Boca Grande and the pirates were quick to capture it. Aboard were a Spanish princess (whose name Panther Key John could not recall) and eleven of Mexico's fairest

* Actually Gasparilla means little Gaspar although there is no mention of his being short

daughters who were going to Spain to be educated. In the hold was a cargo of gold carried in copper chests.

After killing all their male protectors, the outlaws took the women to Charlotte Harbor and there the eleven young Mexicans were divided among the cutthroat crew. Gasparilla kept the imperious little princess for himself and becoming enamored of her, at first treated her with the deference that was her royal due. As she continued to rebuff his advances, however, his courtliness vanished and finally, in a rage, he drew forth his cutlass and cut off her head.

Panther Key John drew a map of where the unfortunate victim was buried and in recent years, the skeleton of a beheaded woman was found there.

After the United States began a massive campaign to clear the Gulf Coast of outlaws, all the big-time buccaneers met on Sanibel to consider the problem. Most decided to get out while the getting was good but Gasparilla, Baker, Caesar and old King John were not yet ready for retirement. Two years later, however, Gasparilla began to feel the hot breath of the U.S. Navy on his neck and decided, at the age of sixty-four, to divide his wealth of some $30 million with his crew and sail away to some place where he could live on his ill-gotten gains under an assumed name.

It took some time, to collect the treasure from six different hiding places and while this was in process, a diversion intervened. In spring of 1822, a large English merchant ship was sighted off Boca Grande Pass and unable to resist taking one more prize, the aging buccaneer decided to go after it. Pierre LaFitte* was said to be with him at that time. At about four in the afternoon, the two captains, each in charge of a boat and

* Pierre LaFitte, a licensed privateer, probably was in Missouri in 1822. He died of natural causes in 1844 and was buried in St. Louis. The last years of his more flamboyant brother, Jean, however, are shrouded in mystery. He may, or may not, be buried near New Orleans.

thirty-five men, emerged from Charlotte Harbor. Gasparilla, first to overtake the fleeing ship, was ready to board it when suddenly it changed before his eyes. Quickly the English ensign was lowered and replaced with the Stars and Stripes while guns, uncovered on the deck, began to fire away. With his craft full of gaping holes and sinking, Gasparilla knew he couldn't get away and wrapping a piece of anchor chain around his waist, he leaped into the water.

With the exception of the cabin boy, the crew was hanged from the yardarms but the men left back at headquarters to guard the prisoners managed to escape to the mainland, among them Panther Key John.

LaFitte, who had watched the whole thing from afar, fled to the Manatee River and his ship was taken there next morning. Whether he himself escaped is not known.

For thirty-five years, the sunken ship could be seen lying five miles off Boca Grande Pass, but eventually, sand covered it. So ended the LeMoyne version of the Gasparilla legend, for such it is.

In 1924, another writer, Phillip Gosse, in his *Pirate's Who's Who*, repeats the Gasparilla story almost exactly as it appears in the Bradlee book except to relate that "the famous pirate" met his end in 1821. Gosse, who admits he received his information "in a desultory way," adds a little more. He says that the Caesar mentioned as being at the pirate's conference had his headquarters on Sanibel and, more important, that José Gaspar sometimes called himself Richard Coeur de Lion. If so, we have evidence that he was not just a figment of Panther Key John's imagination.

September 10, 1821, Commodore David Patterson reported the seizure of the ship *Orleans* in the Bahamas by a piratical corvette mounting fourteen guns. The pirates, who seemed to be Spanish, appropriated the cargo valued at $40,000; but after holding the ship for

111

two days, they relinquished it to return to their own craft, endangered by a rising wind. Before leaving, however, their gentlemanly leader penned a letter in French and delivered or sent it to a Naval Officer who was a passenger aboard the captured ship:

"Sir: Between buccaneers, no ceremony; I take your dry goods, and, in return, I send you pimento: therefore we are now even: I entertain no resentment.

Bid good day to the officer of the United States, and tell him that I appreciate the energy with which he was spoken of me and my companions in arms. Nothing can intimidate us; we run the same fortune, and our maxim is, 'that the goods of this world belong to the brave and valiant'.

The occupation of the Floridas is a pledge that the course I follow, is conformable to the policy pursued by the United States.

(Signed) Richard Coeur de Lion"*

It is food for thought that a Key West newspaper reported that in November (1822?) the British schooner *Speedwell* arrived at Nassau with eighteen pirates captured by the trickery of disguising as a merchantman. Fifteen or sixteen pirates jumped overboard and were killed.

Regrettably, the Gasparilla story cannot be proved nor entirely disproved by what we know today. It is true that by 1819 the mangrove islands of Florida's southwest coast had become havens for runaway slaves and were infested with pirates, slavers and the very dregs of society. Horatio S. Dexter was sent to investigate the situation in 1823 and he was told by the

---

* Gardner W. Allen, *Our Navy and the West Indian Pirates*, P. 87.

Seminole of Charlotte Harbor that there were several settlements of runaway slaves on islands around there. They were supplied with food and a variety of weapons by grim-visaged white men whose vessels mounted two and three guns. The Indians were not permitted to set foot on these keys (and who would want to?), but the white men came to them to exchange powder, lead, rum and molasses for Indian cattle.

These reports and his own investigation convinced Dexter that remnants of pirate bands still operated unchecked in the Charlotte Harbor-San Carlos Bay area and, on his recommendation, the schooner *Terrier* was dispatched from Key West to reconnoiter. But the Florida outlaws were past masters of the disappearing act and the Navy found nothing of a suspicious nature. The Americans also investigated the Spanish fisheries which had been charged with slave-running, gun-running and smuggling on a large scale. Here, too, everything seemed to be in order.

The English had held Florida a scant twenty years, losing it in bits and pieces to the Spaniards who fished in troubled waters during the American Revolution. They, in turn, ceded it to the United States in 1821. By that time, the Cuban-Spanish fishing camps were well established and doing a thriving business. Their picturesque boats came into the great cornucopia of San Carlos Bay-Charlotte Harbor in August, and, until the end of the season in March, they fished the waterways and open Gulf, taking enormous hauls of drum, pompano, sole and sea trout which then were dried and salted at camps on shore and taken to Havana for sale. Mullet, caught by Indian employees by net, were valued for the roe which, along with that of drum and sheepshead was smoked—a delicacy much in demand in Cuba.

Undoubtedly, it was the fisherman's prosperity as well as the fact that they were foreigners that triggered the resentment of some Americans whose nationalism took some ugly forms. At the time Florida became part of the United States, settlers were encouraged to present their claims for the land they had been living on and several Spanish fishermen hastened to do so. Witnesses were produced who testified that many of them, such as José Caldez and José Pais, had resided on their land at least as early as 1812, but the Board of Commissioners, a flagrantly biased body, demanded official records which, of course, could not be produced. Americans who had settled more recently were quickly awarded their property, but every Spanish claim was denied. Since other ways of getting citizenship were never explained to them, the Spaniards eventually lost their property.

Ten years later, there were four Spanish fisheries in the Charlotte Harbor-San Carlos Bay area and again authorities received complaints, this time that the Spaniards, by staying in business, somehow deprived American citizens of making a living. Consequently, the Revenue Cutter *Marion* was sent forth from Key West, aboard her a collector of customs, William A. Whitehead, who was to investigate the fish camps and make his report. A young man, friendly and fair-minded, he kept a journal of his survey which began soon after the cutter dropped anchor in Charlotte Harbor, November 25, 1831.

Whitehead and the Captain visited the first camp, at the north end of Pine Island that afternoon and found only a pack of friendly, barking dogs there to greet them. The dwellings were typical of such places, about fifteen feet square, the roof and sides of thatched palmetto, inside a built-in loft for corn, a hanging shelf with a few pieces of pottery and two or three stools. In one of the huts there was a wooden figure of an angel, perhaps the figurehead from some old ship, and this Whitehead thought to be a place of prayer. Assuming that everyone had gone fishing, the men left their cards at the door of the chief fisherman and returned to the *Marion*.

At five o'clock the next morning, the young custom inspector set out with the Second Lieutenant and four men in a small boat to investigate the other three fisheries. They arrived at the southwest end of Josefa (Useppa) Island and the Caldez camp just before breakfast and were greeted on the beach by José Caldez, its seventy year old owner, whom Whitehead had known for some time. He seemed overjoyed to see them and insisted that they sit down to a meal of cooked fish, potatoes, onions and bread, all cold, laid out on a gunny-sack. To this their effusive host added coffee, hastily made, and a butler-waiter—himself! With the greatest of care, he inspected the plates, cups and saucers placed before them, removing with his fingers any offending spot, and while there were no forks, he generously drew forth a knife from his belt "which very probably had, but a few minutes previously, been employed in slaying some noble fish."* This he carefully wiped on his shirt and offered to his guests. Hungry and vastly entertained, they thoroughly enjoyed their meal.

There had been Spanish fisheries in the vicinity of Boca Grande Pass at least as early as 1765.** Sr. Caldez told of visiting his island before America's Declaration of Independence and he had lived there for forty-seven years. It was a quaintly beautiful place of fifteen to twenty palmetto-thatched dwellings, work and storage sheds sheltered by tall coconut palms and fringed with orange and lime trees, papaya, strangler figs and a fruit called hickok plum. It was much like other camps with

* Thelma Peters, "William Adee Whitehead's Reminiscences of Key West." *Tequesta:* XXV, p. 35.
** E.A. Hammond, "Spanish Fisheries of Charlotte Harbor." Fla. Historical Quarterly, Apr. '73, P. 356.

its small but thriving garden of vegetables and melons which provided, with the local fish and seafood, a wholesome diet for the fishermen, their families and the Spanish Indians who worked seasonally for them. The products of their labor, salted fish and turtles, were taken to Havana on the two schooners of Sr. Caldez, one of which was named the *Josefa.*

Some of the fishermen had married Indian women, fully sanctioned and legal under Spanish law, and their children, brown and naked, played boisterously in and among the living huts. It was the custom to take them as infants to Cuba where they were baptised then return to the islands where the families stayed over the slack season. Older brothers and sisters often stayed on in Havana to be educated.

After an all-day sail on an unusually hot, still day, the inspection party arrived in Punta Rassa where there had been a fishery for thirty-five years. In 1831, there were twelve buildings with about fifty people, men, women and children, and as usual, hospitality was not lacking. The Americans were served a good meal—with forks—"but alas! the knives were now gone." After a sociable evening, they retired to simple but comfortable sleeping accomodations to which the camp's owner had contributed his own cot.

The last fishery was a mile or so up the Caloosahatchee but the head fisherman was not in so the stop there was brief. The party returned to Caldez's camp where the midday meal awaited them. Whitehead explored an Indian mound composed entirely of oyster shell and was told by the old fisherman that the Indians who had lived there 150 years before had been all but exterminated. Caldez had learned from a former resident of Useppa (white or Indian, he didn't say), that there had been a long war which culminated in a final, ferocious battle. After it, the remnants of the tribe had escaped in seventeen canoes to Cuba where their descendants still lived.

In spite of outward appearances and friends like William Whitehead, the life expectancy of the Spanish fisheries was very short in 1831. Whitehead returned to Key West to report that he found no intrusion on anybody's rights but in spite of his efforts, a harsh and sweeping law was enacted, designed to drive out the Spanish fishermen. Under its provisions, foreigners supplying other than territorial markets were required to pay an annual license fee, five hundred dollars, and a two thousand dollar bond. Heavy fines were imposed on those fishing without a license and trading with the Indians became illegal, any master caught doing this to lose his vessel and pay a five hundred dollar fine.

The day after the law was enacted, George C. Willis was appointed to protect fisheries and collect customs at the end of the world—Charlotte Harbor. When he was refused a raise in pay from a dollar and a half a day to two dollars, he resigned. His replacement was Dr. Henry B. Crews, a frontier entrepreneur.

Crews and his wife moved onto Useppa where a house had been built for them just a quarter of a mile from the Caldez camp. While any watchdog would be unpopular, Crew's abrasive personality and heavyhanded methods immediately caused trouble. In July, 1835, he refused permission for a cargo already cleared by customs to be unloaded at Useppa and Whitehead suspended him. The case was under investigation when the Second Seminole War blazed forth in December 1835 with the massacre of Major Dade and his scouting party somewhere northeast of Tampa.

The Indian unrest which led to the Seminole Wars stemmed from a very basic tenet: When one group moves into the territory of another group, the stronger will dominate. This "law of the jungle" was in full play as American settlers moved into Florida, gradually taking over Indian lands and finally becoming so numerous, and therefore powerful, that they could demand the best land of the Indians and eventually all of it. As the Seminoles began to feel the effects of this intrusion, they reacted with hostility and the settlers, fearing for their lives, demanded and got the protection of their government.

Because we like to do things by the book, Congress enacted the Indian Removal Act and Andrew Jackson signed it in 1832. A delegation of Indians was taken to inspect the site of their new home in Arkansas and the Indian Territory. Although they did not like what they saw, they were bribed and pressured into signing treaties.

Back in Florida, the Seminoles were moved on to a reservation with land so poor that even territorial governor William Duval objected to it. Even this eventually was encroached upon. After a series of ineffectual treaties and broken promises, the Indians said, "No more." They retreated into the Everglades and when efforts to remove them from Florida continued, they fought back. Caught in the crossfire were the Spanish fishermen.

On April 1, 1836, while Henry Crews was on a hunting trip to the mainland and his wife was in Key West, twenty-five marauding Seminole braves under Chief Wyhokee attacked Useppa. The revenue collector's establishment was pillaged and burned and the Crews' personal property stolen along with a new revenue boat. The Caldez camp, too, was plundered and two periouges filled with refugees from there were found at the entrance to Charlotte Harbor by boats from the USS *Vandalia.* The young officer in charge, Lieutenant Powell, was taking his men to investigate when they encountered still another boatload of frightened people. These he advised to return for the women and children they had hidden. After finding none of the raiders still on Useppa, he returned the fisherfolk to their homes.

Later, the mutilated bodies of Dr. Crews and his boat

hands were found at the mouth of the Sanybel River (Caloosahatchee) and no one felt safe. The Spanish Indians were accused of the murder but there was no reason to suspect them other than the fact that they were thought to have hated the man. They also feared the Seminoles and left with the Spaniards for Passage Key in Tampa Bay where Capt. William Bunce took them into his fishery.

It is ironic that the Spanish fishermen put themselves into the hands of the very authorities who were intent on removing everyone with even a trace of Indian blood from Florida. Within the following few years, families were torn asunder as some of their wives were claimed as relatives by vindictive Seminoles and along with children of mixed blood, virtually torn from the arms of their loved ones and removed to the west. Many of those taken away were actually American citizens, some of the men registered as American seamen who had served several years on the Sloop *Enterprise*. The Spaniards pointed out that they had served many times as pilots to the Americans and had never lived within reservation boundaries nor been subject to Indian laws.

At first, there seemed some hope. In 1836, General Scott at Tampa and Colonel Gadsden, framer of the treaty of Payne's Landing, both agreed that the Spanish Indians should be exempt, but their successor disagreed. In 1838, a petition signed by twenty-one Spanish fishermen was sent to the Secretary of War protesting the injustices, declaring that while the Seminoles had run amok, the island Indians had continued true to their allegiance. Therefore they should be entitled to the protection of the United States government. They asked to be allowed to return to their island homes or, barring that, be permitted to take their families to another country.

For unfathomable reasons, this petition was turned down and eventually one hundred and fifty Spanish

Indians, men, women and children, were herded onto ships with their Seminole enemies. With them were seven Spaniards, caught up in a tangle of red tape, who were taken as far as New Orleans and there they remained.

The Spanish fishermen, lacking the means and heart to stay in business, eventually abandoned their island settlements. Even an American accused of being a friend of the Spanish Indians became a victim. In 1840, William Bunce's Tampa Bay fishery was destroyed on the orders of General W.K. Armstead.

There is a poignant epilogue to this black chapter of American history. The *Fort Myers Press* in March, 1906, told the story of Captain Raymond Fairfax, who had come to Sanibel with soldiers during the Wars of Indian Removal. The men found an old Indian chief living there with his tribe who doggedly insisted that he had been born on the island and there he would die. Refusing to budge or be bought off by "even shiploads of money," the old man finally was sent away by the "Winchester route." After his execution, the rest of the tribe quickly left Sanibel.

Typical thatched home. From Scotia Bryant Collection.

(Courtesy of Anne Bryant)

121

Sanibel's first American Colonists, 1833.

Chapter IX

THE TOWN OF SANYBEL, 1833

When the United States began negotiating with Spain in 1819 to obtain Florida, it was not clear, at first, who actually owned the Gulf Coast islands. At that time a Virginian, Richard S. Hackley, a consul in Cadiz, had not yet concluded his business transaction with the Duke of Alagon from whom he was buying a large tract in the southwestern part of the peninsula. The Alagon Grant included the coastal mainland from Pavillion Key to the Withlacoochee River, but its western boundary was vaguely drawn. It was generally believed that the offshore islands were included, however, and it was with this assumption that the purchase was completed.

In 1831, with the title still clouded, Hackley sold an option for part of his property to a group of New York investors, the Florida Peninsular Land Company, who had organized for the purpose of establishing a settlement in south Florida. Fifty shares of stock were created, one share equalling about 1,800 acres of land, and each of these originally sold for five hundred dollars.

The prospective buyers had been given a choice of three sites between Cape Roman and Tampa Bay. In spring, 1832, their agent, Colonel George W. Murray, was sent to find the best location for a town. He sailed from New York on May 18th aboard the brig, *Tallahassee*, arriving at Key West on June 9 and at once began to organize his small expedition. His first purchase was a sloop, the *Associate,* and to sail it he signed on Capt. William Bunce and a crew of five. Joined by Hackley's brother, William, and P.B. Prior, the group sailed from Key West on June 27. For more than a month they explored the lower Gulf Coast with special attention to the San Carlos Bay area and Sanibel Island.

The Associate returned to Key West for supplies and refitting in mid-August but was gone again by the end of the month, this time sailing as far north as Tampa Bay. They again landed on Sanibel Island in late September. Noting its good harbor, equitable climate and rich soil, the men agreed that this was the ideal place for their settlement.

Two towns were proposed, Murray and Sanybel, and both requested and received incorporation papers. Only Sanybel, however, actually materialized along with P.B. Prior's sugar cane plantation which eventually was put in near the mouth of the Caloosahatchee. It failed and Prior eventually returned to Key West.

In the fall of 1832, however, the town's backers were highly optimistic and workmen were taken to Sanibel to build the five palmetto thatched huts with floors of shell and sand that were to be temporary shelters. Meanwhile, the undertaking was getting nationwide publicity through the efforts of the Key West physician, Benjamin B. Strobel, who also was editor of the *Key West Gazette.* He already had decided to join the colonists when he wrote a letter September 2 to the *Charleston South Carolina Courier* describing Sanibel and its environs. It was published October 19 and reprinted in newspapers all over the country. This letter and five others, which appeared in the *Charleston Evening Post* between July 17 and 23, 1833, contain almost all we know of the town of Sanybel.

Strobel put out the last issue of his newspaper on September 5, 1832, and returned with his wife and

124

children to his native Charleston. Apparently, his trip to New York in November was for the purpose of buying into the group of investors but he was back with his family at Christmas time. By January 10, he had returned to Key West.

A man intensely interested in the world around him, Strobel was an astute observer of it, a capable writer and a fine, amateur naturalist who frequently collected specimens for the well-known churchman-naturalist John Bachman. On November, 11, Bachman wrote their mutual friend, John J. Audubon, that Strobel had sailed for New York. He would stay there three weeks then settle on "Sinebal"Island, Florida. He added, "He has been industrious in bringing me out a box of birds, skinned by himself." Another letter, dated January 30, 1833, informed Audubon that Strobel had gone to Sanibel, "a portion of Florida where you have never been."

Dr. Strobel was at dockside when the schooner *Olynthus* hove into sight, aboard her twenty or thirty eager men and women from New York, and he was with them when the vessel sailed from Key West. The sloop *Associate* followed some distance behind and all went well that day and night. Eight miles from Sanibel, however, a seaman carelessly giving the wrong sounding caused the ship to go aground. At three o'clock in the morning, with the *Associate* nowhere near, she thumped on a sandbar, heavy surf washing across her decks and through the stern ports. For several hours consternation grew as the passengers peered into the night, searching in vain for the running lights of the little sloop. Then, just in time, the *Associate* caught up with the foundering scooner and anchored a short distance away. Capt. Bunce sent a small boat to take off most of the passengers and these he deposited on Sanibel.

Happy to be at their destination, the colonists were

undismayed at the simplicity of their living quarters—but perhaps not quite prepared for "the reception committee"—swarms of voracious fleas, apparently brought in by work crews. Nevertheless, they unloaded their belongings and built a fire on the beach as others went in search of fish and oysters. By nine o'clock, the *Olynthus*, floated free by an incoming tide, sailed into the harbor, sails set and colors flying, with the hardy souls who had remained aboard her. In a jovial mood, Sanibel's first American residents settled down to a hearty breakfast of fish, oysters and coffee.

The rest of the day was spent in unloading baggage and supplies and stowing them in the palmetto houses. Dr. Strobel and about twenty men and women selected one of these as a dormitory and as night fell, they made their beds on the floor, the doctor reclining on his Buffalo skin, and smoking his "segar." Cheerful and comfortable in the rough but roomy building, they "indulged in merriment at the day's disaster."

It was not long, however, before there was even more to laugh about. Distant thunder soon became a crashing storm, directly overhead, and the skies opened up. "Now came the sport!" Rain in torrents fell on the campsite and while the roof of the house proved watertight, the floor became a lake of floating bedclothes as streams of rain water cascaded through it. When it was finally over, the settlers dug a drainage ditch door to door in their house. With the floor damp-dry, they lay down whatever they could find that was not soaked through and again retired, this time to slip into the oblivion of the totally exhausted.

The irrepressible Dr. Strobel arose early the next morning and taking his gun, went to explore the island, following a fresh water branch (Sanibel slough) for several miles. He came upon some blue-winged teal ducks and easily brought down eighteen. But retrieving them was quite another matter. Wading into

126

eighteen inches of water, he sank deep in muck and with each load of ducks, was obliged to crawl out on hands and knees. As he reached for the last ones, he stepped on the back of an alligator lying on the bottom and as the creature lashed about, he made a hasty retreat, resolving never again to play his own dog!

The days that followed were thrilling to the nature-loving Dr. Strobel as he energetically explored Sanibel from point to end, correctly estimating it to be about twelve to fifteen miles long and from one and a half to two miles wide. He declared the harbor the handsomest he had ever seen and the beach the most beautiful. Here on the south side of the island, great quantities of "elegant" shells washed ashore with every tide and perhaps thinking of his own, Strobel judged it a wonderful place for children to run and play or anyone to ride in the evening. We picture him, cigar in hand, strolling along this wide strand, enjoying everything and missing nothing from the smallest sea shell to the largest sea bird.

On the north side of the island, the ridges of shell were then a little higher than today, six or eight feet above the level of the bay, and the beach quite narrow. Mangroves crowded the western shore but Sanibel was not otherwise densely wooded. The interior of the island was an extensive grassy plain, so level that one could see for miles with only a few palmettos intervening. The landscape of 1833, in fact, was not vastly different from that of a half century later and Strobel accurately predicted that the ridges which lay parallel to each other the whole length of the island would produce excellent crops.

After exploring Sanibel, Strobel turned his attention to Punta Rassa which was insular then, and five to six miles long, one half to one mile wide. The large fishery there employed a great many Spanish Indians who went in their canoes to seine off island beaches. They were taught useful arts and provided with food, clothing and an occasional nip of whiskey by their Spanish employers whose wisdom of some two hundred years had produced an excellent inter-relationship. During the off-season these Indians of mixed tribal blood made camp on the mainland or some nearby island where they planted gardens of corn, pumpkin, sweet potatoes and sugar cane and lived off the land and the sea.

It is significant that the town of Sanybel was established in San Carlos Bay at a time when other parts of Florida were seething with Indian unrest. The Spanish Indians were viewed quite differently than the Seminoles and Strobel did not hesitate to accept an invitation to attend an "Indian Ball" at Punta Rassa. Late in the day, he was transported there in a canoe paddled by Indian fishermen.

The evening began with dinner at the house of the chief fisherman, the menu mouth-watering, even today. Strobel was served pilau made of rice and fowl, broiled wild pigeons, fried fish, venison, excellent white bread and strong coffee, and after it, was presented with six very good Spanish cigars. When the moon rose, flooding the camp with light, soft and ethereal, the Indian Ball began.

The first dance was somewhat like a Spanish fandango in which the performers threw themselves into a number of attitudes and positions, but the second transported them all into the shadowy past of their tribal origins. It was danced by eight or ten women, each of whom strapped a leather band just below her knee from which hung six or eight box turtle shells filled with seed called Indian shot. They formed a ring and paced slowly, throwing their bodies this way and that as they circled again and again making no sound. Then, the leader of the dance began to rattle her shells, still circling, and as they reached the same spot, so did the other dancers until all were jumping, springing and

128

spinning, the noise of the rattles almost deafening, the mood wild, primitive, exciting. Gradually, their speed slackened, the dance became slower, the rattles quieter until nothing was heard, then again building up to the crescendo. This continued until about eleven o'clock when, at last, the ball was over.

Dr. Strobel, clutching his cigars, was conducted to a storehouse where a small fire burned in the center of the room. To one side a bed had been prepared for him and here he slept soundly until morning when the voices of women and children awakened him. As these received their daily allowances and men cleaned and salted down the fish taken the day before, Strobel explored Punta Rassa. He came upon some unusual birds which were feeding with a flock of turkey buzzards on fish entrails. Borrowing a gun from the head fisherman, the inveterate collector shot and skinned two of them. Later, they were identified as Caracara Eagle, (*Polyborus cheriway auduboni*) only one speciman of which previously had been found in the United States by John J. Audubon, who had discovered the prize near St. Augustine.

There were no inhabitants on "Captive" Island in 1833, but there had been, identity unknown. During their exploration of it, Strobel and other men from Sanybel discovered a palmetto house, long since deserted, a few stalks of corn and some pumpkin vines still left in the remnants of a garden. This explained the wild hogs which roamed the island and had been seen on the beach when the men crossed the narrow pass the day before. They had hunted them without success for an hour or so before sunset, then camped for the night on high, sheltered ground.

It was dawn of the following morning when the doctor was awakened by the sound of an animal routing through cooking utensils. Picking up his double-barreled gun, he stepped to the door and blasted away at an enormous hog which proved to weigh about 150 pounds.

Captive Island was outstanding for its beautiful cove or harbor which was formed by an indentation of the sea and it, too, had good, arable land, as did Boca Grande. The explorers finished their tour at Caldez Island where they visited with Sr. Caldez and viewed the fifty-foot bluff above the sound where the Inspector of Revenue had built his house.

In February of 1833, the temperature hovered between 70 and 75 degrees, dropping into the 50s and 60s during the typical winter storms. It seemed to Strobel that the climate was responsible for the robustness of Sr. Caldez and the very good health of the people at the fisheries and the American settlers who, by mid-July, numbered thirty or forty, none of whom had ever been sick. As a doctor, he reasoned that the island would be equally beneficial to convalescents and perhaps he suggested this to the company for a large hotel was contemplated. A doctor would be in attendance to cater to sick and/or transient persons and it would offer wholesome recreation such as horseback riding and sailing. This spa was to be provisioned by island farmers and fishermen but like the rest of the Sanybel dream, it never materialized.

Strobel's practiced eye had noticed that plants grew profusely on Sanibel, even in winter, and he mentioned an indigenous Poppinac tree, Mimosa Farnesiana, "in full bearing," morning glories and wild cotton. This "cotton tree" suggested to him that the growing of Sea Island Cotton commercially could be feasible. In his final letter to the *Charleston Evening Post*, Dr. Strobel reiterated his faith in the agricultural potential of Sanibel and added that fisheries, too, could be profitable ventures. He had observed the Spanish Indians hauling a seine onto the beach of Carlos Bay and was amazed to see that in one sweep, they had netted 115 sheepshead and sixty odd fish of other kinds. Oysters and clams could be procured by the dozens of bushels and at the proper season, green turtles crawled the beaches. There were ducks, turkeys, curlews, flamingos and so much deer that a large haunch of venison could be purchased from the Spaniards for a quarter.

Nevertheless, for all his glowing accounts, he knew that the town of Sanybel could not flourish without a successful mainland settlement and that both must have markets for their produce. He envisioned steamship service from northern cities and small boats plying the Caloosahatchee between the plantation there and the harbor of Sanybel. He felt sure that the Gulf coast cities would clamor for the superior fruits and vegetables produced by the farms of the settlers.

Much of Strobel's dream came true, but not in his lifetime. He did not stay on Sanibel long enough to see the bright hopes fading but returned to Key West in March, 1833. He was challenged to a duel there in which he mortally wounded his opponent, David Pinkham, a deputy to William Whitehead. Strobel immediately boarded a revenue cutter commanded by a friend of him and was taken to Charleston, his family soon following. He resumed his medical practice there and, apparently, never returned to Florida.

Seventy or eighty more settlers were expected to arrive the fall of 1833 but it is not known if they did so. The settlement limped along, petitioning in vain for a lighthouse in December of the same year.

There were thirteen resident petitioners: John Harris, James D. Pell, Francis Watlington, Hy Bennett, Thomas Higinbothan, Phillip Hillegas, George Trotter, William A. Pitcher, Margueron, Horace Robbins, Stephen McNamara, P. McDermott and Thomas Deveaux.

Of these, only Captain Watlington, pilot and wrecker, seemed to be well-known in Key West. His home on Duval Street, built in 1832, was a household of women—his wife amd their seven accomplished daughters: Hannah, Sarah, Emeline, Marie, Mary, Florence and Lilly. All of the girls made good marriages except Lilly, who remained single and was still living in the family mansion in 1912.

The Watlingtons entertained frequently and it is doubtful that any of the ladies ever set foot on Sanybel. Perhaps Captain Watlington fudged a bit calling himself a resident.

John Harris and George Trotter, apparently, were from New York City and William A. Pitcher's home was Catskill, Greene County, New York. There was a William A. Pitcher of Key West who was a Union volunteer in the Civil War, whether he be the same, a relative or neither is not known.

Deeds were registered by other investors. Jacob Rutsen Van Rensselaer of New York City owned Lot 45 and, as did others, a fiftieth of the public land at Pt. Ybel. Issac and Sylvia Bice of Catskill, New York sold Lot 34 to Jacob Plasso but Lovell Kimball, who bought ten lots, kept them for awhile despite his jaundiced view of the islands possiblities.

Kimball, an enterprising man of thirty-odd years, was from Watertown, Jefferson County, New York. He was the stepson of his uncle, Dr. Lovell Massey, who sent him to college to study medicine.

Kimball never became a doctor but instead studied science and worked out the process of making maleable iron from cast iron, winning a gold medal for the feat. Upon graduation, he went into business with his brother making cassimere but the business failed when a flood swept away part of the building in 1821.

Eventually, he gained a reputation as being a man of sharp business practices, too sharp some said. He was accused of deliberately flooding out the land of a man named Sprague which supposedly brought "Sprague's Curse" down upon his head. He was sued twice with one case carried to the Illinois Supreme Court. The plaintiff, Amasa Cook, was represented by a young lawyer named Abraham Lincoln. Kimball won the suit.

In view of the pirate in him, there could be some truth in the family story that he was attracted to Florida because he heard there was gold there. In 1979, two brothers in Key West found some nuggets while drilling through some limestone. Could it be that Ponce de Leon, De Soto and Lovell Kimball were on to something?

Whatever the reason, he bought the lots on the island he called "Cinnabell" and in 1832 sailed from New York for Key West with his brother, his wife and their eight children. At Key West he chartered a sailing vessel and set out to explore his property. The two men rowed ashore smack into a mangrove swamp and hordes of mosquitos. Concluding that Sanybel was uninhabitable they returned to Key West to await transportation to New York. While there Mrs. Kimball died of cholera.

Kimball was in Greene County, New York, in 1833 and built the first maleable-iron foundry there. He built other foundries, too, before leaving for Illinois where he established the town of Marseilles on the Illinois River. The plat of the town was recorded in 1835. He chartered the Marseilles Manufacturing Company in 1836 but it was wiped out by a flood the same year. His mill which was built in 1841 burned in 1842 and, when the insurance company refused to pay, townspeople tended to blame his bad luck on "Sprague's Curse." He died of cholera in 1849.

Finally, all of the colonists left Sanibel but exactly when remains a mystery. In April, 1836, Acting Sailing Master Stephen C. Rowan, pursuing marauding Seminoles, found none of Sanibel but there is no mention in his report of white settlers. John Lee Williams, however, exploring the town at a later date, wrote that one elegant house had been built there and several smaller ones, "but at this time, 1837, it is nearly deserted."

The choice of words is intriguing. Powell reported at the end of November, 1836, that all of the fisheries in the area had been deserted, but the Williams account, after the specific reference to Sanybel in 1837, goes on to describe the Caldez ranch as a going concern of twenty houses. It is not unlikely that the Spaniards returned there after the 1836 raid to attempt to make a go of it and perhaps not all of the Americans had left Sanibel at that time. By 1844, however, no one remained in the island settlments for the U.S. military had deemed it unwise to leave anyone there possibly to trade with the Indians.

There is an interesting sequel to the Sanybel story. Each deed recorded in Key West in 1832 contained property descriptions not only of the Sanybel lots but those along the Delaware or Gallivan's River, near Caxambas, and along the Sanybel River, today's Caloosahatchee, as well. Offered as a reference was a map conveyed or to be conveyed, made by Daniel Ewan, City Surveyor of the City of New York. There were to be three copies of this, one held by Richard Hackley, one by Jacob Rutsen Van Rensselaer and a third deposited in some public office in Key West.

No such map has been found in Key West but in 1977, by happy coincidence, two maps of Sanybel, 1833, were recovered in Oswego, New York. An antique dealer looking over items to be sold at an estate auction recognized the island as Sanibel where friends Bette and Stearns Williamson lived and had their business, The Westward Shop. Since they, too, dealt in antiques, he telephoned to see if they wished him to bid on the maps. After authenicating the town with this writer, the Williamsons bought the maps and after 144 years, returned them to Sanibel. Only 350 numbered prints were made to offer for sale and an original was presented to the

City of Sanibel.

Aside from its great historical and antique value, the Sanybel Map is a work of art, truthfully and carefully executed. The contours of the island have changed somewhat but the natural features are much the same. The J.N. "Ding" Darling Sanctuary is still "Ground subject to Flood" and the soil of the ridges did produce for the husbandman, the homesteader of the 1880s, the fine crops envisioned by the surveyor, Edward Armstrong.

Sanibel Island light-station. 1884

Ann L. Winterbotham

Chapter X

CASTOR BEANS, MULLET AND
THE LIGHTHOUSE

With the departure of the Sanybel settlers, the Cuban fishermen and the Spanish Indians, the islands of Carlos were all but deserted. A blockhouse, erected at the Caldez rancho after the Indian raid of 1836, became Fort Casey in 1850; and in January, 1838, Fort Dulaney was built at Punta Rassa. The term "fort" was loosely applied. Like other military posts in the area, this supply depot contained only a block house and a warehouse, the soldiers stationed there sleeping in tents pitched on the ground. Understandably, these were vacated during the wet, buggy months.

After the Harney Point massacre in July of 1839, Dulaney was spruced up with a barracks, which was demolished by a hurricane in the fall of the same year. Nevertheless, in midsummer, 1841, the fort again was upgraded with a large barracks, warehouses and a hospital, but still ill-fated, it was struck by another storm the following October. This time, two soldiers lost their lives as the new buildings were swept away by one of the worst hurricanes ever to hit Florida's Gulf Coast. After it, the Army abandoned Punta Rassa and went down the Caloosahatchee to select a site more suitable for the new garrison. This they named Fort Harvie, but it, too, would have its ups and downs before it was rebuilt as Fort Myers and eventually evolve into today's city.

Florida became the 27th state on March 3, 1845, and a few months later, today's Lee County became part of Monroe County, the county seat at Key West. There was no one in residence on Sanibel and Captiva when Florida seceded from the Union in 1861.

Fort Casey had been abandoned by June, 1857. Punta Rassa came alive with the start of the Civil War, becoming a shipping point for south Florida. At first, cattlemen sold their stock to the Confederate Army but when the Cubans offered to pay more, blockade running became a large and lucrative business. Two local residents, Jacob Summerlin and James McKay, Sr., formed a partnership to deliver cattle to Havana where they sold it for inflated prices and immediately bought hard to get commodities for the folks back home. So flagrant was the operation that it was announced ahead of time on which day McKay's side-wheeler, *Scottish Chief*, was expected to dock and farmers and ranchers were at the landing ready to give their I.O.U.'s in terms of cattle for the flour, sugar, calico and shoes that had become life's luxuries.

All of this anti-Yankee ingenuity came to a jolting halt when General John Newton, Commandant of Key West, got wind of the goings-on. A Union force of nine steamers, three schooners, and several hundred men were sent to police the Gulf coast, among them a young officer from Deer Isle, Maine. Ensign William H. Reed, who was part of a landing party which inspected Sanibel Island, established his family there twenty-three years later.

At the site of old Fort Dulaney, a barracks once again graced the landscape, this time on high pilings. Throughout the Civil War it served as a base for the Sanibel Island Blockading Fleet.

By 1867, telegraph lines had been laid all the way

to Punta Rassa and, by Act of Congress, the International Ocean Telegraph Company (later absorbed by Western Union), was permitted to take over the point. A young telegraph operator, George E. Shultz, arrived to set up an office at one end of the old barracks. Since he didn't need all of this rough but commodious edifice, he permitted the cattlemen to bunk down in the rest of it, serving them meals, if they wished, for $1.50 a day. This arrangement met no competition at all until 1874 when Jacob Summerlin and his son, Samuel, the first of the cattle barons, put up their own hotel, called Summerlin House, a few hundred feet away.

Florida was readmitted to the Union in 1868 and that same year, a well educated Connecticut Yankee planted a castor bean plantation on Sanibel.

William Smith Allen was born in Enfield in 1823, leaving there as a young man for Ithaca, New York where he met and married Jane Sprague. The couple moved first to Georgia, where William taught school, then on to Jacksonville, Fla. where he was a bookkeeper for the Fairbanks Sawmill Company.

With the outbreak of the Civil War, the young family found themselves quite alone with their Union sympathies and they decided to go to Key West where George Allen was a collector of customs. William became his brother's deputy collector and with him, owned and operated Allen's General Store at the corner of Duval and Front Street. William served as mayor of Key West under military rule during the Civil War and at one time was clerk of the United States District Court. A man of medium height and broadly built, he was brainy, genial, impulsive and hearty. He also had a strong tendency to butt in and take over situations, uninvited. This earned him the nickname of "Buffalo." When his wife, Jane, died in September, 1869, he was left with three young sons, George, fifteen, John and Dwight. Probably it was then that he went to Sanibel to put in a castor bean plantation.

Castor oil, used extensively for medicinal and industrial purposes, was in short supply at the end of the war and noting that the poisonous beans grew wild in Florida, the two brothers decided to go into the business of growing them. A plantation was put in at the eastern end of Sanibel Island, perhaps at the site of the old town where there would be a good well of potable water. At about that time, the forty-five year old William Allen was hired by Jacob Summerlin, by then a legitimate cattle exporter, to build a causeway through the swamp that separated Punta Rassa from the mainland.

William S. Allen, assistant marshall and farmer, and his son, George, age sixteen, farm laborer, were the only residents of Sanibel when the census taker came through there in 1870. It is believed that they stayed three more years, leaving after the devastating hurricane of October 6, 1873, which sent sea water surging across the island.

With their crop destroyed, the Allens had no choice but to set sail for Key West. Putting in at Chokoloskee Bay, they found John Weeks farming at the mouth of a river and Allen was greatly impressed by the lushness of his garden. Leaving some tools with Weeks, he took his son to Key West then returned almost immediately with money and supplies. He bought out the squatter claim of two men, Clay and Lowell, and built a small house at the site of today's Rod and Gun Club. Subsequently, he cultivated a large tract along the stream which would become known as Allen's River, the name changed to Barron River in 1923.

As a community grew up around him, William Allen became Justice of the Peace, marrying, burying and maintaining order until 1889 when he went to Key West where he died in 1891. His former farm hand, George W. Storter, who had bought him out, became the founder of the town of Everglades.

Meanwhile, back on the islands, Terevo Padilla, commercial fisherman, had established fish camps on Sanibel and Captiva. He saw their wealth in the grassy bays and inlets where the mullet ran in season in enormous schools like living, moving islands, noisy enough at night to awaken the soundest sleeper.

Padilla, who came from the Canary Islands, had lived in Cuba and Key West before he established his family on La Costa Island, north of Captiva. His ranchos each had a complement of about twenty-five men under a foreman and operated from October to February when the mullet were fat with roe. As in the old days, the camps were closed in spring and summer.

The Sanibel fishery was located on "the harbor" near the site of today's Seahorse Shop beside an old well that probably had served the Sanybel settlers, William Allen and thirsty seafarers for hundreds of years. Palmetto-thatched cooking and working sheds were built as well as a warehouse and quarters for the fishermen. There was little if any gardening but everyone ate well. Some food was brought in, wild guavas and heart of palm were there for the taking and the men cooked fish, birds and gopher turtles over charcoal burning in large pots.

Long seines reeled up on huge spools were kept on the beaches and these were used to net the hundreds of pounds of mullet taken each day. The fish were filleted and with the roe, packed in salt in wooden kegs which Sr. Padilla took by boat to Key West.

The fisheries were in business at least twenty years, probably evicted from the islands in the early 1880s. The Cuban smacks that once bought their bait mullet continued to fish the snapper and grouper holes miles off shore and were a common sight laying at anchor in San Carlos Bay well into the 1960s. These forty-ton sailboats, neat and picturesque, each had a fish well in the hull through which the sea water could flow freely, keeping the catch alive until taken to market in Havana.

141

Surveyors for the U.S. Government had completed a map of the Caloosahatchee region in September, 1879, but people wishing to homestead on Sanibel found that the land had been withdrawn January 9, 1878, for the purpose of establishing a lighthouse reservation. An enterprising Pennsylvania businessman, Mr. M.S. Quay, also coveted the land. He offered to buy all of Sanibel but that needed for a lighthouse and Estero Island as well, but he was turned down on both requests.

A lighthouse on Point Ybel had been sorely needed since the colonists of Sanybel petitioned for it in 1833, but it was not until the Wars of Indian Removal that Washington officialdom showed any interest. On December 10, 1856, the Lighthouse Board requested that Sanibel Island be reserved for lighthouse purposes but the General Land Office took no action until the request was repeated December 31, 1877. Within nine days, the Land Office had acted favorably on it and Sanibel was closed to private ownership.

The Lighthouse Board now was ready to go hat in hand to Congress. They argued that there was no lighthouse between Key West and Egmont Key at Tampa Bay although Florida west coast shipping, already considerable, was steadily increasing. Six steamers and many sailing ships regularly were plying the route between Key West and Gulf ports. Punta Rassa had become a busy cattle shipping point and vessels made their landfall and took their departure from the southern point of Sanibel, which, therefore, was the logical place for a lighthouse. The Board recommended that forty thousand dollars be appropriated for its construction.

But only the horses moved fast in Washington and it was 1883 before Congress approved the plans for a light station. The necessary money, now $50,000, was made available and the District Engineer surveyed the site, recommending that the east end of the island be permanently reserved. The question arose of state ownership under the Swamp Act of 1850 and it was not until August that Florida relinquished its claim. Finally, on December 19, 1883, all of Sanibel Island became a reservation by Executive Order.

The work of Point Ybel began the following February with an imposing wharf built on creosoted pilings—162 feet long with a "T" thirty by sixty feet. The foundation for the lighthouse was completed and the frame dwellings nearly finished within three months but the iron work for the tower, along with that for the light at St. Blas, was still en route from Jersey City. Unfortunately, the schooner with the shipment aboard was wrecked just two miles from Pt. Ybel and while some of the cargo was put ashore, the rest of it sank with the vessel and was abandoned by the ship's master.

It was the lighthouse engineer who saved the day. Immediately, he sent to Key West for help and within a short time, the tenders *Arbutus* and *Mignonette* arrived with a diver. The crews, the working party, the diver and the engineer himself went into the water and managed to retrieve all of the lost pieces but two small gallery brackets. Construction was resumed while a firm in New Orleans made duplicates of the missing parts and by the end of the summer, the job was done.

The entire structure was 104 feet high and well-suited to the flat, exposed terrain of "Level Island." Its slender, inner cylinder, braced twenty feet off the ground by an iron column, was supported by a pyramid-shaped frame of latticed wrought iron which offered little resistance to high winds. The French-built giant lens was mounted in brass and revolved, by means of intricate clockworks, around a fixed frame. Thus, the Sanibel light was first a revolving beacon and not until it was converted to acetylene gas did it become a flasher.

Sanibel light station was activated August 20, 1884. On that night, a tender entered the tower and climbed the 127 steps of the spiral stairway to the iron watch-room and the lantern above it. When he lit the wick of the great lamp, ships sixteen miles at sea saw its powerful beam for the first time.

Until the early 1940s, the light was fueled by kerosene oil and required almost constant attention. Every morning, the keep and/or one of his assistants, climbed the tower to the lantern where he extinguished the flame, trimmed the wick, polished the lens, wound the clockworks and drew the curtains around the plate glass enclosure to guard against the damaging rays of the sun. In the afternoon, the lamp was filled with oil, pumped and lit.

Dudley Richardson came from Key West to be the first lighthouse keeper, with him his assistant, John Johnson. Richardson received his appointment November 24, 1884, but probably he was on hand before that. Presumably, with wives and children, these men were the only residents of Sanibel until 1888 when they were joined by Henry Shanahan, who came in his sailboat from Key West with his wife and two small sons. He replaced Johnson in 1890 and stayed on to become keeper when Richardson resigned in 1892. Shanahan served for twenty-two years and established the first permanent family on Sanibel.

Over the years, the lighthouse became a refuge from hurricanes, some of which sent surging sea water to the top step of the keeper's quarters. Once, a Cuban fishing boat was cast ashore and its crew drowned. Unable to learn their identity, the islanders buried the men on Point Ybel.

Usually, the Cuban smacks took refuge in the harbor during the big storms and their crews joined the islanders in the lighthouse, there to entertain with the music of Spanish guitars and voices raised in song. At other times, picnics were held in the shade beneath the quarters and dances on the porches above. The keeper's quarters had still another function. Since Henry Shanahan's mother-in-law was an expert midwife, several babies were born there, most of then little Shanahans.

During World War II, the light was converted to acetylene gas with a sun-valve which utilized the rays of the sun to turn on and off the beam. Six tanks of gas, each weighing 225 pounds, were hooked up together and it took two men to change even one of them.

Chief Bo's'nmate William Robert England, Jr., the last resident lighthouse keeper, was transferred in April 1949, after three years on Sanibel. The responsibility for maintaining the light was assumed by the men of the Coast Guard Light Attendant Station which was established in Fort Myers. The keeper's quarters became headquarters for the J.N. "Ding" Darling National Wildlife Refuge in 1950. In 1962, the light was converted to electricity and problems soon developed. A mercury switch failed and the light was dark for a week, shattering the perfect record of seventy-eight years and a succession of faithful lighthouse keepers.

Intrepid through three wars, numberless storms and even the failure of modern technology, Sanibel light might be expected to flash on forever. In October, 1972, however, the Coast Guard announced that unless its usefulness could be proved, the historic beacon would be turned off. At a subsequent public hearing, this was done to everyone's satisfaction and the light was permitted to shine on. By that time, the French-built lens had been replaced, but some of the plate glass enclosure remained and the signal was the same. Still, the good, old days were gone forever. The light frequently was out of commission, during the summer of 1973, a sort of barometer of a lot of things gone wrong on Sanibel.

Sanibel Light and Keepers Quarters were officially listed on the National Register of Historic Places November 22, 1974.

The U.S. Fish and Wildlife Service decided not to renew its lease in 1980. Therefore, the U.S. Coast Guard announced in August, 1978, that the department had requested that an 1883 Executive Order placing the reservation under its jurisdiction be revoked. The federal government would keep the fifty-by-fifty-foot piece on which the lighthouse and keepers quarters stood. The rest would become surplus property. It was unlikely that it would be placed on the open market. After the federal agencies, Florida came next in line and would have an option to buy the tract to add to its parklands. Nevertheless, to insure its preservation, the City of Sanibel notified the Coast Guard that it wished to buy it. The Coast Guard was not willing to sell the property but it agreed to lease it to the City of Sanibel which would maintain it and house its employees in the keepers' quarters. The lease was signed in 1982.

Abia Vaughan Wiren

Courtesy of Bertha and Vaughan
Pearson

Pastor Andrew Wiren

Courtesy of Bertha and Vaughan
Pearson

Matthews Wharf on San Carlos Bay, 1896.

Chapter XI

THE PIONEER FAMILIES—EAST SANIBEL

Under the provisions of the Homestead Act of 1862, an American citizen, or one in the process of being naturalized, could acquire as much as one hundred and sixty acres of free land providing he or she was head of a family or over twenty-one, resided on the property or cultivated it for five years and paid proving up fees. Veterans of the United States Army were given special preference.

Until it was repealed in 1891 settlers also could take advantage of the Preemption Act of 1841 which permitted them to locate a claim of one hundred and sixty acres and after six months of residency purchase it for as little as $1.25 an acre.

Fort Myers had been opened for homesteading since the completion of the government survey in 1879, but because of transportation difficulties and federal restrictions, there were few people on the off shore islands.

The situation changed, however, when the railroad was extended to Punta Gorda in 1885. The following year, the steamer *Alice Howard*, scheduling three trips weekly between there and Fort Myers, brought both settlers and visitors into the San Carlos Bay area. St. James City, at the south end of Pine Island, became a fairly sizable community and with the construction of the San Carlos Hotel, Pine Island enjoyed modest fame as a tourist resort.

Settlers had been living on Sanibel under the pre-emption and homestead laws at least as early as 1884. It was to enable them to perfect their titles that the Acting Secretary of the Interior issued the order which released for private ownership all of the island except Sections 20, 21, and 29, the permanent lighthouse reservation at Point Ybel in 1888.

Henry Shanahan, born in Ireland, was a short, strong man who seldom was seen without a clay pipe, stem broken short, jutting from his mouth. He arrived in Key West in the early 1880s, aboard a fishing boat on which he was cook, and went to work at the lighthouse there. He married an American girl and the couple had three children, two of whom, Eugene and Webb, came with them to Sanibel. The eldest child, Grace, much older than the boys, never lived on the island.

Shanahan applied for the position of lighthouse keeper when Richardson resigned but because he could neither read nor write, the Lighthouse Board, at first, refused him. When the doughty Irishman made it clear he would not stay on as assistant, however, the usual educational standards were waived and his appointment was made official May 21, 1892. He was paid the princely sum of $640 per year and became one of the most able and meticulous keepers ever to serve on Sanibel.

Shanahan's first wife died shortly before the turn of the century leaving him with seven motherless children, Eugene, Webb, Henry, Flossie, Nell, Mattie and Ada. In 1900, he married Mrs. Irene Rutland, also widowed, who had come to Sanibel with her husband and children in 1896 after the Big Freeze had destroyed their citrus grove in West Apopka, Florida. Unwell even at that time, Othman Rutland died the following year. His widow, faced with the necessity of providing for her family, went into the business of raising turkeys.

There were five little Rutlands, Pearly, Katie, Marguerite, Newton and Clarence, and when their mother married Henry Shanahan, the combined family numbered twelve, eventually thirteen with the birth of Grinelle. Somehow, there was room for everybody in the keeper's quarters where they lived in happy confusion for more than fourteen years.

As the boys grew up, they helped tend the light. Eugene became assistant in 1906 and keeper after his father died in 1913. Webb and Henry lent a hand as did Clarence Rutland, who was assistant from 1918 to 1926. Henry, Sr. served until his death in 1913. He was buried in Key West.

The homesteaders, a diverse and colorful group, included three ministers. The first to arrive in 1884 was Pastor Andrew A. Wiren (pronounced Vi²-rain) of New Sweden, Maine. He was born in Sweden in 1841 and emigrated to America as a young man of twenty-six. He spent four years in Michigan then served as the first pastor of the Lutheran Church of New Sweden, arriving a year after the colony was established in 1870. The colonists had built their "Capitol" on a hill, a two-story building which contained storage rooms, offices for the Commission of Immigration and a big upstairs room which was used for church services, town meetings and the school which Pastor Wiren established as soon as he arrived. He gave English lessons to all who required them and provided his seventy-seven young students with a sound elementary school education.

Andrew Wiren was living in Woodland, about halfway between New Sweden and Caribou, Maine, when he met Abia Vaughan, the young blond daughter of Washington A. Vaughan, a pioneer and businessman of Caribou who built the first hotel, Vaughan House, in 1860. A local landmark, it repeatedly burned and was rebuilt over a span of ninety-four years. Abia was born in Caribou in 1857. Her mother died when she was seven and she did not get along well with her stepmother whom she considered too strict. When she fell in love with Andrew and wanted to marry him, her father, with three daughters under his roof, gave his consent perhaps with a sigh of relief. Abia was sixteen when they married in 1873.

The couple had five children, Washington, Estella, Alice, Ralph and an infant who died at birth. It was a happy home but for Pastor Wiren's health which steadily declined after he contracted tuberculosis. He was a sick man when he resigned his ministry in 1881. The family was living in Caribou when Ralph was born there in 1884. Shortly after that, because he had been told that Sanibel's climate would be good for his health, Pastor Wiren moved his family to the island.

The Wirens homesteaded 160 acres of land which extended along Periwinkle Way and down to San Carlos Bay and for a time they lived near the beach. Eventually, they built a small frame house along the main road but their years on Sanibel were not happy ones. Estella was only ten years old when she was badly burned and had to be in bed for a very long time. She had been trying to get a fire going when a bottle of kerosene exploded in her hand. Andrew's health was very poor and in the fall of 1890 he died of tuberculosis. He was buried on his land.

Abia returned to New Sweden with her children shortly thereafter and they were warmly welcomed. A new house was built for them and in 1891, she was appointed postmistress, a job she held for ten years. She sold off portions of her Sanibel property, some to Mary Bailey in 1894, to Rudolph Jenny in 1896 and the piece where their home had stood to W.D. Swint in 1913. By that time, Osman Rutland was buried beside Andrew Wiren beneath the palmetto trees. Abia died in 1922 and was buried in New Sweden.

Samuel Barber Woodring, was a descendant of Samuel

Wotring, who came to Pennsylvania in 1749 to claim his royal land grant in Whitehall Township. He was a Union soldier stationed at Key West during the Civil War and after it, returned to Pennsylvania where he married Elizabeth Rauch. The couple had three children there, Anna, Carl and Samuel.

Woodring was a blacksmith in Allentown when he decided to take his family south and for several years, they moved from place to place in Florida. When the builders of the resort on Pine Island advertised for help, he went there and made all of the iron pieces for the San Carlos Hotel. His wife, Anna, became chief cook and manager of the employee annex.

When his work was finished at the hotel, Samuel Woodring again became an itinerant blacksmith, traveling to the island communities in his own sailboat. A point at the northern end of Sanibel greatly attracted him and after he and Anna had explored its wild, untouched beauty, he resolved that he would one day own it. When the land was released for homesteading, he laid claim to 160 acres of today's Woodring's Point.

Woodring brought in lumber in summer, 1888, and the large, frame house was ready to move into November 1. The following January, Flora Sanibel was born there and a fifth child, Harrison, came along five years later.

As Samuel continued his work on the islands, Anna took in an occasional boarder and the children attended the first island school, reached by walking through the sandflats. When her husband died in 1900, Mrs. Woodring turned the family home into a boarding house, which became well known for the excellence of her cooking.

The children had left home by 1923 when she sold the place to winter residents and moved to Fort Myers to live with Flora. She died there in 1933.

As Samuel Woodring built the family home, another

homesteader was erecting a small, palmetto-thatched shack on Commodore Creek. Edwin Reed, called Commodore by his neighbors, lived on a pension received through his service in the Union Navy. He lived alone and very simply on the products of his fruit trees and garden and such fish as could be netted or caught from the end of a single-plank dock which extended into Tarpon Bay. A gentle, kindly man, he read voraciously and sent money regularly to relatives in St. Louis. When he died, no one came to claim the body and it was his neighbors who fashioned the rough, pine coffin and buried him on Sanibel.

By coincidence, another man of the same last name also homesteaded on Sanibel, arriving there shortly after the Woodrings.

William Haskell Reed, born in 1829 at Whitfield, Maine, grew up on coastal Deer Isle, where his mother's family had lived since 1786. His father was a doctor but Will took to the sea at an early age and had his own sloop by the time he married Lucy Elizabeth Thompson. He built a rambling house on Eggomoggin Reach and the couple's three children, William Sumner, Florence Lucy and Eugene, were born there.

He joined the Union Navy in 1864 and as an Ensign served on a gunboat of the Gulf Blockading Fleet. When "The Rebellion" was over, he returned to Deer Isle and again went to sea. He was master of the brig *Itasca* when an accident occurred while landing at Fire Island, New York, which claimed the lives of five of his crew. Deeply saddened, nonetheless, he continued as the ship's captain until the family moved to Portland where he worked as a shoe salesman.

Predictably, the job proved far from his natural bent and Will Reed did not stay with it very long. He went to Punta Gorda, Florida in 1887 and when Sanibel was opened to homesteading, he and his eldest son, William Sumner, investigated the island. Captain Reed laid claim to 160 acres along San Carlos Bay, southeast of the Woodring property, and as soon as a house was built for them, Mrs. Reed and the two younger children joined them. Their joy in the new adventure was short-lived. In April, 1889, Eugene was drowned when he fell from his sailboat.

Captain Reed and Will built homes and a dock from which the captain sailed his sloop *Lucy*, carrying freight and produce between Punta Gorda and the islands. His wife died in 1894 and a few years later, he went to Deer Isle, Maine, and went into business in Stonington. He married Jennie R. Haskell there in 1901. By 1910, he was back on Sanibel where he died in 1921.

William Sumner Reed became Sanibel's second postmaster in December, 1894, succeeding Laetitia A. Nutt. His post office was in his father's house next to the Reed dock. He called it Reed after himself until April 1, 1895, when it became Sanibel. After the captain's house was destroyed by the 1926 hurricane, a very small post office was built next to Will's house. It served Sanibel until 1943 when a new postmaster, Scotia Bryant, opened her post office at the ferry dock landing at lighthouse point.

Will Reed was postmaster for forty-four years, during which time, he and his wife, Charlotte, raised four daughters, Lelia, Carrie, Florence and Hazel. His sister, Lucy, married Bert Daniels and with her children saw him killed by a drunken farmhand in fall, 1907. He left his widow an unusual legacy. The pepper crop was very fine that year and with the money she made on it, Lucy, with some help from her father, was able to buy "The Floating Palace," a houseboat hotel. It was put ashore at the Reed place and renamed Sanibel House, it became a popular small hostelry. Lucy remarried in 1910, her second husband, O.L. Richardson, who bought the Mackie homestead land and put in Richardson Subdivision.

In late fall, 1888, Robert and Salome Dunlop and their three youngest children, Roberta, Claire and Charles, arrived at the lighthouse dock. They had come to homestead 160 acres of land in the interior of Sanibel which was not then densely wooded. To reach their claim, they followed cart tracks across the reservation and on a piece. This narrow road eventually became Periwinkle Way, named for the flowers which bloomed so profusely beside it.

Both Robert Bailey Dunlop and his wife, Salome Forrer, were of old, American families. The Dunlops came from Argileshire, Scotland, in 1750 to settle in Augusta County, Virginia, where Robert was born in 1835. The Forrers were Swiss, descendants of Christian Forrer, who came to Pennsylvania in 1750 as a boy of thirteen and stayed on to become a well known clockmaker. Salome, two years older than her husband, married him in 1851 and they had eight children, three of whom died in infancy. The two eldest, Mary Elizabeth and Daniel, were grown in 1889 and did not accompany their parents to Sanibel.

During the Civil War, the Dunlop plantation in Virginia was well-protected by the Confederates who needed the tannery which was on the premises. Nevertheless, when the war was over, the family left there for Gainesville, Florida.

Robert Dunlop lived but a short time after coming to Sanibel. He fell ill and died in August, 1889, and was buried on the property. His family stayed on, the teenage children taking such jobs as were available. Charles worked for one dollar a day at odd jobs at The Sisters Hotel, sometimes picking up an extra quarter selling fiddler crabs to such tourists as Thomas A. Edison. At one time, he was night watchman at Pt. Ybel for the International Ocean Telegraph Co. A telegraph cable, which was being laid from Key West to Punta Rassa, came ashore there and for a few hundred feet was underground. It was by way of cable that America would hear of the sinking of the *Maine* in 1898.

For a while the future looked bright for the family. In December, 1894, Charles had a fine crop of tomatoes for which he was offered a large sum. The following day, temperatures plummeted and with hundreds of other farmers, he was ruined by the Big Freeze.

Mrs. Dunlop received her homestead certificate in February, 1895. Not long after that, she left with the children for Boxwood, Virginia, where she died in 1910.

Charles Dunlop became a dentist and practiced in Brooklyn, New York. He retired in 1955 and came to Sanibel to live with his niece, Miss Pauline Wilson. He died in Tallahassee in March, 1962.

Mrs. Laetitia Ashmore Nutt would seem an unlikely pioneer of a remote little island of fishermen, farmers and smudgepots. A widow of aristocratic bearing, sharp of mind and eye, she had a no-nonsense air about her that bespoke school teacher—which she was. Strong, positive and resourceful, she came to Sanibel in 1889, with her daughters, Cordelia, Laetitia Lefon and Nannie, her brother, James Ashmore, and her eighty-year-old mother-in-law, Ann T. Nutt. All but the elder Mrs. Nutt took up homesteads along the gulf beach. The ladies built a large house, aptly called The Gables, which was both home and boarding house. James Ashmore, who had been a Confederate Army officer during the Civil War, built his house on adjoining property.

Laetitia Ashmore was born in Woodford County, Kentucky, in 1835, one of the fifteen children of Laetitia Lafon and William Edward Ashmore, an educated family with close, affectionate ties. She was twenty-two and very pretty when she married Leroy Moncure Nutt, an aristocratic Virginian.

When her husband joined the Confederate Army in 1862, Laetitia followed with their three small daughters

157

Laetitia Ashmore Nutt—1857.

Photo courtesy of United Daughters of The Confederacy.

and as he moved through the Southern battle grounds,
so did his wife and children, taking rooms as close as
possible to his camp. When the Arkansas post fell to
the Yankees, Captain Nutt was captured and until he
was exchanged for Union prisoners of war, his wife
stayed with him in prison.

Laetitia Nutt was indomitable during the war years
but the defeat of the Confederate forces dealt her an
embittering blow. For the rest of her life, she was
unforgiving of the North, Northerners and President
Lincoln, whom she blamed for all the woes of the South.

After the war, the family went to Shreveport, Louisiana, where Leroy Nutt became a well known lawyer and was elected to the state senate from Caddo Parish. The girls grew up in an atmosphere of genteel affluence and culture and eventually, Cordie and Lettie fell in love. Unfortunately, they never married for Cordie's choice, an Army officer from the North, and Lettie's station agent suitor were equally unacceptable to their mother. Nannie, quite late in life, married Sanibel homesteader, Nels Holt.

Captain Nutt died in 1882 and a few years later, a fire destroyed the Nutt home and most of its magnificent furnishings. Faced with financial ruin, the ladies had little choice but to homestead. Since Lettie was ailing, they chose the healthful climate of Sanibel Island.

Mrs. Nutt was appointed Sanibel's first postmistress July 3, 1889. She took boarders and day students into The Gables and in 1898, taught the island school. Her daughters became teachers and with her, they organized the Fort Myers chapter of the United Daughters of the Confederacy. She died in 1914 and was buried in the little family cemetery at The Gables which already contained the graves of James Ashmore and Mrs. Annie T. Nutt.

The sisters remained on Sanibel and continued to teach. Gentle Miss Cordie, intellectually brillant and dedicated to good works, helped organize Jones-Walker Hospital for Negroes in Fort Myers as well as Lee Memorial, of which she was a director. She organized the Sanibel Civic Club, which evolved into the Sanibel Community Association, and donated the land for the Community House. Lettie, quick and peppery, was an ardent conservationist and active in island affairs almost all of her long life.

In 1915 Cordie and Lettie moved into Palm Cottage selling The Gables to an Episcopal sisterhood, The Community of the Transfiguration of Cincinnati, Ohio.

The Order used the house for a winter home especially for the Mother Superior who was not well. When the Nutt sisters no longer could care for themselves, they were taken to the Order's retreat house at Bat Cave, North Carolina. Cordie died at Lee Memorial Hospital in Fort Myers in 1934; Nannie died out west in 1939 and Lettie died in Bat Cave in 1945. All were buried in the family cemetery.

Reverend George O. Barnes came to Sanibel in 1889, toward the end of an illustrious career. He was an evangelist of great eloquence and power, learned, witty and charitable. A tall, handsome man, he was a natural actor who moved without awkwardness on the platform and cast his spell through his magnificent gift of expresssion—yet no one could doubt his Christian commitment.

Because of his journeys into backwoods Kentucky, the *Louisville Courier-Journal* called him the Mountain Evangelist and printed one of his sermons each day. At the height of his career, thousands flocked to hear him. The sick came to be anointed with oil, and when any of these claimed to be healed, the newspaper published their names and addresses.

George Barnes was born in 1827 in Danville, Kentucky, the youngest of the four children of Maria Smith and James C. Barnes, a Presbyterian minister. In 1846, he graduated from Center College in Danville and went to work in the office of a well known Kentucky lawyer, only to volunteer a few weeks later for the Mexican War.

Barnes emerged unscathed with a reputation as a wit and a prankster—and a burning desire to become a minister. He entered his father's alma mater, Princeton Theological Seminary, and upon graduation, married a Kentucky girl, Jane Cowan. The two were sent as Presbyterian missionaries to India where their three children, Marie, William and Georgia, were born. They remained there almost twenty years.

Returning to the United States because of ill health, the Rev. Barnes soon found himself a controversial figure. He was much too unorthodox for the small Kentucky church to which he had been assigned and it was only a matter of time before he was he was on a collision course with the Kentucky Synod. Because of his doctrinal differences of opinion, he was tried for heresy and permitted to leave the Presbyterian Church. Shortly thereafter, he left for Chicago where an admiring friend had built an independent church expressly for him. There, he joined Dwight Moody for a series of meetings. It was the great Moody who recognized his special qualities and persuaded him to become an evangelist.

The family was back in Kentucky by 1877, the outcast now acclaimed. Marie traveled with her father over the winding mountain roads; bringing her organ with them in the horse-drawn cart, she added her music to the religious services conducted in the small, isolated communities. At the revivals in the cities and towns, both girls sang and as George Barnes' eyesight began to fail, Marie read the scriptures for him.

Eventually, they took their crusade all over the United States. In 1883, with his beloved daughter, Marie, George Barnes made a very successful world tour. In spring, 1889, the family was in Punta Gorda, Florida, where the evangelist had been invited to speak. Their arrival on Sanibel at the end of that week was totally unplanned.

They were cruising with friends aboard a sloop when it went aground in San Carlos Bay. To pass the time until the tide floated it off, the passengers decided to explore a nearby island—Sanibel. Thrilled by its pristine beauty, they inquired about homestead land. That same year, the parents and each of their children laid claim to a 160-acre tract. For George Barnes, Sanibel was the

Promised Land and he would always believe that God had guided them there.

The family first lived in the middle of their property in a house they called Palm Ranch. In 1890, they built a cottage type hotel which they named The Sisters because it lay at the junction of the land of Marie and Georgia. Mr. Barnes' church, the Church of the Four Gospels, was built after 1895 where the four corners of the family property met. The first on Sanibel, it was severly damaged by the 1910 hurricane and eventually torn down. The stained glass windows were put into Georgia's home and the pews moved into the little brown church on Periwinkle Way after it was built in 1917.

The Sisters became a fashionable and popular resort, known for its Indian cuisine and the hospitality of its owners. Georgia met and married a guest from Kentucky, Edward Duncan, and a home, Thistle Lodge, was built next to the hotel for them. Will married and was widowed while his children were very young and eventually married again; but Marie remained a spinster and raised her brother's son, Ferguson.

Reverend Barnes became an Episcopalian late in life but never was ordained in that church. His wife, Jane, died quietly in her chair in 1901, and not long after her death, he left the island. It is believed that he went to Zion City, north of Chicago, and joined the Doweyites, a religious sect that stressed divine healing. In 1908, he returned to Sanibel where he died. Both he and his wife were buried in Danville, Kentucky.

Marie Barnes became interested in the work of evangelist Aimee Semple McPherson and moved to California in the early 1920's. Georgia joined her there and the two sisters died in San Diego.

The hotel was renamed Casa Ybel shortly after the turn of the century. The Duncans managed it for some years. Will Barnes took it over in 1910 and stayed there until he died in 1923. At that time, Charlie Knapp bought the property which included a dozen buildings and 306 acres of land, a mile and a quarter of which was Gulf beach. He paid nineteen thousand dollars. It was sold to Dayton Hotels, Inc. in 1945.

In 1971, Howard Dayton, president, sold the hotel to a group of investors headed by Naples developer and attorney, Walter Condon, who changed the name to Island Beach Club. Condon lost the property in a foreclosure action March 31, 1976. Old Sanibel Cemetery, which had never been dedicated, was located at the back of the tract. Dayton donated it to the City of Sanibel in August, 1977. It would be preserved as a park.

Dayton Hotels, Inc. sold the land to Mariner Properties in June 1977 for $2.4 million. The name of the hotel once again became Casa Ybel. For a few months there was hope that Thistle Lodge would be restored and preserved as a historic landmark. Sally Cist Glenn, who had lived there, planned to move it to another location and renovate it for her family's use. However, the problems involved proved insurmountable. The island Water Association had declared a moratorium on water hookups and refused to make an exception for Thistle Lodge. Consequently, Mrs. Glenn could not secure financing and she had to abandon her dream. The structure was demolished in January, 1978.

The buildings of the old Casa Ybel were removed from the property and in 1979 modern condominiums were built there.

The Reverend George S. Fitzhugh was an Episcopal minister and an erudite man, well known for the excellence of his sermons. He was on Sanibel several times, the first in 1890. He came from Maryland by way of Pine Island with his wife, Angeline, his two sisters, and the children, George, Edward, Lena and Mary. They homesteaded three one-hundred-and-sixty-acre parcels along Periwinkle Way.

Father Fitzhugh conducted services in Fort Myers, Punta Gorda and sometimes, on Sanibel in Mr. Barnes' church. He traveled by horse and buggy, a rather stylish contraption later bought by the Bailey brothers for their mother.

The family left Sanibel before the turn of the century but in the 1920's, Edward returned with his wife Margaret and children Lee and Mary.

George Madison Cooper, born in Screven County, Georgia, in 1844, was sixteen when he joined the Confederate Army as a drummer boy. He served four years as a musician then returned home to face the difficult days of reconstruction. The Coopers, an educated and distinguished family, had been established in Screven County since the early 1790s and the town of Cooperville was named after them.

George Cooper was well-read and musical. A man well ahead of his time, he held broad views on religion and politics and supported the Socialist candidate, Eugene Debs, in the 1904 Presidential campaign. He was a widower with four children, Hugh, Helen, Mell and Marie, when he came to Florida in 1886. He established a sawmill on Yellow Fever Creek, across the river from Fort Myers and built a home nearby.

He married another Georgian, Mary Anne Davis, in 1888 and three years later the family moved to Sanibel where Captain Cooper laid claim to 160 acres of homestead land. Their two-story frame house was finished just in time for the new baby, Genevieve, who was born in April, 1891, at the lighthouse. One other child, George, also was born on Sanibel.

Like the Dunlops, Cooper was a truck farmer. He was successful in raising tomatoes, peppers, eggplant and a "money crop," watermelons. In time, he added three tenant houses and a packing house then built Tarpon Bay Road to get his produce to the long dock that was there.

He owned and operated several boats including the two masted *Three Brothers,* later replaced by a schooner with three masts which he sailed to Honduras to trade in mahogany and other exotic goods. The motor launch *Genevieve* made runs up the Caloosahatchee, while the *Marie Cooper* carried crates of Sanibel vegetables to Mobile, bringing to life the vision of Dr. Benjamin Strobel, who predicted such commerce in 1833.

George Cooper was the first justice of the peace and, probably, the first mail carrier. He went to St. James twice weekly to pick up the mail and bringing it home, placed it on top of his wife's sewing machine. Residents came individually and on foot to collect it.

Until 1910, the Cooper packing house was the island's polling place. Except for two years in Tampa, 1900-1902, members of the family occupied the farmhouse until the property was sold in 1913. John Bruaw, a farmer from Pennsylvania, bought it for six thousand dollars and with Elmer Fentrow, continued to farm the land. With another farmer, James Johnson, they built a packing house at the end of the pier at Tarpon Bay. Produce was shipped from there until the building became a store in 1921.

After selling their land, Captain and Mrs. Cooper, with Genevieve and Clarence, moved to Fort Myers where Cooper continued to operate a launch on the Caloosahatchee. He died there in 1916. His wife died the following year.

Florida's southwest coast attracted a number of sea-faring men from Maine, among them William H. Mackie, whose eighty-one acres of homestead land stretched along San Carlos Bay, north of Bailey Road. He came with his wife in 1891, leaving a son behind in Key West. He built a house and did a little farming.

The captain was a rather swashbuckling type who enjoyed telling tales of his earlier days as a ship's master. Among other things, he had run slaves, picking up his cargo on the beaches of North Africa where the Negroes were corralled and sold for one dollar a head, sometimes by their own chiefs. Mackie told hair-raising stories of restive captives, incipient uprisings, death and despair; and of the sharks that followed the ship, awaiting the corpses that, daily, were cast overboard.

Mackie received his homestead certificate in 1896 and shortly thereafter returned with Mrs. Mackie to Key West.

Samuel Ellis was a retired British Navy sailor who had worked with Samuel Woodring on the San Carlos Hotel and was married there while Mrs. Woodring was in charge of the Annex. His wife, the former Safiah Underhill, was a widow with one child, George. The family lived on Estero Island until 1891 when they moved to Sanibel where they homesteaded 157½ acres of land along Tarpon Bay which adjoined the homestead of Commodore Reed.

Short, stout and pugnacious, Ellis was never a pillar of society and spent little time farming. Most days, he could be seen sailing about the bay, jug at his elbow, while back at the palm-thatched homestead, Mrs. Ellis did the work with the help of young George. Not known for his social graces, he, nonetheless, showed a certain English aversion to being called by his first name. "My name's got a handle," he would growl. "Use it!"

Mrs. Ellis, tall and angular, was an Indian from the middle of Florida, a quiet, kindly woman, wise in Indian lore and a competent midwife. She delivered the baby of Aurora Woodring, then insisted that the young mother swallow a potion made from deer horn, scraped from an ancient and dusty relic on the homestead porch.

Smithsonian anthropologist, Frank Cushing, visited the Ellis place in 1895, investigating a Calusa burial mound which the owner had discovered on his property. In his paper delivered before the American

Philosophical Society in November, 1896, he remarked on his hospitable reception there and described the homestead as very picturesque, the thatched houses set on the low, flat stretch of sand admist clumps of palmetto and luxuriant lime, orange and other fruit trees. In a day of digging, he secured several skulls and a few pierced shell ladles, and left Sanibel with a note from Mrs. Ellis which was to introduce him to Mrs. Johnson on Mound Key.

After the death of her husband, Mrs. Ellis divided the Tarpon Bay property with George Underhill, who brought his wife to the island and raised his family there. Eventually, Safiah Underhill Ellis died and was buried next to her husband on their land.

George O. Barnes had great powers of persuasion and on frequent trips to Kentucky, he extolled Sanibel, declaring that he had found paradise. Among those who heard him was Mrs. Jane V. Matthews, a childless widow who saw life on a tropical island as both adventure and opportunity. Small, plump and determined, she left her home in Cincinnati, Ohio for Sanibel in the early 1890s and homesteaded 160 acres of land along the Gulf beach, adjoining the Nutt property.

Mrs. Matthews built houses for investment and two piers which she dedicated to the island in February, 1896. The dock on San Carlos Bay, as it turned out, mistakenly was built on government land, but the Lighthouse Board grumpily admitted that removing it would do more harm than good and permitted it to remain. With a plantation store at the end, it became a busy shipping point and was the center of island activity until the 1926 hurricane swept it away.

A second dock, with a bathhouse midway and a pavilion at the end, extended several hundred feet into the Gulf east of Mrs. Matthews' home. Frequently washed out and rebuilt, it finally succumbed to the storms of the '20s.

In 1895, friends of Mrs. Matthews, William and Har-

167

riet Matthews, rented the cottage next to her. With them were their four children, Annie Meade, Douglas, Charlotta and Clark. "Aunt Jane," actually unrelated to the family, was a frequent visitor and when she suggested paying to have her meals with them, it seemed a very sensible arrangement. By the end of the winter season, so many people had asked to do the same that the Matthews found themselves in the home restaurant business.

Jane Matthews died shortly after the turn of the century, leaving her homestead property to a niece, Julia Sanford, and a bequest of five hundred dollars to "Hallie" Matthews. Since Julia had no interest in the island, it seemed logical for the two to swap inheritances and this they did. Hallie immediately began giving away pieces of beachfront to friends, asking only that they build winter residences there and take their meals with her. Eventually, Jane Matthews' two-story home became lodgings for an increasing number of guests— and The Matthews Hotel was a reality.

William John Matthews, born in Indiana in 1856, grew up in Louisville, Kentucky, and attended Kentucky Military Institute, then a college, from which he graduated with honors. He married Harriet Wood, small, energetic and outgoing, who was born in Carollton, Kentucky, the same year as he, and educated at an Episcopal convent. In 1895, they were living in Louisville where William worked as an auditor for the Southern Railroad.

By that time, Mr. Barnes' hotel on Sanibel was well known in parts of Kentucky. When Will's father was slow to recover from an illness, it was decided to take him to The Sisters. The visit changed their lives, for only grandfather and Uncle Edward returned home at the end of the vacation.

Casting about for a way to make a living, William Matthews first went into farming with two friends, but the undertaking proved a dismal failure. The men

168

returned to Louisville and the Matthews had innkeeping thrust upon them.

They were ideally suited for hotel work. William, tall, brownhaired and easy going, viewed life and his fellow man with bonhomie, tolerance and humor and he delighted in good conversation. Hallie, bustling and efficient, was everybody's friend and was loved by everybody all of her long life. The hotel enjoyed a fine reputation and by 1917, it had outgrown its simple accommodations. The Barracks built then, was easily the most impressive structure on Sanibel with its three stories, four porches and thirty-one rooms. A dock, in front of it, washed away twice but the barracks remained in use, remodeled, until 1970 when it was torn down to make room for new construction.

William Matthews died in 1927 and was buried in Louisville. With the help of her daughter, Charlotta, Hallie continued to run the hotel, which was renamed the Island Inn in 1937. She died on Sanibel in 1950. The hotel remained in the family until 1957 when it was sold to the Island Inn Company.

Ernest Royal Bailey came to Sanibel in May, 1894, to investigate the feasibility of farming. He took a room with Mrs. Nutt, fifteen dollars a month with board, leased a six-acre field from Ed Duncan and began dickering with Nels Holt to buy land. With the prognosis good, in spite of heat and mosquitos, he was joined in August by two of his brothers, Marion Harrison (Harry) and Francis Pryce (Frank), and in the fall, by their widowed mother Mary Beers Bailey. None of them had ever been farmers.

At the height of the gold rush in 1849, Samuel Major Bailey of Richmond, Virginia, only son of an only son, boarded a clipper ship and sailed around the horn. He stayed in California long enough to find a few gold nuggets, one of which became a handsome ring; then, heading home, crossed the Isthmus of Panama on the back of a donkey.

In 1854, Samuel married Mary Beers, a well-educated young lady from Virginia, whose grandfather, a Connecticut sea captain, had come from England in 1706. The two had nine children, seven of whom survived childhood. Samuel carried on the family business, the manufacture and distribution of tobacco products such as Bailey's Best and Pride of the West, well known brands of plug tobacco.

Samuel drove an ambulance during the Civil War and his business suffered as battling troops burned and trampled the tobacco fields. Nevertheless, the family stayed in Richmond until some years after a fire destroyed their large warehouse. They moved to Covington, Kentucky in 1878.

Samuel Bailey died in 1885 and the business was passed on to his eldest son, also named Samuel, who inexpertly ran it to the ground. By 1894, Mary Bailey had decided that she and her three youngest sons, Harry, twenty-seven, Ernest, twenty-three, and Frank, twenty-one, should seek a new life on Sanibel. She had heard of it from Jane Matthews. At that time, Frank was a clerk in a steel rolling mill in Cincinnati, across the river from Covington.

The family, well-read, intelligent and outgoing, were well received on Sanibel and there were few civic or social affairs that didn't include one or all of them. Mrs. Bailey, of aristocratic bearing and stylishly turned out, was a woman of strong will and pioneering spirit who ruled the roost as long as she was in it. She died in 1913.

Harry, easy going and convivial, had been a secretary before turning farmer. He married Miriam Pasteur, who taught school on Sanibel in 1919, and moved to Fort Myers soon after. They had no children.

Ernest, an active layman of the Episcopal Church, loved the theater and was himself an actor who always spoke in accents fine. Often, he was up and away with some theater group or enrolled in a college course that happened to interest him. A proponent of healthful living, he didn't ride when he could walk and never missed his daily "sunbawth" at the end of Bailey's dock. In 1919, too old to be a soldier, he served with the YMCA in France for the duration of World War I. He never married.

Frank, a genial man with a quiet sense of humor, was dependable, hardworking and the most reponsible of the brothers. He married Annie Meade Matthews in 1919 and they had three sons, Francis P., Jr., John and Samuel. Frank, a founder of the Community Church, became a school trustee and justice of the peace.

For the Baileys, the years on Sanibel were not without setbacks. The Great Freeze destroyed their first garden as snowflakes drifted through the air and long icicles hung from the wooden cisterns. They replanted and were doing well by 1898. Nevertheless, Ernest went to Cuba to farm experimentally, hoping to undersell the U.S. market. The enterprise ended in a tangle of red tape a year later and, deciding that "the game is not worth the candle", he returned to Sanibel.

In 1899, the Bailey brothers bought out Will and Charles Geraty and Steele Doyle, who had been operating a plantation store at the end of Jane Matthews' wharf on San Carlos Bay. At about that time, their combined enterprises, which included groves and gardens, became the Sanibel Packing Company. It proved the most durable of island businesses.

The 1926 hurricane destroyed the Matthews wharf and the buildings on it disappeared into the bay. Soon afterward, Frank and Ernest put up a new building, some distance up the beach, which became a general store. A county dock was constructed in front of it.

The store, called "Bailey's," also served as an emergency center for people with problems and a social center for those awaiting the steamers. Shady and musty-smelling, it contained a variety of intriguing things to buy—or search for. Bamboo poles leaned in an out of the way corner and somewhere there were bathing slippers, postcards, fish hooks and Klim. At one end, Frank worked at his desk under a light suspended from the ceiling, his eyes protected by a green sunshade. Ernest's desk was next to it and on one or the other was a cantankerous telephone used to send and receive telegrams, often incomprehensibly garbled.

Tragically, Mrs. Bailey died in 1935, leaving her three sons to be raised by their father. Harry died in 1943, Frank in 1952 and Ernest in 1954. All members of the family were buried in the family plot in Richmond, Virginia.

Francis P. Bailey, Jr. took over the store after his father died and modernized it. It was moved into a new location in 1966.

George Riddle came to Sanibel with his father, James, in 1895. after the Great Freeze had destroyed their groves in Umatilla, Florida. They bought eighty acres of land along Casa Yble Road and planted it in vegetables and citrus. James Riddle, who homesteaded Silver Key and adjacent land, left the island two years later. His son stayed on, built a house for his wife Clyde and two small daughters, Florette and Irene. He bought forty more acres on Tarpon Bay Road and by 1904, had a store there.

Riddle became a school trustee and for one term, a Lee County Commissioner. Other children came along—Louise, George, Jeannie Clyde, James, Blanche and Marion—their home was enlarged and the family was deeply involved in island affairs. It was the 1910 hurricane which brought them financial disaster. The family survived the storm in their packing house, the little children tucked into the vegetable bins, but the gardens were a total loss.

George Riddle tried washing the salt from the soil but never again was he able to raise good crops on his land. In 1914, he gave up and moved the family to Fort

172

Myers. Mrs. Riddle died in 1923, her husband in 1946.

James Hugh Johnson came to Sanibel in 1898 because he had heard that it was one of the largest truck farming areas in the South. The Big Freeze had wiped out his groves on Lake Placid, Florida, and he was forced to go to work in a crate factory. But he wanted to return to farming and, while on Sanibel, he worked for Frank Bailey.

He was no stranger to hard work. The thirteenth son of Florida pioneer William Johnson, he was fifteen years old when his father died in 1884. With older brothers grown and gone, James became head of the houshold working in the groves to provide for his mother, Georgeana, and younger siblings.

By 1901 he owned a farm with a house on Periwinkle Way to which he brought his wife Beal and their sons Ray, Belton and Fred. Eventually, the coconut palms he planted there gave name to a restaurant, Coconut Grove, built on the site by John Kontinos in 1957.

Tragedy seemed to stalk James. Beal was in Georgia with her sister in 1904 when she and her baby died in childbirth. Georgeana came to care for the children and stayed with James until he married Anna Higdon in 1907. Their daughter Elizabeth was born on Sanibel and in 1912, a son, Earl, who was just three months old when his mother died. In 1914, when James married Emma Young, a widow with two children, the Johnsons became one, big happy family.

Along with other island families, they faced financial ruin when the 1921 hurricane pushed sea water over their fields, killing everything and making the soil unfit for cultivation. James, Emma and the two youngest children moved to Dr. Franklin Miles' farm on the Caloosahatchee. Misfortune still dogged their footsteps. James contracted measles, then pneumonia, which so undermined his health that he no longer could do the heavy work of farming. The family moved into Fort Myers where Emma took boarders into their house on

Jackson Street. James was living with Belton, who had remained on Sanibel, when he died in 1935.

Belton enlisted in the Naval Reserve during World War I and, afterward, became a commercial fisherman, a fishing guide and a boat pilot. He married a young widow, Miriam Williams, in 1942 and her daughter Jeanette became as dear to him as if she were his own. They moved to Captiva where Belton worked for eight years for winter resident Alice O'Brien as captain of her yacht. Well known and well loved, he was ninety years old when he died in 1986.

Meanwhile, Earl Johnson had returned to Sanibel to fish commercially. Later, he worked at South Seas Plantation on Captiva as groundskeeper and security guard. He retired amidst fond farewells in 1977.

Mary Dos Santos Bowen, 1878.

Courtesy of Helen Bowen Hileman.

Oliver Fellows Bowen, 1887.

Courtesy of Helen Bowen Hileman.

Captiva Cemetery, established 1901.

Chapter XII

THE PIONEER FAMILIES—WULFERT, CAPTIVA AND BUCK KEY

During the 1890s and well into the 1920s, the Wulfert area of Sanibel was a busy farming community. The name originated with the post office which was named after no one and no place anybody had ever heard of—except presumably, the post office inspector.

Originally known as Dwight Settlement, after an early arrival, dissension arose among the inhabitants when the post office was established February 2, 1897. Jennie Doane, the first postmistress, noted that Sanibel Post Office once had been named Reed after its postmaster and she saw no reason why hers should not become Doane. Understandably rankled, Mason Dwight objected, and the fat was in the fire.

The matter was still unresolved when the postal inspector came to look over the new facility. No one remembers his name, except that it was not Wulfert, but he was a man of limited patience. He warned that he would wait only overnight; then, if the residents had not decided on a name, he would decide for them.

Day dawned with no agreement and this unknown gentleman stepped forward. The name of the new post office, he declared, was Wulfert—and with that he wrote up the papers and departed—with no explanation of any sort.

Oliver Fellows Bowen, a Mississippi River boat pilot, and his wife, Mary Dos Santos, were first to homestead there. They arrived in 1887 with their children, Marguerite and Harold, and laid claim to eighty acres of land. They had come from Port of Spain, Trinidad, in their own sailing vessel which was loaded, not only with their household effects, but with lumber, slate shingles and even nails with which they would build their house and barn. Oliver also brought agave, called century plant, scions of which still grow there. He had hoped that the sap might prove to be a substitute for rubber. The project failed and Mary would say that the only time Oliver made money on Sanibel was when he killed a large rattlesnake and sold the hide.

Bowen was born in 1828 in Akron, Ohio, where his father was a metal forger. As a young man he felt the lure of the Mississippi and as he had an uncle, Sam Bowen, in Hannibal, Missouri, he went to live with him. He became apprenticed to Horace Bixby, known up and down the river as the best pilot there was and when he became certified, he came home to the adulation of his younger cousins, Will, Sam and Bart and their friend, Samuel Clemens, who would gain fame under the pen name of Mark Twain. He was, indeed, a dashing figure, his eyes bright blue under the broad-brimmed pilot's hat. As was his right, he wore white shirt and trousers, dark coat, flowing tie and a gold watch with chain and fob that distinguished his trade. He would wear no other, even on Sanibel. His cousins and Sam Clemens, perhaps inspired by him, also became pilots.

Another uncle, Francis Bowen, gained notoriety in New York as the last man to be hanged for running slaves. He was at the time captain of the *Nightingale,* the once proud clipper ship which had fallen on evil times.

Bowen's first marriage was annulled after an unsuccessful elopement. His second, to Eliza Sones, produced a son, Richard, in 1861. When the Civil War reached the Mississippi, he was pressed into service as a pilot in the Confederacy's River Defense Force. He served aboard the *Gen. Van Dorn*, a converted gunboat which played a major part in the Confederate victory in the Battle of Plum Bend in April 1862. The Union Navy made a better accounting of itself when the two forces met again at Memphis. The *Van Dorn* was the only Confederate gunboat to survive this terrible battle which sealed the fate of the Confederate Navy. Bowen piloted it down the Mississippi then up the Yazoo River to safety. He was paid off and honorably discharged June 24, 1862.

He returned to the river when hostilities were over and when the Venezuelan government bought a paddle-wheeler he delivered it to Caracas. He was a widower by then with Richard in the care of relatives so he stayed on. He was living in Port of Spain, Trinidad, when he met Mary Dos Santos, a handsome woman sixteen years younger than he was. She was born on Madiera Island off the coast of Morocco. Her parents, Presbyterians in a Catholic country, had fled religious persecution when she was a girl, crossing the Atlantic Ocean to Trinidad in an open whaling boat. When Bowen married her in 1878 he married a strong woman well able to cope with hard times and hard work on Sanibel.

Mary ran the farm at Wulfert, growing vegetables for northern markets with little help from Oliver. Fastidious about his white trousers, he didn't work in the fields but often delivered produce and eggs to the San Carlos Hotel on Pine Island. Sometimes he then would sail down the Caloosahatchee to Fort Myers where Thomas Edison, the great inventor, often could be found fishing for sheepshead off his dock. The two would discuss Bowen's experiment, for Edison, too, sought a rubber substitute.

179

Mary had learned lacemaking as a child on Madeira and when their youngest son, Albert, was born in 1890 she made him an exquisite pair of tiny lace stockings. He would remember the happy time on Sanibel when the children swam in the bayou, went fishing and played with the wooden animals carved by Harold.

But his father's health was failing and he spent more and more time in his hammock slung between two trees next to the well. When he died February 17, 1894, Mary followed to the letter the burial instructions he had left for her. A workman, Frank Mitchell, filled in the well almost to the top, then enlarged it to accommodate the coffin. The Mississippi River boat pilot was laid to rest in his favorite spot and after the funeral, Mitchell put a concrete slab over the grave. Later, Richard Bowen placed a tombstone there.

Richard had been working as a mining engineer in the Kimberly diamond mines in South Africa. When he arrived on Sanibel he offered to support the family in exchange for the homestead land, an offer Mary gratefully accepted. Marguerite and Harold went to live with their Aunt Chinty in Oberlin, Ohio. Mary stayed in Wulfert to complete the homestead requirements then took Albert with her to Trinidad. She died in Los Angeles, Californina, in 1922.

Mason C. Dwight, who came with his wife in 1894, bought 112 acres of land which he put into citrus groves and produce. His partner in the venture was Thomas Holloway, a bachelor Englishman, who took care of the farming end of the business. Over the years, Dwight served as shipping agent, storekeeper, and after Jennie Doane, postmaster.

The Dwights had no children. Since Mrs. Dwight was in poor health, they hired a housekeeper, Mrs. Julia Carson, whose son, Robert, then fourteen, worked in the groves.

As at Captiva, shallows close in kept the steamers

Lewis and Jennie Doane.

. From their family album

from docking at Wulfert and all freight, mail and passengers arrived and departed by way of the bulkheads, about a mile and a half off shore.

The mail carrier at that time was Lewis Austin Doane, husband of the determined Jennie, a short, slight man with a drooping mustache and an anxious expression. He was born in North Dana, Massachusetts in 1844 and was eight years older than his wife. They married in 1883 and had one child who died in infancy.

Jennie Doane, a pretty brunette in her younger days, was a staunch believer in dress reform and women's rights. She posed for her wedding photo in a dark, tailored, calf-length dress over matching long pants. On other occasions, she was attired in a dress or skirt and bloomers which reached the tops of her high button shoes. This was her costume, with few modifications, all her life.

The Doanes had lived in Vineland, New Jersey, and Ocala, Florida, before homesteading on Sanibel in 1897. They raised chickens and had a garden. Their neighbors believed that they had come to Wulfert to establish a spiritualist colony with the Dwights and Dr. O.N. Bancroft, a chiropractor, who also homesteaded. This undertaking never materialized but the Doanes continued their beliefs. They frequently held seances during which tables moved and ghostly voices spoke. They got on well with the other residents and were honest, unconventional folk who kept their coffins at their home some time before they were needed. Robert Knowles, who lived on Buck Key as a child, recalled going with his mother to the Doane house and was served breakfast there—six walnuts rolling around on a plate.

Lewis Doane died in 1921 and was buried in the Captiva cemetery. Some years later, Jennie was laid to rest there beneath a monument carefully inscribed with the family's vital information—except the date of her own death, March 26, 1929.

Josiah Dinkins, who filed his claim in 1898, lived in Wulfert for 28 years. He was a steamboat engineer, married late in life to an enormous, pleasant woman who, some said, had been the Fat Lady in a circus. Dinkins had many acres in citrus fruit and feuded with his neighbor, Father Stahley, a retired Episcopal priest, who was mean as sin and a little senile. Dinkins died in Fort Myers at the age of ninety-five.

Some of the Wulfert homesteaders stayed but a short time. Robert Bowman, after whom the beach is named, never completed his homestead requirements and David Hope left after receiving his certificate in 1898. In 1902, there were ten families in the community. There was never a church but in 1901, David Sumner taught nineteen students in the home of S.L. Roberson. In 1902, a schoolhouse was built for them. It was attended until it combined with the Captiva school in 1917.

The storms of the 1920s badly damaged the gardens

and groves at Wulfert. After the 1926 hurricane, most of the farmers sold out to Clarence Chadwick who put the whole area into lime groves, vestiges of which remain today.

Although the population of Sanibel continued to increase, Captiva had few permanent residents before 1900. The homestead of Judge Powell, whose brother had been part of the plot to assassinate Lincoln, adjoined the government reservation at Captiva Pass, and the claim of the Bain brothers was next to it. South of The Narrows, which became Redfish Pass in 1921, only William H. Binder was in residence in 1888. He was alone there for ten years, a willing Robinson Crusoe in his tropical paradise.

Binder first landed on Captiva as a boy, quite by accident. An Austrian, he was en route to New Orleans on a German freighter when it wrecked off Boca Grande. Unable to swim, he clung to some floating planks and eventually was carried by the currents into the shallow water off Foster's Point. He stayed on Captiva, living on wild fruits and seafood, for some weeks, gaining weight. He gathered timbers with which he improvised a small boat. This he paddled to Pine Island where he found people who helped him to return home.

William Binder was thirty-eight years old when he returned to Captiva in 1888. Because he had served in the U.S. Army and was in the process of becoming naturalized, he was permitted to homestead 160 acres of land, roughly at the midsection of Captiva as it is today. He was known as a man with a musical education, and perhaps, a career in grand opera. He played a silver flute with sweetness and skill, but supported himself in his declining years by selling off parts of his homestead property. A widower, he occasionally was visited by his son. But mostly he lived alone, becoming prickly and unsociable as the bed of sandspurs which surrounded his little frame house. He died and was buried on Captiva in 1933.

George W. Carter, a tall, spare, blue-eyed man, had spent most of his life on the water. He was born in Georgia in 1840 but moved to Florida as a young man and worked there as a professional fisherman and boatman. He married Elizabeth Brewer and the two had eight children, three of whom died in childhood. The other five were young adults in 1898 when the family moved to Captiva to homestead 160 acres of land, now part of South Seas Plantation.

A Mr. Montgomery, who had abandoned the property without completing his homestead requirements, wanted to return to it and fiercely disputed the Carter claim—at times, with a loaded shotgun. But George Carter, quiet and tenacious, refused to relinquish his legal right and divided his land among his three sons, James, Knight and Jesse. Primarily, the brothers were fishermen, but after building their homes, they put in a truck garden and a grapefruit grove and eventually built a long dock from which to ship their produce.

The Carters had two daughters, Mary Jane, called Mamie, and Alpine. Mamie, petite and pretty, was a widow with two small children when she married Tobe Bryant in 1898. Alpine remained a spinster and with the elder Carters, lived with Jesse, who had married Bessie Gibson in 1907. Their comfortable frame house today is part of the dining room of South Seas Plantation hotel.

The old folks died within a few months of each other in 1914, but the brothers remained on Captiva until 1921. On October 25 of that year, a devastating hurricane pushed nine foot tides over the islands and for several days the Carter gardens and those of their neighbors lay under a lake of salt water. When it drained off, groves and gardens were dead or dying. Faced with financial ruin, the Carters left the island to find work elsewhere. All but Jesse went to North Carolina. In 1923, the brothers sold their land to

Tobe and Mamie Bryant with five of their children. Captiva.

Photo from Scotia Bryant Collection.

Clarence B. Chadwick of Denver, the inventor of the protective paper with overprinting which is used for bank checks.

Chadwick came to Captiva in 1923 on a vacation trip with his wife Rosamond who had been a nurse and became a concert singer. In poor health at that time, he became increasingly arthritic and within three years was confined to a wheelchair. A glassed-in, heated swimming pool, fed by sea water, was added to his home and this, with frequent sunbaths, eased his stiff limbs— but not his acerbic personality. Tightfisted with money, he was abrasive and unpopular. Rosamond, however, was kind and outgoing and once saved the life of little Edward Willis who had swallowed kerosene.

There were towering coconut palms on the Captiva property and Chadwick planted more, creating a coconut plantation from which he hoped to harvest copra. When the 1926 hurricane killed citrus groves at Wulfert, he bought most of the arable land there and acreage on Pine Island, replanting it in limes. By 1940, he was building cottages on the former Carter homestead for people who worked for him, visualizing it a community with a pier and a post office. It never thrived and the property eventually was sold for a hotel, appropriately named South Seas Plantation.

After Clarence Chadwick died in 1947, his widow moved to Fort Myers, where they maintained a house, and was active there until her death in 1961.

Wilson Langley Bryant was better known as "Tobe," a nickname bestowed on him by his father, who thought him stubborn as Tobe, the family mule, He was born in Lake City, Florida in 1871, the eldest of seven children of Granville Worthington Bryant, who had married twice and twice was widowed. The family had been in Florida since 1812 and were descendants of an Irish nobleman who emigrated to Georgia for political reasons in the 1700s.

Tobe, a big man with a square, determined jaw, had had one year of college and liked to spend his spare time, what little there was, reading. He was working as a well driller in Useppa when he and Mamie Curry were married and their first child, Elizabeth, was just three weeks old when they moved to Captiva in 1899. The family homesteaded 160 acres just south of the Carter property, their first home a palmetto hut on Bryant's Bayou. Eventually, there were ten children, Ollie May and James Curry, Elizabeth, the twins William and Hunter, Jesse, George, Johnnie, Mary Jane and Joseph.

Tobe grew sugar cane and made syrup at his own mill, planted avocados, vegetables and fourteen acres of citrus fruit, some of it on "oil ridge" which seemed to shed rain water as fast as it fell. In 1903, he ran for State Representative on the Socialist ticket and was defeated.

In 1917, with his family bursting at the seams, Tobe

built a larger house a half mile from the Gulf beach, wisely putting wooded areas, a swamp and oil ridge between them and high tide.

G.W. Bryant and his older children, Hunter, Karl, Corely and Lula, came to Captiva in 1901, at which time he and Karl bought land from Tobe and farmed. Lula and Corley did not stay but Hunter became the island's first postmaster in 1901, his post office a small, plank house on the bulkhead about a mile from shore. He moved to Fort Myers in 1903 and became county tax assessor. Karl married Rosa Kennon after her family moved to Captiva in 1902. They lived with their four children, Scotia, Granville, Kenneth and Robert, part time on Captiva but mostly in Fort Myers where Karl operated a restaurant, then a movie house and a bowling alley.

Early in 1921, Tobe's farm was worth more than thirty-five thousand dollars; in October a hurricane ruined it. The Chadwicks bought it in 1923 for nine thousand dollars. The Bryant home, remodeled, became their winter residence, grandly renamed the Manor House. Now on the beach, it is part of South Seas Plantation resort. The artesian well which Tobe dug on an oil ridge is harder to locate. Still flowing, it is a quarter of a mile out in the Gulf, a curiosity to the boaters who pass over it.*

For a time, Tobe endured the embittering experience of working as a farmhand for $1.50 a day on land which once had been his. He left to take a job at the fish house at Matlacha. He was working in Miami as a carpenter when he fell from a scaffold, breaking his leg at the knee, an injury which would cause him to limp for the rest of his life. He was a Glades County Commissioner at one time but he and Mamie were living in Fort Myers

---

* Over the years, wave action has carried away hundreds of feet of Gulf front property. Erosion remains Captiva's most pressing problem.

187

when she died in 1950. He also died there, in 1961.

The Narrows was the last property to be homesteaded on Captiva. Fort Myers attorney Walter F. Mickle built a large home there in 1909 for his wife, Lucy, and their eight children, Mack, Maurice, John Margaret, Chubb, Lucy, Helene and Ward. For seven years, Mickle commuted to the island on weekends as he continued to practice law in Fort Myers. The family moved to Fort Myers in 1916, lived briefly at St. James, then returned to the city.

The Mickle property had been sold and there was no one living in the old house in 1921 when a hurricane swept through The Narrows. It became Redfish Pass. Walter Mickle died the same year. His wife died in 1947.

Two hundred yards off Captiva's southeastern shore was Buck Key, named for the large deer that frequented it. It was little more than a mile long and perhaps less than half a mile across, yet, ridged with Indian mounds, it supported the homesteads of three families and a bachelor uncle.

The first to arrive in 1896 was Herbert Dwight Brainard, a dairy farmer who was born in Canada in 1856. Because he had not been well, he and his wife sold their farm in Quebec Province and moved to Buck Key with their children, Gordon, an adopted son, and Ann, then five years old.

Before leaving home, each of the children had been given a gold piece by their grandparents and Ann still had hers when the family moved into their new home. An endearing little girl, sensitive and responsive, she loved to row across the channel with her mother and watch the sun set from a small, wooded knoll on Captiva. Because it was her favorite spot, she decided to buy it with her gold piece, and to everyone's surprise, William Binder agreed to sell it to her.

The Brainards planted citrus groves on Buck Key and

A "Log Rolling" on Captiva. Neighbors helped each other clear their land and made an outing of it. Scotia Bryant Collection.

(Courtesy of Anne Bryant)

during their five years there, Mrs. Brainard gave birth to four blue babies who died in infancy. Their greatest tragedy, however, occurred after they had moved to Captiva in 1901. Ann, who had stepped on a nail, contracted tetanus and died within a week. Her grieving parents buried her on her own land. It became Captiva cemetery.

Hattie Brainard, all her life the Good Samaritan, became the the island midwife and put her doctoring talents to good use. She was appointed Captiva's postmistress in 1903, and served thirty-five years. Her post office was a box-like enclosure in her own home which in the early years was no more than a thatched hut.

Gordon Brainard married May Kennon and the couple had young children when he died as a result of a tragic escapade the night of April 1, 1912. With his friends, he had sneaked up on the camp of some black workers and as the men sat around their campfire, Gordon suddenly yelled and began firing into the ground at their feet. As the others ran for cover, one of the men picked up a grub hoe and hit Gordon over the head with it, killing him almost instantly. Gordon's friends carried him home and a posse was formed to bring in his assailant, but the men had slipped away and none of them was ever apprehended.

Herbert Brainard was fifty-eight when he died and was buried with his children in Captiva Cemetery. Hattie had become interested in spiritualism through her friendship with Jennie Doane and it was because of this that she eventually married a second time. A relative in Wichita, Kansas suggested that Hattie correspond with a friend, Alvin Gore, who shared that interest, and the two became "pen pals." They met for the first time on Captiva in 1915. Appropriately, it was the mailman, Robert Knowles, who brought him ashore. The meeting went well and a wedding soon followed.

The Brainard's frame house contained the post office and in 1925, it was enlarged to become the Gore Hotel. It was blown apart by Hurricane Donna in 1960 and burned shortly thereafter.

Alvin died in 1934, Hattie in 1945. She was eighty-two. Both were buried in Ann's little cemetery to which Mrs. Gore had donated another acre of land.

The northern end of Buck Key was homesteaded by Henry Perry Knowles, a Georgia farmer, who came with his wife, Julia, in 1897. Like their neighbors, the Knowles grew grapefruit, still new in the United States and much in demand on the northern markets.

They had only one living offspring, a son, Harvey Edward, who was thirty-two years old when he brought his wife and son to Buck Key in 1898. Traveling from Inverness, Florida, in a covered wagon, Edward sold the contraption in Punta Gorda to buy steamship tickets and arrived on Captiva almost broke. With his last fifty cents, he bought a hoe and went to work for Tobe Bryant.

With the help of his neighbors, Ed Knowles built a thatched hut and for some months, his two year old son Robert enjoyed playing in the sand and shells which were all there was to the floor. Unfortunately, it burned down and the family moved to Buck Key where a frame house was built. They moved to Arcadia in 1900.

Mrs. Julia Knowles died in 1909, and Henry was alone on his one hundred and forty-four acre farm on Buck Key. Edward eventually returned to Captiva and was farming there with his wife when his son arrived to take a job as mail carrier. Robert stayed two years, then left to continue his studies. He received his teacher's certificate in 1917 and was drafted in 1918. He spent a year in the Army then married and returned to Captiva to teach school. He and his wife were living in Buckingham, Florida when the 1921 hurricane destroyed the Knowles' Captiva farm. Mr. and Mrs. Edward Knowles moved to the east coast of Florida in 1922.

Captain and Mrs. George Ormsby, their daughters, Ida Will and Louise, arrived on Buck Key at about the same time as the Knowles. They homesteaded the south end of the island and George's bachelor brother, William, homesteaded sixty-seven acres next to them. He received his homestead certificate in 1903. Both properties were planted in citrus and other tropical fruits.

It was largely through the efforts of the Ormsbys that a school district was organized on Buck Key in 1897. In February, 1898. twelve students, drawn from Wulfert and Captiva as well as Buck Key, were hard at work in the little schoolhouse on his property. Their teacher was Miss Fannie Porter. For four years, it was the only public school available in that area. In 1903, George Ormsby drew funds of two dollars and fifty cents a pupil for the seven who remained but his teacher left him before the year was out, and it is assumed that the children then transferred to Captiva.

The hospitable Ormsbys hosted community outings of all sorts and church and Sunday School classes were held at their place. A beautiful spot, it was a favorite destination for island excursions. From time to time, Mrs. Ormsby took boarders into their two-story home.

For one winter session, January through May, 1914, Professor Clarence Snyder of Chicago used the buildings for his "Outdoor School." George Ormsby died in 1914 and his widow and daughters left the island.

Over the years, the natural vegetation returned to Buck Key and it was very beautiful. However, the island was zoned for rather high density construction and it was feared that it would be overdeveloped. Sanibel-Captiva Conservation Foundation in cooperation with The Nature Conservancy contacted the property owners and each was asked to consider preserving the land in its natural state. One of them, Mrs. Elena Duke Benedict, responded munificently. She donated her two hundred acres, worth more than one million dollars to The Nature Conservancy in honor of her family. Benedict Wildlife Sanctuary, her gift to the American people, was dedicated in January, 1979.

Teddy Roosevelt on Captiva. L. to R.: Fishing guide, (name unknown) Roosevelt, Mrs. Julia Dickey, Col. Coles and Dr. John Dickey. Photo courtesy of Mrs. Dorothy Dickey.

Thistle Lodge at Casa Ybel Hotel. 1924.

Chapter XIII

FARMING, HURRICANES AND THE TOURIST TRADE

In 1898, the Revenue Cutter, *McLain*, patroled the waters around Sanibel and Captiva and the U.S. Signal Corps took over the operation of Sanibel Light. An observation tower was erected at the south end of Tarpon Bay Road, but except for the influx of seven young men, considered a social windfall by the young ladies of the islands, the one-hundred-fourteen-day Spanish-American war produced nothing in the way of excitement.

That same year, a telephone line was extended from the cable office on Punta Rassa to the Sanibel lighthouse and on to The Sisters Hotel. It was operative by mid-June.

Sanibel, Captiva and Buck Key were flourishing agricultural communities by then; their chief products grapefruit, tomatoes, peppers, eggplant and watermelon. John Morris, then farming on Sanibel, wrote the *Lee County News* that he had grown 880 crates of peppers and 972 crates of eggplant on less than two acres of ground and grossed $2,695 on them. He also shipped 4,240 crates of tomatoes. Other farmers, too, did very well and in 1919 grapefruit grown by the Bailey brothers brought the best price of the season ($6.30 a box) on the New York market. The industry peaked just before the 1921 hurricane when the islands were shipping more than 150,000 crates of produce a year. This storm, followed by the 1926 hurricane, virtually ended farming as a lucrative business on the islands.

Most growers were served in the very early days by the steamers of the Plant Line which departed every morning except Sunday from each end of the Fort Myers-Punta Gorda run. The most palatial of these, the sternwheeler, *St. Lucie*, was brought to Fort Myers from the Mississippi in 1896. Double-decked and 120 feet long, it had twenty-four staterooms, a large dining salon and running water.

When the Atlantic Coastline Railroad was extended to Fort Myers in 1904, the Kinzie brothers, George and Andrew, with their Kinzie Brothers Steamship Line, won the contract to carry the mail to the islands. Their first boat, the little wood-burning steamer, *Belle of Myers*, was bought from the Harvey boatline. It was followed by the sternwheeler, *Success* and the *Gladys*. The first *Dixie* was built at Cronton-On-Hudson, New York, in 1914. The brothers traveled to New York in December, taking with them a black deckhand, Dave Price, who was to help them bring the new boat south. Unfortunately, delay followed delay and it was January 16 before the trim little steamer left Brooklyn, only to have to put back with engine trouble. The shakedown cruise of the sturdy *Dixie*, beset by fog, ice, snow and gales, was a true odyssey which finally ended at Fort Myers at the end of February, 1915.

The *Dixie* cut through the waters of San Carlos Bay and Pine Island Sound, often with a bone in her teeth, until requisitioned by the Army during the first World War. With true, patriotic fervor, she ferried troops in New York harbor.

The second *Dixie*, a larger boat, became the lifeline of the islands. Besides mail, passengers and freight, it carried such items as fresh meat, milk and, two days a week, ice in twenty-five, fifty and one hundred-pound chunks which were deposited on Bailey's dock to melt away until claimed—sometimes too late.

The Sanibel Packing Company, always referred to as Bailey's store, was the only general store at that time but other small, neighborhood "convenience stores" had come and gone. The Riddles had a little grocery store near Tarpon Bay, the McIntires one on the road to Captiva and there was a store of sorts at Wulfert. Will Geraty operated a plantation store at the end of Matthews wharf until the Bailey brothers bought him out in 1899, and in 1900, the Reverend George Gatewood, the circuit preacher, had a small establishment in the same building as the post office at Reeds' place. He and Mrs. Gatewood provided islanders with all the necessities—and sometimes a little more. On one occasion, the front steps became a dentist's chair as he succesfully extracted an aching molar from the jaw of Mr. McIntire. The packing house at the end of the long dock at Tarpon Bay, dark and cavernous, was used for a store in the 1920s.

On May 1, 1889, there were twenty-one houses and forty families on Sanibel with a total population of one hundred. A petition to establish a school district there, submitted the previous December, was accepted by the Board of Public Instruction and the County School Board offered to provide materials for a 16 x 24 x 12 foot schoolhouse, costs not to exceed seventy-five dollars, which island residents would construct. It would be years before they would agree again on anything.

Mrs. Nutt, who had reneged on her promise to build a schoolhouse at her own expense on the beach, expected to teach the public school and wanted it located near her home. Those who lived up that way liked the idea, but the east end families did not and arguments dragged on. Finally, the County Superintendent selected a site about 1½ miles from the lighthouse and in 1892, East

Sanibel school was built.

Meanwhile, the so-called West Sanibel School was organized in Mrs. Nutt's home, and in December 1891, Miss Lettie Nutt was hired to teach it, her monthly salary two dollars and fifty cents per pupil. Although this school was to have been discontinued in 1897, apparently it simply was relocated and in 1899, there were three tax supported schools on the island. Mr. Wilhelm received twenty dollars that year for the use of the second floor of his packing house and in 1901, Mrs. Nutt was hired to teach at "south" Sanibel school, held in a building at The Matthews.

Mrs. Belle Boyd, who was the first teacher in the new school at the east end of the island, was out of a job when the schoolhouse blew down in September 1894. The same year, Mr. Pell was paid fifty-four dollars and fifty cents to build a new school on his land but for some reason, this caused a furor and as Ed McIntyre called for backbone and forbearance, the School Board sold it for twenty-seven dollars and fifty cents and built another.

This third schoolhouse, then located at the corner of Bailey Road and Periwinkle Way, was moved by rollers and a winch up the island in 1903, and is today the Pirate Playhouse. A one-room schoolhouse in the finest tradition, it had a platform up front where classes of two and three pupils took turns saying their lessons. Halfway, there was a woodstove which warmed the room in winter and sometimes heated cocoa and soup, while at the back lingered the faint smell of fertilizer from a sack kept there to nourish the schoolyard garden.

There was no school for black children until 1927 when island farmer, James Johnson, offered their parents the use of the old Baptist church, located on his property. In 1929, Lee County bought the building from the Florida Baptist Convention for $1,500. Miss Hazel Hammond taught there until 1933. The school was closed from 1940 to 1946. Miss Angelita George was the first principal.

The old white schoolhouse, enlarged and with plumbing installed, was in use until the Sanibel-Captiva Elementary School was built in 1963. In fall of 1964, it became the first public school in Lee County to be totally integrated.

On Captiva, a schoolhouse twenty by thirty feet, was built in 1901, near the Gulf beach on the Binder property. Classes were held January 5, 1901, with Mrs. T.M. Wilkinson as teacher. By 1906, there were seventeen pupils.

The building doubled as church with services held there when the circuit preacher came through, usually about once a month. On such occasions, the families arrived on foot or by mule-drawn wagon, bringing enough food to last all day. They picnicked between morning and evening services and as the children ran and played, their elders sat in the shade of the spreading seagrapes. The men were off to one side swapping stories while their wives swapped recipes and any newsy, little bits of gossip that might have come their way.

When it appeared that most of the students were Bryants or their cousins, a new school was built about a half mile from Tobe's house. The school combined with the Wulfert School in 1917, but in 1921, it was swept away by a hurricane.

The first building, damaged and abandoned, was eventually restored, largely through the efforts of Mrs. Hattie Gore, and it once again became a church. It was sold by the county in 1921 to the Methodist Conference. In 1947, a committee of Captiva residents purchased the property. Enlarged and remodeled, the old school-church is now the Chapel-By-The-Sea.

As Sanibel and Captiva became more productive, the jungle was reclaiming much of Buck Key. Only the Ormsbys were permanent residents there in 1904 when

German-born Bernhard Eyber bought land at the northern end and with his son, Richard, put in a grapefruit grove.

Eyber worked as a bookkeeper in a New York drug store. He was not well and the climate of Captiva was recommended to him by a pharmacist, Walter Turner, of Fort Myers. A reflective man who loved nature and books, Bernhard Eyber was restored by Buck Key. Not so his wife, Clara, and daughter, Charlotte. Fresh from the refinements of New York, the ladies found the thatched hut, mosquitos, and isolation most depressing and soon left for Punta Gorda where they worked for Ernest's Department Store, designing clothes and sewing for the well-to-do.

When Charlotte married Andrew Kinzie in 1907, Mrs. Eyber returned to Buck Key. Two years later she became manager of Captiva's first hotel, Captiva House, known also as Dickey Hotel and Eyber House. It was a large, three-story structure lacking in all the conveniences. Sponsored and financed by winter residents, John R. Dickey, Dr. Hicks and Dr. Deadrick, all of Bristol, Virginia, it was an inn until June, 1914, when Clarence Snyder bought it for his boys' school.

Dr. Dickey, a pharmacist, his wife, Julia, and their sons, Herman, Carl and Ernest, were Captiva's first winter residents, arriving for their first season on the island in December, 1906. Corely Bryant, who met them at the bulkhead, found they had brought a maid, five trunks and enough supplies for a small army.

As luck would have it, the wind was blowing hard that day and the small, over-loaded boat soon went aground. With no choice but to wade, the passengers slogged their way to shore and three and a half miles to the new house. The next day, bad news awaited them. The boat, tied up at Carter's dock, had swamped and sunk during the night, taking with it all of the Dickey's provisions. Sea water got into the rice, the flour, and the sugar. Labels came off the cans and clothes and bedclothes were streaked with dye from the boxes they were packed in. In all the sodden mess, just one item remained dry—a casting net in a tin container!

Despite their rough initiation, the Dickeys returned to Captiva every winter and, like the Matthews, gave some of their land away to friends who built on it. The Dickey boys were educated in their own little, red schoolhouse. There was a classroom on the ground floor and an apartment above for their tutor, who came with them from Virginia. Miss Reba Fitzpatrick, who taught them for many years, was given a piece of land at the south end of the property and the boys built a little house for her there. In 1925, her piece was sold to Mr. and Mrs. F. Bowman Price, Jr. who built a cottage type hotel, 'Tween Waters Inn, in 1931. Miss Reba's small house became the entrance to the dining room.

Since the first awesome storm altered the coastline of the emerging island years ago, Sanibel and Captiva have experienced hurricanes. Florida averages one a year. There is one chance in twelve that this tropical cyclone, with winds of 74 mph or higher, will hit the Fort Myers area. Of Florida's greatest hurricanes between 1888 and 1966, six have come through the islands, probably the most violent of them the 1910 Big Storm.

Captain William H. Reed, eighty-one years old at that time, described the night of October 17 in his journal. Sea dog that he was, he worried not for himself but for his son, Will, who had gone off in a boat with Sam and Harrison Woodring and some stranger who wanted to be taken to La Costa. As it turned out, the men holed up on Pine Island and were much safer than the people they had left behind.

The wind had been increasing throughout the day on Monday and by early afternoon, San Carlos Bay was a boiling pot, spilling over into a long line of breakers that rolled over the Reed dock and crashed onto the beach behind it. By 3:00 P.M. the wind was howling through the coconut palms, whipping the fronds to shreds, the rain had begun to fall and the sky took on an eerie, yellow look. As the tide went out, there was another unsettling sight. Except for the channel which ran around the end of Woodring's Point, the water had gone out of the bay and Pine Island Sound and one almost could have walked to St. James.

The Reeds had been busy all day, securing the boats, boarding up windows and laying in extra food and supplies, and by evening, fifteen anxious people had taken refuge in the homestead. The fringe winds of the one hundred mile wide hurricane reached them at about ten o'clock, and by eleven o'clock, winds that exceeded one hundred ten miles per hour bore down on the cluster of buildings, moaning and shrieking like some wild beast. Time and again it slammed into the captain's house which shuddered and shook and finally cracked under the impact.

Tired and scared, the islanders crawled on hands and knees to Will's place, but when one of the windows blew in and driving rain drenched them, they decided it would be best to go to a small wash-house at the back of the property. Moments later, the captain's house crashed down on the wash-house and the fifteen weary people, miraculously unhurt, took shelter under some trees. As they huddled there, Will's house collapsed into a pile of rubble and one corner of Lucy's Sanibel House was knocked off its foundations. With nowhere else to go, they started for the interior of the island.

There was a road of sorts behind the post office which went through the sand flats to Periwinkle Way, a distance of about one and three-quarter miles. Although it was knee-deep in sea water, it was decided to chance it and with the men carrying the children and supporting the women, the bedraggled little band set out. The wind still plucked at them with furious gusts and frequently they were toppled by it, but they fought their way on until close to their destination. Suddenly, the wind dropped and within minutes they were walking through moonlight, ghostly and still. For about a half an hour, the eye of the storm passed over them. They had reached the Mitchell home, and safety, before the hurricane began blowing full fury from the opposite direction.

On the gulf side of Sanibel, the Mitchell Lilley family anxiously watched the sea water rise around their beach cottage, perched high on long pilings. With porch and steps gone they were marooned on a manmade island—as four porpoises cruised playfully around them. The children, Elise, Emily and Mitchell, Jr., far from being frightened, considered it all a great adventure.

When the water receded, Mr. Lilley climbed to the ground and was relieved to find that Mamie, the mule, had survived the storm, although the shed which had sheltered her had blown away. The wagon, too, was intact and this he positioned beneath the house as his family jumped into it.

There was but one way to get to the lighthouse—the beach—but they had to ford the sandbars to get past the chasm dug out by the raging Sanibel River. They found other survivors there. One man, cut and bleeding, had climbed a palmetto and spent the night there. Perhaps the weariest of all was a small deer, which wobbled in, too exhausted to be afraid.

At six o'clock in the morning of October 17, Arthur Gibson and an engineer started down the Caloosahatchee with mail for the islands. Since the weather was too bad for the steamer, the men took a thirty-four foot launch and in spite of the rough water, they managed "the swift completion of their appointed rounds" by midafternoon. They were leaving Captiva bulkhead when the fringe winds of the hurricane caught up with them and it was only with the greatest difficulty that they were able to get to Wulfert, where they tied up the boat and took shelter in a small, vacant house on shore.

The men slept through the storm but sometime during the night, the launch broke loose and sank, scattering the mailbags all along the beach and into the swamp. Somehow, the boatmen retrieved all thirteen soggy sacks and hung them on the mangroves to dry. Then, cleaning the muck and debris out of the boat, they patched a little, straightened the rudder and eventually, got the motor running.

The mail and the mailman finally got back to Fort Myers—twenty-seven hours late. Unfortunately, this was not the end of Arthur Gibson's troubles. There were so many complaints about the condition of the mail that the Post Office Department had to come to his defense. An official letter sent from Washington declared unequivocably that Arthur Gibson was in no way responsible for an Act of God.

At noon on Monday, all the residents of the south end of Captiva began streaming into Eyber House, except old Judge Powell, who stayed in the upper room of the Dickey schoolhouse, reading his Bible and trusting in the Lord.

Mrs. Eyber had become anxious as the weather, unsettled since Friday, became increasingly worse and her son, Richard, had to give up an attempt to board up the windows as the wind snatched the hammer from his hand. As more and more people crowded into the hotel, the Eybers handed out blankets and all but went through their winter supply of food. Still, except for the inevitable squalling infant, all went well until the first crisis. Shortly before midnight, a section of the roof gave way and a torrent of rain water cascaded down the two flights of stairs.

The eye of the storm provided an opportunity to make repairs but the weary islanders had no more than sopped up the rain water when the storm began afresh, even more violently because it was out of the exposed southwest. Climbing onto chairs, they watched incredulously as the waters of the Gulf and the waters of the bay met in the middle of the living room!

As the walls began to lean dangerously, it was the consensus that another shelter must be found and the little company started out waist-deep in surging sea water for the Dickey house. Some of them were standing on the porch when Richard, fumbling with the keys, suddenly yelled a warning and pushed them out of the way. He, too, leaped to safety just as the roof fell in.

It was a shaken, wet, frightened group of people who stood in the lee of the house as the wind increased to a high pitched yowl. At that moment, they saw a pinpoint of light from Judge Powell's small room and in seconds, they had climbed the rickety stairs, and burst in on the old gentleman. With one hand on his Bible and the other steadying a kerosene lamp, he surveyed them sternly. "Why do you come to me?" he demanded. "Don't you trust in the Lord?"

For the rest of the night, the men, women and children sat in the wavering lamplight praying and singing hymns. The tiny house held its own against the wrenching winds and as the storm moved away, they slept. They awoke to a clear, sunny day perfumed with the scent of broken leaves and flowers. There was destruction everywhere they looked, but good news, too. A man believed to be lost had survived the night in the limbs of a tree and Bernhard Eyber was safe on Buck Key. The 1910 hurricane, worst in island history, had taken no lives.

As always after a disaster, bargain hunters came shopping. On Captiva, Frank A. Lane, a speculator from Connecticut, found the four-room Munsey "hotel" demolished and with Dr. Franklin Miles, bought the property which extended from bay to Gulf. The low land on Pine Island Sound was dredged and filled for lots and a small hotel was built there. A two-story building was added in 1914 and the complex was named Fishermen's Lodge. It burned down in 1948.

Former president Theodore Roosevelt first came to Captiva in 1914. His interest in wildlife led him to join the party of Colonel Russell Coles, who was experimenting with tanning the skins of fish, such as manta rays and sharks. Teddy had stepped off the train at Punta Gorda amid fanfare and speeches, then stepped onto a sort of floating fish camp set up on a barge. This was towed to today's Roosevelt Pass where it was anchored and used both as laboratory and living quarters.

The expansive Teddy received the entire local populace with his usual heartiness but perhaps his favorite caller was eleven-year-old Margaret Mickle who arrived unannounced and dripping wet. She had started out in a leaky rowboat which began to sink halfway. Her companion, Paul Gore, jumped overboard and swam to shore but Margaret, holding a borrowed camera over her head, swam to the barge and was helped aboard. When the ex-President heard a childish voice inquire, "Where's Teddy?" he emerged from his cabin and viewed the little girl with great amusement. She was invited to stay for dinner and afterward accompanied home by both Roosevelt and Coles.

After he left Captiva, Roosevelt sent Margaret a .22 rifle, a pair a fish skin slippers and an autographed picture of himself. The two friends corresponded for several years.

Roosevelt returned to Captiva with Colonel Coles in 1916. Genial as always, he was entertained at the Snyder School for Boys, then strolled down the road to take tea with Dr. and Mrs. Dickey. It was a short, working vacation and his last on "The Ark" in Roosevelt Channel

The school, still new on Captiva, probably would have

Ross Mayer, Sr., left, with Roy Rider. Chalked on car top: "Sanibel Island. 200 lbs. of fish in 20 min. 2/11/24."

been in the old Schultz Hotel on Punta Rassa had the place not burned down shortly before the staff and the students were to occupy it. With no alternative, Professor Snyder, founder-headmaster, took his boys first to Ormsbys' on Buck Key and then in January, 1915, to Eyber House. The building was improved, a tennis court put in and, eventually, another building added.

Synder School was both elementary and high-school, catering to boys of well-to-do families from all over the United States. The purpose was to live and study outdoors as much as possible and for that reason, they followed the sun, holding the fall and spring sessions in the mountains of North Carolina and winter sessions on Captiva. With an annual cruise on a schooner, yacht or houseboat, outdoor sports, excursions and social occasions of all kinds, it was as idyllic as a school could be. It closed in 1926, and the buildings burned down some years later.

With American involvement in World War I impending in 1917, the boys at the Snyder School were drilling on the tennis court and on Sanibel, the non-denominational little brown church was completed in June. The following year, perhaps as a result of the Coles expedition, a shark factory, the Ocean Leather Company, was built on the bay side of Sanibel. A private, and malodorous, enterprise, it employed fishermen to catch sharks and bring them to the factory where the skins were tanned, the livers rendered into oil and fins made into glue. It lasted only two or three years.

The first bridge between Sanibel and Captiva was built in 1918, but it remained a harrowing trip to get to it across washboard roads. In late fall, 1919, a storm blew the old Dulaney house on Sanibel off its high pilings and set it on the car of Ross Mayer, winter visitor, damaging neither very much. It stayed on the ground and eventually became a little hostelry, known forever after as Hurricane House. It burned in 1963.

There was a labor shortage in Lee County during the war years and this followed by the 1921 hurricane greatly reduced island population. Isaiah Gavin, who established the first black family on Sanibel, worked for one dollar a day and was glad to get any kind of job.

Business picked up somewhat with the Florida Land Boom of 1924 as three platted subdivisions appeared on the island: Sanibel Center on Main Street, Sanibel Gardens on the old Cooper property, and Sunniland del Mar, complete with roads and "street" signs, at The Rocks.

At the height of all this optimism, MacGregor Boulevard was extended to Punta Rassa and in 1925, a man named Cogsdale put in a ferry which ran between there and Reeds' landing. The 1926 hurricane wiped out the business as well as the Florida boom. Two years later, the Kinzie Brothers bought the small ferry, the *Best*, and began regular runs to Sanibel. The first landing was near Bailey's dock, the second and last near lighthouse point.

The boat was more than a mere carrier of cars and passengers, mostly because of its captain, Leon Crumpler. A genial man, reliable and competent, he dispensed the news as he collected the fares and judiciously advised the tourists. Except when it was in drydock (and a tug-drawn barge took over) or during the most awesome hurricanes, the *Best* made all its trips. At night or during any emergency, it was always ready, the sound of its engines reassuring to those who awaited it.

The steamers passed from the scene in 1936 and the motor launch, *Santiva*, captained by Ray and Cleon Singleton, carried mail, freight and passengers to the islands. The *Best* was joined by the bigger ferries, the *Rebel*, the *Islander* and the aptly named, *Yankee Clipper*. Their last run was the day the Sanibel Causeway opened, May 26, 1963.

The Sanibel River, 1973

Chapter XIV

THE YEARS OF CHANGE

Prohibition posed no major problems on Sanibel and Captiva, mainly because it was largely ignored. A Coast Guard Cutter patrolled at night in search of rum runners but seldom caught any, while on shore, at least three illicit stills, deep in the mangroves, continued to produce bootleg whiskey for local consumption.

There were few arrests, the best remembered occurring some years after the 18th Amendment was repealed. In the 1940s, the manager of the highly respectable Island Inn asked Frank Bailey, then justice of the peace, to investigate strange noises on the hotel grounds. Bailey caught the scent of fermenting mash and followed his nose to the source of the trouble. Caught red-handed was an enterprising islander, busily operating his still behind the servant's quarters.

The 1926 hurricane, with very destructive fourteen-foot tides, hit the islands September 18. There was the usual exodus of those who suffered heavy property damage. That same year, the Sanibel Community Association was organized by Curtis Perry, a winter visitor from Maine, who became its first president. A plump, kindly bachelor, he spent winters at The Matthews Hotel, where he painted sunrises and sunsets—nothing else. In 1926, he walked Sanibel end to end soliciting funds for a building and in 1927, it was constructed on land donated by Miss Cordie Nutt. When Perry died on the island several years later, his friends put up a plaque in his memory.

Dances were held at the Community House, (music by radio, admission ten cents), plays, lectures and, inevitably, a shell fair. It had been the custom of The Matthews and the Casa Ybel to set aside one day each winter for guests to display their collections and in 1927 it became a community affair. In the early days, only native shells were shown and these were arranged on cotton in a cardboard box, labeled, if at all, with such colorful common names as Scotch Bonnet, Chinese Alphabet and Lion's Paw. Shellcraft, needlework and baked goods were sold and the local ladies served lunch. One year, island produce was displayed and Francis Bailey's chickens, but always the main theme was shells and marine life.

Dr. Louise Perry (not related to Curtis) directed the show until 1941. A medical doctor from Asheville, North Carolina, Dr. Perry studied malacology as a hobby and established her reputation in that field with her first book, *Marine Shells of the Southwest Coast of Florida,* published in 1940. A winter resident since 1924, she was well known for her generosity and aid to the black people and her willingness to tend the injured and ill in any medical emergency. She was eighty-three when she died in Asheville, North Carolina, in 1962.

Except for the years of World War II, the Shell Fair has been held annually.

Sanibel's first library, a few shelves of dog-eared books, was in the Community House. As it grew, it was moved three times, first to a line of offices known as Town Square, which was leveled by a tornado in 1972. By that time, the library was on Periwinkle Way. Its permanent home, Sanibel Public Library, designed by Sanibel architect, Frank Vellake, was built on land donated by Florence and Gerald Martin and opened in

October 1973.

The Captiva Civic Association, established by 1936, began as a women's organization, the Captiva Beautification Club, organized by Mrs. John R. Dickey. The ladies had begun a library, a few shelves of books in Mrs. Dickey's house, but most of these were given away when she died in 1947. For several years, Captiva residents relied on the Book Boat of Mr. and Mrs. Roger Amory of Boca Grande, which made periodic stops on the island. When the Captiva Civic Center was built in 1960, the few shelves allotted to donated books soon were overflowing and the need for a separate room was apparent. Captiva Memorial Library, built onto the meeting hall, was dedicated February 1, 1970.

It was also the winter of 1936 that Edna St. Vincent Millay checked into Shanahan's Palm Hotel on Sanibel shortly before it caught fire. She was on the beach when she turned to see it ablaze, realizing that everything in her room was lost, including the manuscript of "Conversation at Midnight." Eventually, she rewrote her poems from memory and published them in 1937.

The seclusion of Captiva also attracted famous people. Anne and Charles Lindbergh frequently rented a house from Herman Dickey, their privacy guarded as zealously by islanders as by themselves. Violinist Albert Spalding, gentlemanly and delightfully outgoing, had a winter home there where he practiced faithfully after his morning "skinny dip" in the gulf.

The islands' first newspaper, which appeared December 8, 1934, was a mimeographed weekly (winters only) called *The Sanibel Islander* until December, 1935 when it became *The Islander*. Published by H.S. "Nick" Carter, it was put together by a volunteer staff, more willing than able, and lasted three seasons until Carter's death in 1937.

In 1961, four issues of the single-page *The Islander's Newsletter* were sent free to boxholders by the Sanibel

Island Improvement Association. There was no real newspaper, however, before *The Sanibel-Captiva Islander*, published weekly by Duff Brown at Fort Myers Beach, first appeared November 15, 1961 and for years it was supported by advertisements. It was challenged briefly in 1963-64 by an excellent, island-based weekly, the *Record*, published by James H. Toughill. The *Record* failed, we believe, because it cost ten cents. *The Islander* had no further competition until November 16, 1973 when the *Island Reporter* appeared, its editor, Don Whitehead. With a paid circulation of more than 7,000 it received many awards, including Best Florida Weekly in its circulation category.

The primary concerns of local people changed very little over the years. The first *Islander* editorialized about washboard roads and inadequate or unenforced conservation laws. Committees were formed but, then as now, it was the roads which received token improvements.

The conservationists badly needed a champion with influence in Tallahasse and Washington. They finally found one in J.N. "Ding" Darling, an ardent, articulate defender of wild creatures and the natural environment. His speech to an overflow audience at Fishermen's Lodge February 17, 1937, was the turn of the road for Sanibel and Captiva. With a sense of history, *The Islander* of the following week bore a cover sketch by Matt Clapp of two faces, the Spirit of Captiva and the Spirit of Sanibel, between them the lighted candle, "Conservation."

Jay Norwood Darling was a political cartoonist who always hankered to be a doctor. Dubbed "Ding" by childhood companions, he carried the nickname all his life and so signed his famous cartoons. Born in Norwood, Michigan, in 1876, he was educated at Beloit College. He went to work as a reporter for the *Sioux City Journal* in 1899 and in 1901 became its cartoonist when he

Tom Wood as seen by "Ding" Darling.

Courtesy of Charles LeBuff.

submitted to his editor a cartoon of an irate lawyer caning his opponent in court. From 1906 until he retired in 1949, he was staff cartoonist for the Des Moines, Iowa *Register*. His wit and talent earned him two Pulitzer Prizes, in 1924 and 1943, and he was named "Best Cartoonist" by leading newspaper editors in 1934.

Ding's strongly conservationist viewpoint, reflected in his work, attracted the attention of President Franklin D. Roosevelt who asked him to head the U.S. Biological Survey (todays U.S. Fish and Wildlife Service). In 1934, Darling took the low paying job, giving up cartooning, which had paid $100,000 a year. Despite frequent tilts with Interior Secretary Harold Ickes and over zealous land developers, he was an effective administrator for twenty months, acquiring $20 million in federal funds for conservation projects and adding more than 4 million acres to the federal system of wildlife refuges.

He first arrived on Captiva in March, 1936, and with his wife Penny spent two weeks at 'Tween Waters Inn. Deeply impressed with the island, the two returned the following year drawing a trailer, the Bouncing Betsy. They eventually built a winter home at the end of a dock with a drawbridge on it, which was pulled up when Ding was working. Much of the time, however, they stayed in a cottage at 'Tween Waters leaving their house to guests.

Darling continued to draw and worked hard for conservation. He was a leader of the Izaak Walton League, a founder of the National Wildlife Foundation and served on the board of directors of the National Audubon Society between 1936 and 1939. Meanwhile, he helped the islanders and it was largely through his efforts that Sanibel and Captiva and contiguous waters became a wildlife refuge by a special act of the 1939 Florida Legislature. At that time, an Inter-Island Conservation Commission, empowered to enforce state and federal game laws, was formed. It included Dr. Lousie Perry,

Mrs. W.J. Matthews, Webb Shanahan, Ernest Bailey and Allen Weeks.

Ding Darling died in Des Moines February 12, 1962, and a few days later, his friends on Captiva and elsewhere received his final cartoon. It depicted a cluttered and cobwebbed office and the wraith-like figure of Ding himself disappearing through the door with a jaunty wave of the hat. The caption read, "'Bye now—it's been wonderful knowing you." His secretary, sworn to secrecy, had kept the drawing many years, sending it out after his death to a list of friends—as he had instructed.

Sanibel National Wildlife Refuge was officially established in 1945 and included all of Sanibel and the southwest tip of Captiva. It was administered by Gerald Baker, manager of the Everglades National Wildlife Refuge. In 1949, Tom Wood, U.S. Fish and Wildlife Service, became the first resident manager. Wood, a resourceful, outspoken former Navy pilot, would stay for twenty years on Sanibel, his very strong feeling toward conservation matching those of an admirer who became his friend, Ding Darling.

There was no staff in the early days but Jake Stokes, local fisherman, served as part-time patrolman. The designation of refuge did no more than ban the hunting of certain animals to which migratory birds were added by Presidential Proclamation on December 21, 1945. Obviously, greater restrictions were needed if Sanibel and Captiva were to retain the flora and fauna for which they were famous. There were 1,900 acres of State-owned mangrove and hummock land on Sanibel's northern shore which Florida agencies had been selling off in bits and pieces for development. Ding Darling had strenuously objected to this and since 1936 had tried in vain to have this part of the island set aside as a permanent refuge, a national monument, perhaps for tropical birds. Eventually, he felt quite hopeless over the blindness of Florida and turned his back on it, selling every inch of ground he owned there.

It remained for the members of the Sanibel-Captiva Audubon Society to pick up the standard and they did so in 1959, with a campaign to preserve these ecologically valuable wetlands. The guiding hand at that time was Roy A. Bazire, president, a man of great ability, vision and achievement. Also at the forefront were Willis and Opal Combs, whose home, Woodmere Preserve, was the first natural arboretum on Sanibel.

In the early months of 1960, the organization forged ahead, gathering signatures on a petition and digging out the legal descriptions of the property involved. They were helped by John Storer, president of Florida Audubon Society and by Nature Conservancy. Storer, friend and ally, presented this material to the Trustees of the Internal Improvement Fund in Tallahassee in March. In November, Willis Combs wrote Ding Darling and in reply received a letter wishing them well but reflecting much cynicism and bitterness. "Governor Holland (now Senator)", Ding wrote, "was the only one who ever gave us the least hope during his administration of the governorship. He tried to be of help but the bloodthirsty real estate promoters and seemingly all of the state representatives and local businessmen were on the opposite side of the fence."*

It is the ultimate irony that the great conservationist's death made his dream come true. It was only days later, in February, 1962, that John E. Evans, press-aide to Governor Farris Bryant, addressed those attending the Sears Foundation awards banquet. He proposed the creation of a memorial on Sanibel in recognition of Ding Darling's contribution toward the conservation of Florida's natural resources. Sanibel-Captiva Audubon had been waiting for such a breakthrough and program

* Ding Darling to Willis Combs, November 23, 1960.

218

chairman Opal Coombs was quick to respond by letter. "What could be more fitting," she asked, "than the creation of the refuge Ding had so ardently sought?" She mentioned the petitions still languishing in official channels and enclosed, most pointedly, a copy of Ding's letter to her husband. Almost immediately, there was an encouraging reply with the suggestion that her organization "drum up" statewide support for the project.

To this end, the Jay N. (Ding) Darling Memorial Committee was formed March 6, 1962, its purpose to work toward the creation of the refuge. Chairman Emmy Lu Lewis and Captiva resident, Harold Bixby, flew to Tallahassee with Tom Wood several times during April to present their case to state officials. At the end of the month, the Governor's Committee on Recreational Development, after an inspection of the area, recommended that the land and waterways be dedicated under the protection of the Florida Board of Parks and Historical Monuments. It was a monumental achievement.

By that time, the drive through the sanctuary had been built. It was the brain child of Tom Wood and Wayne Miller of Lee County Mosquito Control Board as part of a mosquito control program. Water was impounded and fill was dredged for a four and a half mile long dike, the top of which was leveled to serve as a road. One man did all the work, Colon Moore, whom islanders called "Virtuoso of the Dragline." He used a compass and his own unerring instincts to complete the job in twenty-seven months. However, the equipment was not quite up to the challenge of Hardworking Bayou. There Moore found coquina rock and deep water and had to detour around it. Wood dubbed the place "Colon Point."

The drive was not an instant success. As dry season followed very wet, car after car got stuck in the soft sand as mosquitos swarmed and tempers grew short. Eventually, the surface hardened and it became one of Florida's most popular natural attractions. Between September 30, 1977 and September 30, 1978, 314,888 vehicles drove along the road.

The U.S. Fish and Wildlife Service administered the Sanibel Wildlife Refuge and later J.N. "Ding" Darling Sanctuary from the fifty-four-acre Lighthouse tract which it leased from the U.S. Coast Guard in 1950. Also, it leased one hundred acres of land on Tarpon Bay Road from Sanibel pioneer, Francis P. Bailey, Sr. and bought it in 1954, for fifty dollars an acre. Ding Darling already had paid for a free-flowing well there which provided water for wildlife. Eventually, there also would be a bird watching tower.

In 1963, Dr. Louise Perry donated 3.31 acres of gulf front land to the Service as a refuge. These properties formed the nucleus of Ding Darling Refuge, which in recent years had been expanded to include islands in the Caloosahatchee, Matlacha Pass, Pine Island Sound, Charlotte Harbor and Tampa Bay.

In historic 1967 land swap with Florida agencies, Fish and Wildlife Services took title to all state-owned lands within the sanctuary. At that time, at the request of the Jay N. (Ding) Darling Memorial Committee, the name was changed to the J.N. "Ding" Darling National Wildlife Refuge. Three years later, a $1.5 million appropriation from Congress was used to buy up private property within its boundaries. This brought the total acreage to almost five thousand, roughly one-third the area of Sanibel. In 1976, 2,700 acres of mostly mangrove forest within its borders were designated as "wilderness area," thus preserving the habitat of tropical plants and animals. A surprise bonus was the discovery of several ancient Indian mounds, largely undisturbed and hidden by thick underbrush. Official passivity being as it is, J.N. "Ding" Darling National

Wildlife Refuge was not formally dedicated until February 4, 1978. The U.S. Fish and Wildlife Service built a $500,000 headquarters and interpretive center at the entrance on Sanibel-Captiva Road in 1982.

As a footnote, credit must go to an unknown surveyor who slowed down development of the wetlands. His 1875 survey was so erroneous and possibly fradulent that most landowners did not know where their property lines were or even how much acreage was involved. This hero of conservation did his work from a boat anchored offshore, well beyond the reach of Sanibel's notorious salt marsh mosquitos.

The Sanibel-Captiva Conservation Foundation (SCCF), today a power to be reckoned with, also had its roots in Sanibel-Captiva Audubon, or more specifically, the Jay N. (Ding) Darling Memorial Foundation of Des Moines, Iowa. It had been created by the family and friends of Darling for the specific purpose of coordinating the groups which formed after his death to further his aims. Since a primary objective of the Des Moines organization was to establish the sanctuary on Sanibel, the Memorial Committee joined them and banked with them $25,000 which had been raised for that purpose.

At the urging of Fish and Wildlife and Florida's Board of Parks and Historical Monuments, the committee continued to serve as guiding hand. It added to the emerging parklands such things as canoe trails, docks, a bridge and a tower dedicated to Alice M. O'Brien, former Captiva winter resident, whose interest and support furthered conservation causes. Funds to build it were donated by family and friends.

In 1967, when it became apparent that the Fish and Wildlife Service would take over the service, Roy Bazire and Emmy Lu Lewis met in Des Moines with the directors of that foundation to discuss the implications. As a spring snowstorm blanketed the area, the islanders were told that a decision had been made for the Sanibel group to become inactive until a plan was developed for the refuge—news received with some dismay because in the interim, there would be no funding for Sanibel-Captiva projects.

When the two reported back to committee members, they offered an alternative. Instead of losing momentum and perhaps community support, why not go it alone? Although there was some uncertainty among the members, it was decided to "damn the torpedoes"—and they went full steam ahead. The Memorial Committe separated from the Des Moines foundation, its $25,000 was returned and it reorganized as Sanibel-Captiva Conservation Foundation. Incorporated in November, 1967, its first president and chairman of the board of directors was Emmy Lu Lewis. Vice-chairman was Roy Bazire who also became administrative director.

A bold program was initiated from ideas first proposed by Opal Combs. Its first priority was the acquisition of certain strategically located properties which must be preserved to protect the refuge and fresh water wetland along the Sanibel River. This was the slough of 1833, which had been dredged in some parts to allow freer flow of water. Bazire sought and obtained grants: $200,000 from the Mellon Foundation, $25,000 from the Alice M. O'Brien Foundation and $25,000 from the Gannett Newspaper Foundation. Gannett published the *Fort Myers News-Press*.

One by one, other goals were realized. The acquisition of land would be an on-going thing, especially that property still privately owned within the refuge.

By 1976, SCCF owned 207 acres of wooded land along the Sanibel River which had more than three miles of nature trails winding through it. The long-awaited Nature Center was built there in 1977. Designed by Fort Myers architect Wiley Parker, the building contained Foundation offices, meeting rooms, a small library, a shop and various exhibits. Administrative Director Richard Workman, who succeeded Roy Bazire in March, 1973, was heart and soul into conservation. A quiet man of great versatility, he innovated projects and experiments while fighting, it would seem, on every front in defense of the natural environment. The building soon became the environmental nerve center of Sanibel-Captiva.

With a growing reputation of achievement, membership increased to about 2,500 in 1978. SCCF funded the archaelogical digs at the Wightman Site and an extensive survey, "Sanibel Natural Systems" by John Clark of the National Conservation Foundation. Sanibel's planners leaned heavily on this report when drawing up the Comprehensive Land Use Plan. The Foundation also supported Workman and two Captiva residents, Mary Eckler Brown and Michael LaTona, in their efforts to preserve the wilderness areas of two beautiful barrier islands, Cayo Costa and the south end of Upper Captiva. Florida declared these "an area of critical state concern" in 1976, effectively blocking further development. By 1987, the Foundation owned 900 acres of preserve lands.

Other organizations, too, had furthered the case of conservation on Sanibel-Captiva. Caretta Research, Inc. was organized in 1968 by scientific technician Charles LeBuff, of the U.S. Fish and Wildlife Service. In 1964, LeBuff began a program of tagging the huge loggerhead turtles (*Caretta caretta*) which crawled ashore at night in May, June and July to lay their eggs on island beaches. Their numbers were dwindling and in an attempt to reverse the trend, beaches were patrolled and the eggs collected for hatching in enclosures. The emerging babies were kept in captivity until large enough to fend for themselves. By 1979, the operation had expanded to cover Florida's West Coast from Clearwater to Cape Sable.

Care and Rehabilitation of Wildlife, C.R.O.W., maintained a shelter for sick and injured birds and small animals. It would have a home of its own by 1980.

For those looking back, there had been deplorable changes in the landscape since Matt Clapp's drawing appeared in *The Islander* in 1937. But there had been gains also. On Sanibel and Captiva, the candle called "Conservation" was still well-tended.

The Lee County Electric Cooperative first supplied power to Sanibel-Captiva in April, 1941. The move toward electrification began in North Fort Myers where certain residents had become dissatisfied with the *status quo*. It seems that George Judd, a citrus grower, had installed a small generator at his packing plant and for a small fee, supplied power to neighbors within a five-mile radius. Those outside this circle also wanted electricity but on this Judd was adamant. Not only would be not expand his plant; he wanted to get out of the business entirely.

By this time, a committee had been formed and these people went to Florida Power and Light with the request that their service be extended to North Fort Myers. After some deliberation, FPL decided that such a move was not feasible and advised the group to consult the Rural Electrification Administration in Washington. REA advised them to add to their list of prospective customers the residents of Pine Island, Bokeelia, Bayshore, Sanibel and Captiva. When they had enough subscribers to form a workable cooperative, they would be eligible to receive a loan at 2.46 percent interest in order to buy out George Judd.

On Sanibel-Captiva, Ernest Bailey, Julia Worthington and Louise Perry went from door to door, receiving enthusiastic response from would-be subscribers. On the other islands, too, most residents wanted electrictiy. Eventually, the loan was made and on November 17, 1940, Judd signed over his tiny electric plant. Modernized and expanded, it became Lee County Electric

Cooperative.

Sanibel and Captiva were blacked out during World War II and Coast Guardsmen, billeted at Casa Ybel Hotel patrolled the beaches. Bowman's Beach was an air-to-ground target range. The officer in charge was Army Air Corps Lieutenant John Wakefield, who, with five enlisted men, was quartered on Captiva. If anything, the islands were quieter than usual and by 1948, there were only two miles of paved road.

In 1955, however, disquieting news swept the islands like wildfire. Two Miami firms, Cruttenden and Podesta Investments and an engineering company, Brown and Blauvelt, had appeared before the County Commission to request permission to build a bridge-causeway system, by the sale of bonds, not only from Punta Rassa to Sanibel but Punta Rassa to Pine Island to Sanibel and Fort Myers Beach to Bonita Beach.

The following year, the would-be investors persuaded the county to pay about $33,000 for two reports from the Florida State Road Department: a traffic and engineering survey by Hazlet and Erdal of Louisville, and a financial study by Coverdale and Colpitts of New York. Based on a suggested $1.50 round trip fare for cars, the New York firm calculated that revenues the first year of operation (1960) would reach $117,000 and would average $226,000 yearly by 1970. Although moneys collected would total $1,883,000, building the causeway would cost twice as much and the project died.

In July, Cruttenden and Company were back with a new associate, Robert H. Bell and Company, also an investment firm. This time, they were interested in a Punta Rassa to Sanibel span only and suggested that the county pay no more than $20,000 for a preliminary study. Once burned, the county declined.

Hardly had the islands settled down when another bridge proposal came before the commission—this one with a difference. Through a spokesman, Hugo Lind-

Hugo Lindgren, who was responsible for Sanibel Causeway, 1963.

Photo by Fort Myers News-Press.

gren, president of Jamestown Metal Products Company of Jamestown, New York, offered to pay all preliminary costs with no obligation to the county. Construction would be financed through bonds to be repaid with toll revenues and the county would not encumber present or future tax revenues. When and if bonds were sold, Lindgren would be reimbursed while the man who presented his case, Robert S. Baynard, president of the Venice-Nokomis Bank, attorney, real estate developer and builder of the Boca Grande Causeway, would receive a fee, five percent of any bonds sold. Lindgren organized the investment group and his money paid the bills, but in the beginning he stayed very much in the background.

Hardly noticed at first was the route the causeway would take. Instead of the shorter route, that taken by the ferries to Point Ybel, the Lindgren Causeway, some 1,500 feet longer, would dogleg to the end of Bailey Road. According to the engineers, this was because the bay was shallower there and would cost less to fill. When finally constructed, it terminated 520 feet east of Bailey Road on property owned by Lindgren.

The Commission agreed to Lindgren's proposals in March, 1959, and a Bridge Authority was formed of the commissioners then in office: Wilson Pigott, Mack H. Jones, George S. Hunter, Herman J. Hastings and J. Fred Huber. Lindgren pledged money for a traffic study, a hydrological study of the Bay bottom and plans. He also offered the assistance of his attorney in preparing the necessary papers for the validation of the bonds and selling the idea in Tallahassee. As a result, the project received the enthusiastic support of Al Rogero, State Road Board Member for Lee County's district. He assured Chairman Pigott that the stretch of road between Fort Myers Beach cutoff and Punta Rassa, neglected for years and peppered with potholes, would be resurfaced and widened in anticipation of heavy traffic. Although some thought was given to tying in Pine Island, the investors decided against it.

The traffic study, prepared by Walter Smith and Associates of New Haven, Connecticut, was quite different from that produced earlier. Recommending a round trip fare of three dollars for passenger cars, revenues were expected to be $326,428 the first year of operation (1962) with a daily average of 577 vehicles making the crossing. Tolls were expected to generate an average of $449,200 a year for the first five years, rising to $801,668 in 1979. This would total $11,511,833 in eighteen years. With the cost of construction estimated to be $3.1 million the project was judged feasible and the commission decided to proceed with it.

Hugo Lindgren, who so altered Sanibel's history, emigrated to America as a young man from a small village in Sweden. He found work in a furniture factory in Jamestown, New York, and because he had ambition and ability, he eventually had his own business, Jamestown Metal Products Company, which manufactured metal cabinets for hospitals, laboratories and medical offices. In Jamestown, he realized The American Dream—success through his own efforts; if not "rags to riches", at least a very good life earned with hard work.

In the 1950s, he bought a Gulf to Bay parcel on Sanibel, now called Shell Harbor. Then he had misgivings. "Who would want to own property on a remote little island which could only be reached by ferry?" he asked himself. He thought he had made a poor investment and it was simply to enhance the value of his property that he decided to build a causeway terminating on it. He made no bones about it and expected it to speed up development of the island.

Lindgren never lived on Sanibel and his visits usually were for business reasons. He became hero to some and villain to others but he honestly believed that he had served the communtiy more than himself. To an interviewer, he said, "Can you imagine the thousands of tourists that would never have seen Sanibel, the hundreds of lots that would never have been sold, the hundreds of homes that might never have been built if it hadn't been for the bridge and causeway?" It is food for thought that among these homeowners were some who fought the battles of the seventies.

Lindgren maintained that he had lost money. He donated the land on which the Chamber of Commerce building was built and gave right of way through his property to Lee County for a connecting road.

In retrospect, it would seem that a bridge to Sanibel was inevitable. By 1959, cars waiting to cross on the ferry sometimes stretched for more than a mile at both ends of the run. Kinzie Brothers Ferry Line, carrying an average daily load of 257 cars in 1958, considered but then rejected paying $100,000 to buy more boats and equipment. In view of the frequency of the bridge proposals, it was deemed too risky.

Meanwhile islanders, who were not noted for indifference on any issue, took sides. It was not old residents *vs.* new residents, young *vs.* old or even businessmen *vs.* those retired but basically a matter of personal philosophy. Generally, those who opposed the causeway as planned were conservationists, people who loved the islands as they were, enjoying the remoteness and leisurely pace of life. They argued that such easy access would bring heavy development with all its problems, that the causeway would irreparably harm the fishing, shelling and bird life so enjoyed by all and thereby hurt the islands' one industry, tourism. A 1959 poll of the fifty-six members of the Business Association, forerunner of the Sanibel-Captiva Chamber of Commerce, indicated that only four members wanted a bridge but the figures changed in favor of it as the months passed.

The Sanibel Community Association, Captiva Civic Association, and Sanibel-Captiva Audubon adamantly opposed the project and it was mainly from the membership of these organizations that the Sanibel-Captiva Taxpayers League was formed. In 1960, the League, headed by Willis Combs, collected almost six hundred signatures on a petition calling for a referendum on the bridge issue. Most of the signers were voting residents but County Attorney William H. Carmine, Jr. advised that there was no legal basis for a referendum and the commissioners rejected it. When Carmine petitioned the circuit court for validation of the $3.9 million bond issue on January 20, 1961, the league challenged it on the grounds that tolls would be insufficient to retire the bonds, making it necessary to use tax money to do so. Judge Lynn Gerald, rejecting this argument, validated the bonds and although the league appealed to the Florida Supreme Court, his decision was upheld.

The supporters of the bridge, although top-heavy with those involved in some way with development and/or construction also could claim a cross section of island society. They supported the Lee County Commission arguing that everyone would benefit if the islands became more accessible since property values would rise. They wanted to be able to get to the mainland quickly— in times of medical emergencies, for school, sports events, social occasions— and this group circulated a petition in support of the project. With ninety-four signatures, they claimed a majority of island residents.

In an August, 1960, report to the U.S. Corps of Engineers, the U.S. Fish and Wildlife Service objected to the solid fill causeways and the dredging of the bay bottom as being highly damaging to the fish and wildlife resources of the whole area. By obstructing the flow of water, they would lower the salt content not only on San Carlos Bay but adjacent waterways. The bottom plant and animal communities of the area to be filled

Sanibel and Captiva "old-timers." L-R Clarence Rutland, Esperanza Woodring, Charlotta Matthews, Rosa Bryant, Arthur Gibson and Belton Johnson, 1963.

Fort Myers News-Press Photo

231

(one hundred acres) would be permanently damaged while the dredged areas, about 1,100 acres, would be destroyed for a long period of time. This would be permanent if maintenance dredging was done.

The State Game and Fresh Water Fish Commission and the State Board of Conservation concurred with the report and Conservation Director Ernest Mitts recommended that the roadways be supported entirely by pilings, but this was rejected indignantly by the County Attorney as being so exorbitantly expensive as to kill the project. The county commissioners looked for and found some dissenting opinions but it was the Corps of Engineers which settled the matter. Persuaded that the county as a whole would reap economic benefit, it approved the causeway on September 29, 1960.

On October 19, several contracts were approved by the county commission. Robert H. Matts and Associates, designers and engineers of the causeway, would receive a fee of $107,500; Ford, Bacon and Davis would be paid $4,500 a month for supervising construction and Kinzie Brothers Ferry Line would get $30,000 for docks, equipment and agreement to give up their franchise which still had ten years to go. All payments were contingent on sale of the bonds.

A final hearing was held by Robert C. Parker, an assistant to the Attorney General, on November 15, 1961. With feeling running so high, the chairman was unable to control all of those present and the police had to be called to restore order. Parker's report, subsequently delivered to the State Cabinet as Trustees of the Internal Improvement Fund, recommended that the project be approved. In language hardly complimentary to the biologists of the Fish and Wildlife Service and the state's own conservation agencies, he said in part that "no expert testimony had been produced at the hearing which showed with any degree of satisfaction that the construction of the bridge and causeway would seriously

232

or adversely affect the fishing or growth of marine life in this area of the Bay."* As for the other objections raised by the opposition, these were matters for local government to deal with.

On November 28, 1961, the cabinet granted Lee County the 24,000 feet right of way it sought. Shortly thereafter, Cleary Brothers, whose low bid of $4,727,909 had gotten them the contract, began construction of Sanibel Causeway.

On May 26, 1963, Edna and Paul Kearns and their son and daughter-in-law, Dick and Vivian Kearns, gathered guests aboard two ferries for one last nostalgic run as ribbon cutting ceremonies proceeded on the span above. It was strictly a Lee County show. The only islanders present, Floyd Snook and Gerald Martin, were seated in the bleachers. They were two of the four to receive invitations the day before. American Legion Post 38 of Ft. Myers conducted the flag raising and bigwigs from Tallahassee were front and center.

The bridge controversy had ruptured friendships and divided families—even churches—but the battle was over in 1961, when the State Cabinet gave the county right of way to build across the Bay. Both sides took comfort in the knowledge that they could plan their island and control the zoning through the Sanibel Island Planning and Zoning Authority. They could not have foreseen that the act which created it would be invalidated in less than a year—that the *coup de grace* to their way of life would be delivered in court.

The Sanibel Island Planning and Zoning District was the work of the Sanibel Island Improvement Association (S.I.I.A). It was organized by winter resident Edith Kiewitt when it became apparent that a link to the mainland was imminent. Incorporated in March, 1959, its purpose was planned growth and to that end, the

* Fort Myers News-Press, November 29, 1961.

organization hired two experts in the field: Dr. Ernest Bartley of the University of Florida, and Fred Baer. When islanders rejected incorporation in favor of a special taxing district, the two men helped draft the bill creating House Bill No. 2102, which became law in 1959. Elected to the Planning and Zoning Authority were Joseph Gault, chairman, John Kontinos, Lee Roy Friday, James Jack and Richard Kearns. The Authority worked with the planners to prepare and adopt zoning ordinances and a comprehensive plan. It also ruled on requests for zoning changes.

Therefore, it was imcomprehensible when the Florida Legislature seemed to reverse itself by passing another enabling act authorizing county-wide zoning in 1961. Sanibelites were shocked when the Lee County Planning Board gave notice that it would take over Sanibel zoning. A sympathetic county commission advised the authority to continue until a satisfactory arrangement could be worked out. There were frequent meetings with county officials but no agreement could be reached and in August, 1962, the authority, represented by John Kontinos, brought suit to restrain Lee County Planning Board from taking action on the re-zoning of Sanibel. The suit was lost in November when Circuit Court Judge Archie Odom ruled that the 1961 enabling act superseded the 1959 act which had created the Sanibel Island Planning and Zoning District. The Authority's attorney, John Savage, announced that the ruling would be appealed.

On Sanibel, residents decided to seek a new enabling act with powers of zoning only, although by then there were some dissenters. Senator Elmer Friday and Representative Bruce Scott advised that they would not sponsor a local bill without the approval of the county commission. That approval never came. On March 2, 1963, in a three to two decision, the commission voted not to approve a referendum which would have given

Sanibel voters the right to decide the issue. Commissioners P.A. Geraci and Julian Hudson voted for it. Time was permitted to run out on filing an appeal to the Florida Supreme Court and Sanibel lost the right to do its own planning and zoning. Although former Planning and Zoning administrator Andrew Mellody was placed on the Lee County Planning Board in 1964, and was succeeded by Robert Haynie in 1968, the appointment proved impermanent and Sanibel became even more vulnerable to over-development. By that time, the Sanibel Island Improvement Association (in February 1963) had merged with the Sanibel Community Association.

Hurricane Donna roared through the islands on September 10, 1960, with sustained winds of 92 mph and gusts up to 121 mph. Australian pines were tossed like toothpicks across roads and landscape and there was extremely heavy property damage. Power lines went down, docks were swept away and some places on the islands were without electricty for twenty-six days. There were no fatalities.

In contrast, the Civil Rights Movement came quietly in 1962, integration beginning with St. Michael and All Angels Episcopal Church when the Reverend Thomas A. Madden announced that he would no longer serve a segregated congregation. In 1963, the parents of the pupils of Sanibel Elementary School, then all white, requested total integration. It was the first integrated public school in Lee County. A year or so later, the venerable Sanibel Community Association dropped the word *white* from its requirements for membership and in 1970, Mr. and Mrs. James Carl Jordan, sponsored by Mr. and Mrs. Robert L. Dormer, became the first black members.

The islands progressed in other areas. In 1962, Lee County bought two and one-half miles of gulf front beach at the south end of Captiva for Turner Park, paying Walter S. Turner, Jr. $500,000. The Island Water Association was formed in 1965 to bring treated water to the islands from the Pine Island Water Association. Taps were turned on in November, 1966. In 1971, after three years of fighting the billboard lobby and off-island businesses, Sanibel-Captiva Chamber of Commerce persuaded the Lee County Commission to pass an ordinance limiting signs, in number, size, etc., on the islands. The Chamber also raised money to build a public pier in 1973, sharing costs on a fifty-fifty basis with the county.

In 1967, Lee County hired the planning firm of Adley Associates of Atlanta, Georgia, to develop a county-wide comprehensive plan. The zoning proposed for Sanibel and Captiva sent shock waves through the island communities. Buck Key and all of Captiva, except Turner Beach, were recommended for highrise, heavy density construction, as was most of Sanibel. To add insult to injury, a four-lane highway would bisect the sacrosanct Darling refuge. If fully developed, the two little islands would stagger under a population of almost 95,000 people.

Characteristically, islanders did not stand idly by. Sanibel resident Malcolm B. Beattie organized an interested citizens committee and from this evolved Sanibel-Captiva Planning Study Group. It became Sanibel-Captiva Planning Board (SCPB). Supported by a membership of about five hundred, including organizations, its purpose was to promote planned growth which would protect the natural environment. Also, it would represent its membership before state and local bodies. SCPB also made recommendations to the county commission, participated in studies and surveys and issued detailed reports on subjects related to planning.

Aided by dawning environmental awareness in Tallahassee, SCPB and S-C Conservation Foundation would set the course which Sanibel should follow and

Captiva to a lesser extent. It was a mere finger in the dike but it survived because of the strong support of most residents and the leadership, bold and sometimes brilliant, of its first president, Malcolm Beattie, and his successor, Vernon G. MacKenzie. Both were engineers, graduates of Massachusetts Institute of Technology.

In retrospect, it seems impossible that such an ill-conceived plan could have been seriously considered, yet as late as 1970, a map showing the proposed highway hung on the wall of the Lee County Planning Department. Still, some progress had been made. The county commission, then generally sympathetic toward the efforts of the islands to retain their rustic life-style, usually supported the recommendations of Commissioner P.A. Geraci who ably represented Sanibel-Captiva. In October, 1969, Geraci's motion to impose a moratorium on buildings more than thirty-five feet high was passed unanimously by commissioners Julian Hudson, Bruce Scott, Kenneth Daniels and James Sweeney. At a later date, a new classification, *H*, was proposed which would have permitted any community in the county to restrict building heights and it was this larger application which aroused a storm of protest from businesses in any way involved in the construction trade. Actually, other residential areas showed no interest in such a ban and Sanibel-Captiva Planning Board stood alone to present its case at the hearing on February 17, 1970. As three hundred people filled the room and spilled out into the hall, the commission voted unanimously to extend the moratorium to October, 1970. It would be extended again for a scheduled hearing in January.

The commission had been concerned with the legality of height restrictions applied to just one section of the county but in the end, it was Commissioner Bruce Scott, a former State Representative, who resolved the question with a telephone call to the Florida Attorney

General's Office. Assured that there probably would be no legal problems entailed, the height restriction law was passed in February, 1971. Five years later, to simplify its application, the thirty-five foot height restriction was amended to forty-three feet above sea level. To date, it has not been challenged in court.

At the time the high-rise issue was debated the planning board also requested that the permitted number of dwelling units per acre on Sanibel and Captiva be reduced and that construction on the Gulf beach be set back at least one hundred feet from the vegetation line. The commissioners were under heavy pressure from developers and they could not agree on these points. The request was denied.

By July, 1971, Lee County still had no land use plan and as property values skyrocketed on the islands, the planning board persuaded the commission to form a committee to draw up such a plan for Sanibel and Captiva. Appointed to this committee were Commissioner Walter Shirey, who had replaced P.A. Giraci in September, 1970, and Commissioner James Sweeney, two members from Lee County Zoning Board. Sanibel Community Association, Sanibel-Captiva Chamber of Commerce and the U.S. Fish and Wildlife Service each sent one representative. Repeatedly frustrated by delays and disagreements, the work dragged on for two years as developers rushed projects to completion which often were poorly planned, built and located. Building permits, issued years in advance of construction, would cause problems for Sanibel.

However, during that time, the commission ruled that the Sanibel-Captiva Plan need not await the completion of a countywide plan so there was a certain, cautious optimism when it was finally scheduled for a public hearing on July 24, 1973. On July 23, the county attorney was notified of a suit filed against the

Mike Dormer and Lucia Fishburne on Sanibel's beach. 1976.

Photo by Robert R. Dormer.

commission by Sanibel developer Walter Condon who charged that the committee which drew up the plan had violated the Sunshine Law.

By this time, Commissioners Hudson and Scott had been replaced by George Goldtrap and Dick Sayers, both of whom expressed opposition to land use planning which they considered a threat to private enterprise. It was decided not to challenge the suit but instead, County Planner Mac Irwin was instructed to draft a new plan. In September, a week before its first public hearing, Irwin, who alienated many by his stiff-necked opposition to heavy development in environmentally sensitive lands, was fired by Commissioners Sayers, Daniels and Sweeney.

Construction had shot up seventy percent on Sanibel since the previous year and anxious islanders decided to make one last stand. The Rocks Civic Association proposed that a moratorium on multi-family housing be imposed on the island until a comprehensive plan could be implemented. Reaction was instant and predictable. A badly divided Sanibel-Captiva Chamber of Commerce took no stand but several island businesses circulated petitions in opposition, alarmist in tone. Many construction workers, afraid of losing their jobs, signed them. In an unprecedented move, the Ft. Myers-Lee County Chamber of Commerce, predicting county-wide repercussions and economic disaster, sent out petitions to three thousand members and distributed badges proclaiming "Moratorium Means Unemployement." They would bloom like the flowers of spring at the public hearing on October 31, 1973.

There was an air of bread and circuses as workers, some wearing hardhats and all given the day off to attend, joined the goliaths of the construction industry already crowded into the commission hearing room. In the face of such massive resistance, only the islands' scrappy commissioner, Walter Shirey, an honest and

240

capable public servant, favored a slowdown of any sort. Island residents listened in shocked disbelief as Commissioner Dick Sayers advocated an end to building height restrictions and no population cap of any sort for Sanibel and Captiva.

In the end, Walter Shirey made two motions: to impose a partial building moratorium on Sanibel and to seek a new county planner. Both died for lack of a second as the crowd cheered. The foot had come down very hard on the neck of Sanibel. With this act of arrogance, incorporation became a very live issue.

The S.S. Algiers, land locked on Sanibel, 1979.

242

Chapter XV

THE CITY OF SANIBEL

In 1958, islanders had considered the incorporation of Sanibel but rejected it because the population was small. By the early 1970s, however, the scene had changed and with it the mood of the people. In the spring of 1973, a Sanibel-Captiva Planning Board poll revealed that while Captiva residents preferred to stay within the fold of Lee County, which paid the high cost of erosion control, Sanibelites showed a mild interest in incorporation. However, the events of summer and fall caused considerable indignation, the best possible fuel for change. Self determination began to look most attractive.

With a comprehensive land use plan for the county still in limbo, SCPB directors decided to establish an *ad hoc* committee of local residents to explore home rule. The board would lend financial support—then stand back. So began the home rule movement.

Almost immediately, things began to move. Public meetings in October and November led to the creation of the Home Rule Study Group with Ralph Zeiss as chairman. In January 1974 Eileen Lotz, a planning consultant, was hired to make a study of alternatives and her report concluded with the recommendation that only Sanibel should incorporate. With the approval of the Group, she proceeded to draft an incorporation charter which would undergo many revisions before it was presented to a southwest Florida Legislative Delegation, slated to hold hearings at Ft. Myers Beach on February 18. At that time, representing the majority of Sanibel voters, Zeiss would request that the November ballot include a referendum on incorporation.

The island had not reached this point without heated debate. Such epithets as "communist" and "greedy developer" were hurtled back and forth but generally, the meetings were orderly. Opposition came mainly from speculators and those in the construction trade who could foresee stringent restrictions if Sanibel were incorporated. But ordinary citizens also opposed what they saw as a threat to private property rights and the costs of another level of government. Proponents regarded incorporation as the only course left open to them, a last ditch effort to prevent the complete urbanization of the island. They welcomed restrictions and were willing to pay the price.

There was an urgency to Sanibel's flight to freedom because of growing sentiment in the state legislature that Florida was getting too many small incorporated communities. Delay could mean "never" and everyone knew it.* There was some tension, therefore, as both factions appeared to testify at the February 18 hearing, chaired by Representative Paul H. Nuckolls. The meeting proceeded routinely except for the unexpected appearance of Commissioner Dick Sayers, opposing incorporation, who assured the delegation that Lee County soon would have a comprehensive plan. Actually, Lee, the fastest growing county in the United States in 1975, was years away from such an accomplishment. Despite a 1974 state law which re-

---

* A law to limit incorporation to communities of 10,000 people or more was proposed but not passed by the Florida Legislature.

quired all counties and incorporated communities to adopt a land use plan by July 1, 1979, Lee was unable to meet this deadline and requested an extension. By August, 1979, one planner had been fired and three had resigned as the newest proposals failed to get the approval of the county commission.

As Sanibel's incorporation papers proceeded through various channels, the Home Rule Study Group scheduled a March 27 public meeting in order to take a straw vote on incorporation. A few days before, postal customers received two letters, one from Commissioner George Goldtrap and the other from Commissioner Dick Sayers, both strongly opposing incorporation. The Sayers letter, mailed with the return address of the Island Beach Club, then owned by a group headed by Walter Condon, was franked by the Shell Harbor Inn. It referred specifically to "the MacKenzies, the Dormers, the Zeisses and the Art Hunters" of Sanibel. Directly or by implication these residents were accused of "demagoguery," conceiving and nurturing distrust of the county commission, unfairly representing the island and misleading island voters. At about the same time, Condon wrote Representative Nuckolls objecting to the form of the incorporation charter and pointing out what he, as an attorney, considered legal deficiencies.

Although both commissioners denied that they were interfering in Sanibel's internal affairs and were in no way connected with Condon, there were, to say the least, raised eyebrows. Those singled out considered the Sayers letter a left-handed compliment but the episode was one of several tactical errors. With wry humor, the two men later would be referred to as "the fathers of incorporation".

Five hundred people crowded into the Sanibel Community House on the evening of March 27. There were regular ballots for registered voters and "blue ballots" for anyone who wished to express an opinion. According to Florida law, however, only voters could decide the issue and of these fifty-five percent favored a referendum of incorporation in November.

Shortly thereafter, apparently acting on the information in the Condon letter, Representative Nuckolls announced that the incorporation charter must be in bill form and advertised for thirty days. This would have delayed consideration of it past the date scheduled for the State Legislature to adjourn. Immediately, Mrs. Lotz arranged a meeting with Nuckolls and on April 3, convinced him that everything was in order. Consequently, Nuckolls introduced House Bill No. 4001 in the Florida House of Representatives on April 29, 1974. This put the incorporation of Sanibel to a referendum.

There remained battles to be won or lost. In a letter to House Speaker Designate Donald Tucker, Condon complained that he and six thousand other nonresident property owners would be discriminated against if they could not vote in the referendum. When the Subcommittee on Community Affairs held a hearing on the bill May 7, an attorney representing Condon and others offered an amendment which would give property owners the vote. Rejecting this, the Subcommittee and later the full Committee of Community Affairs voted unanimously to approve the bill as written.

Meanwhile, there were the usual differences of opinion within the Sanibel-Captiva Chamber of Commerce. At its annual meeting on May 21, the majority of those present voted to form an "Action Committee", chaired by David Holtzman of Shell Harbor Inn, to oppose incorporation. Representatives were sent to Tallahassee to oppose the referendum—but to no avail. The incorporation bill cleared the House of Representatives on May 24 and the Senate on May 31, 1974. Two weeks later, Governor Reubin Askew permitted the incorporation bill to become law without his signature.

Developers now flocked to the County Building Department which generously dispensed building permits. On Sanibel, intense campaigning began. The Home Rule Study Group, having done its job, gave way to Sanibel Tomorrow, which would coordinate incorporation efforts under the chairmanship of Mrs. Zelda Butler, who would become a member of Sanibel's first City Council. This group and the Action Committee presented separate reports on the costs of incorporation and vigorously competed for the vote. Sanibel Tomorrow was strongly supported by Sanibel-Captiva Planning Board and two loosely formed groups. Save Our Sanibel (S.O.S.), organized by poet-photographer Mario Hutton*, brought letters of support from well-known conservationists all over the country. Sanibel Businesses for Incorporation, organized by real estate broker Robert L. Dormer, bought ads in the local papers to dissent the views of the Action Committee.

The Lee County Commission bowed to the decision of the State of Florida on August 28 and unanimously endorsed a resolution to place the incorporation question on the ballot. But the following week, during a routine commission meeting, Commissioner Dick Sayers unexpectedly proposed a resolution which would make an incorporated Sanibel ineligible to share the revenues from Sanibel Causeway. The resolution was supported in a three-to-two vote by Commissioners Goldtrap and Sweeney. An indignant Walter Shirey called for another meeting and on September 6, Sweeney switched his vote and reversed the decision. Whatever his reasons, Sayer's action was seen as a bla-

---

* In 1977, Hutton presented the City Council with a copy of his will naming the City of Sanibel heir to his estate.

247

tant attempt to influence the vote on incorporation and it angered residents of all persuasions.

Three days later, another Condon suit seeking an injunction to halt the referendum only added fuel to the fire. "Voter backlash" was assured when he filed suit again, this time in Federal Court, claiming that his civil rights would be violated if this election took place. Lee County and a group of island residents challenged both suits which subsequently were dismissed. Although Condon did appeal, he could not then or later invalidate the referendum. On November 5, 1974, 84 percent of Sanibel's registered voters went to the polls to vote, 63.6 percent in favor of incorporation.

Shortly after the vote on incorporation, Sanibel-Captiva Planning Board was dissolved. Its membership combined with Sanibel Tomorrow to form Committee of the Islands (COTI). The new organization would seek to further the best interests of Sanibel and Captiva.

It soon became apparent that there would be no dearth of candidates willing to serve without pay on the new city council. Of the sixteen who ran for office, five were elected December 3, 1974. Porter Goss received 60 percent of the vote, Vernon MacKenzie, 52 percent, Zelda Butler, 51 percent, Charles Le Buff 46 percent, Francis Bailey, 39 percent. All had been prominent in island affairs, were conservationist in outlook and shared the strong conviction that their first priority must be the adoption of a land use plan tailored to Sanibel's special needs. Dissimilar in age, background and special skills*, their performance proved to be outstanding.

The newly elected city council met in a procedural session on December 11 at Sanibel Community House before a large and enthusiastic audience which included county and state officials. Lots were drawn for council seats, each with a predetermined term of

*"Who's Who on Sanibel". A File, Sanibel Public Library

office. Sanibel's native son, Francis Bailey, drew number 1 for a two-year term; Charles LeBuff, number 2, two years; Porter Goss, number 3, two years; Vernon MacKenzie, number 4, four years; and Zelda Butler, number 5, four years. The two who had received the most votes in the November election, Porter Goss and Vernon MacKenzie, were elected mayor and vice-mayor.

It was a long session—eight hours—indicative of things to come. David Bretzke, former manager of Plant City, Florida, was hired as temporary city manager and Mildred Howse, also of Plant City, as treasurer and city clerk. Appointed temporary city attorney was Frank Watson Jr. of Fort Myers, whose services already were needed. Francis Bailey had failed to resign from the Lee County Mosquito Control Board, an elective office, before running for councilman. He resigned on December 19 and immediately was reappointed, pending a special election slated for February 25, 1975. Unopposed at that time, he was reelected automatically.

There were inherited problems. Between election day November 5 and the birth of the new city, December 16, 1974, seventy-four building permits with a total value of $9,618,400 were issued by the Lee County Building Department. Few would conform to Sanibel's new code.

The first official meeting of Sanibel City Council was held at St. Michael and All Angels Church January 6, 1975. At that time, Elinore Dormer's request that a historical committee be formed was unanimously approved. The following week David Bretsky, with Dormer's help, drew up Resolution 75-10 which created the Historical Preservation Committee, City of Sanibel. One of its goals was the establishment of a historical museum.

As the city council got down to business, *moratorium* became a household word. In January, a ninety-day "respite," by any other name the same, slowed down multiple construction and was twice extended. Nevertheless, by the end of April, 1976, three hundred building permits, mostly for single family homes, had been issued by the new city.

Meanwhile, an obvious need had been met on February 25, 1975, with the creation of the Sanibel Planning Commission, an appointive body. Its purpose was to review and make recommendations to the council on matters relating to planning and this necessitated public hearings on all requests for building permits. It was a tough, demanding, thankless job in which the commissioners sometimes were subjected to the outbursts of irate petitioners. However, it was characteristic of those early days that capable people were found who were willing to serve without pay. The original seven-member body included Duane White, chairman, formerly a president of Sanibel-Captiva Planning Board; Ann Winterbotham, vice-chairman, formerly a president of Sanibel-Captiva Conservation Foundation; Joseph McMurtry, Lee Roy Friday, Don Marshall, Anina Hills and Malcolm Beattie. Beattie and Hills resigned after short tenures and were replaced by George Tenney and Twink Underhill. When White was elected to the city council in 1976. Mrs. Winterbotham became chairman.

A few weeks later, Walter Condon threw another bombshell. His suit filed in Circuit Court March 13, 1975, demanded, in effect, that the City of Sanibel prove that it was legally incorporated. For technical reasons, not entirely clear to Sanibel's citizens, Florida's Attorney General Robert Shevin joined him in the suit. The new city was threatened with bankruptcy. Unable to collect taxes its first year of existence, it had been operating on a small loan from Bank of the Islands which had promised an additional $250,000. Reluctantly, the bank's directors withdrew the offer, pending the outcome of the suit.

Needless to say, outrage was the mood of the island but there was little hand wringing. Sanibel watchers were surprised by the very practical and generous response as gifts of money poured into city hall—$307,000 from 124 people by April 17—and a grateful city council decided to issue tax anticipation notes to their legal limit. Within days, they were oversubscribed.

Meanwhile, Mayor Porter Goss and the city's attorney, Frank Watson, flew to Tallahassee where they found Representative Frank Mann's office hard at work on Sanibel's behalf and Representative Paul Nuckolls offering support. Shortly thereafter, the suit was dismissed and since the Attorney General's office withdrew, Condon did not appeal.

Through all this, it was business as usual at city hall, then in offices at Periwinkle Place, as the planning commission received bids and interviewed prospective planners. The firm recommended and eventually selected by the city council in April, 1975, was Wallace, McHarg, Roberts and Todd (to be known as WMRT), of Philadelphia, established by Ian McHarg, whose book, *Design With Nature,* had created new awareness of environmental planning. It had a reputation for successfully defending its plans in court, a very important consideration for already the city had lawsuits waiting in the wings. To aid the city's attorneys, Frank Watson, Roger Berres and, later, City Attorney Neal Bowen, WMRT recommended Fred Bosselman of the Chicago law firm Ross, Hardies, Babcock, Parson and O'Keefe. Bosselman had helped write Florida's community planning law and would prove invaluable.

The Sanibel project was directed by WMRT's senior

partner, William Roberts, who spent much time on the island. On his recommendation, task forces of local people were formed to collect data and sample public opinion. Over one hundred people participated, working through a long, hot summer. But a comprehensive survey of the island's natural systems also was called for and this was provided by Sanibel-Captiva Conservation Foundation which hired John Clark of The Conservation Foundation of Washington, D. C. to do the job. His excellent study. *The Sanibel Report,* began with a kind of poetry: "Islands always seem special. But Sanibel Island is absolutely unique. North America has no shore, no island, no other place equal to it. Nature will not again create such a place."

It soon became apparent that planning Sanibel was much more complicated than expected and could not be done, as first proposed, in six months. Also, the cost had risen from a bid of sixty thousand dollars to $195,637. Along the way, many of those who had opposed incorporation also opposed the emerging comprehensive land use plan and/or planning in general. Concerned Property Owners of Sanibel, Inc. (CPOOS) canvassed for support of a legal challenge, collecting one thousand dollars from Sanibel Motel-Hotel Association and the same amount from Politically Active Property Owners. The latter group, a county-wide organization, advocated a toll-free Sanibel Causeway. CPOOS never brought suit but there were some stormy public hearings. To their everlasting credit, the planning commissioners and the councilmen calmly withstood "the slings and arrows" with the strong support—even admiration—of the majority of voting residents. The Comprehensive Land Use Plan was accepted by the city council July 19, 1976. Somewhat amended, it would stand as a shining example of what could be done with good professionals and a receptive, persevering community.

Meanwhile, the causeway, once again, was a bone of contention. In 1973, Sanibel-Captiva Planning Board looked ahead to funding city government and the real possibility that a bridge free of debt could become a bridge free of tolls. The board backed the efforts of the county attorney to persuade the Lee County Commission to refinance it when the original bond issue was paid off in late 1975. There was some debate but the real issue had always been how the surplus revenues from the causeway would be spent. Some commissioners believed that very little of it, if any, should go to Sanibel-Captiva.

In May 1974, the county attorney filed an eighteen million dollar bonding resolution in Circuit Court. Almost immediately, a group of Sanibel-Captiva residents intervened, charging that the islands were not getting their fair share and that some of the roads to be funded were illegally included. It was noted that the commission could veto any project and the political climate was such at that time that the first to go could well be those on Sanibel-Captiva. Consequently, the county withdrew its resolution and having bought time for Sanibel to incorporate and fight its own battles, the group took no further action.

Negotiations dragged on and the City of Sanibel grew impatient and decided on a dramatic move. An ordinance was passed on May 30, 1975, annexing the causeway and the approach to it. The intent was to have policing powers during emergencies and, admittedly, to give the city more bargaining power. A shocked county government took the matter to court and on July 31, 1975, Judge Shearer ruled the annexation illegal.

All was forgiven by fall and an interlocal agreement was reached giving Sanibel 26 percent and Captiva four percent of the surplus funds generated by the causeway. Both islands were required to use the money on general county projects such as roads, with some consideration for erosion control on Captiva where as much as seven hundred feet of beach had been lost in some areas. On December 16 Commissioner L.H. "Bob" Whan, who had replaced Walter Shirey, presented Mayor Porter Goss with a check for $137,010.38.

Circuit Judge Thomas Shands validated the bond issue July 1, 1976. Sanibel looked forward to funding its capital improvements—only to hit another roadblock. A group of Lee County people, James Nix of Sanibel and Fort Myers residents, Hannah Davis and Marcelle McGovern, filed notice with the state Supreme Court that they were appealing the ruling. Later they would charge that not all of the six road projects were approach roads to the causeway and that refinancing would, in effect, perpetuate the tolls.

The prospect of a free bridge was anathema to most Sanibel-Captiva residents who believed that the number of "day-trippers" would dramatically increase, aggravating problems already present in seasonally heavy traffic, crowded beaches, litter and petty crime. Without tolls, Sanibel, Lee County and the taxpayers therein would most certainly feel the pinch as costs of maintaining the causeway mounted.

It was a year later when Florida's high court remanded the suit to the Circuit Court, setting forth standards for approach roads. Judge Shands reversed his 1976 decision and the county reworked its list of projects. With Sanibel's support, the suit was appealed. Finally, April 12, 1979, the Florida Supreme Court validated the bond issue. Sanibel's share would be $2.7 million.

The causeway was indeed a money-maker. When Hugo Lindgren first proposed building it in 1959, tolls were expected to generate $801,668 in 1979. In 1978, $1,807,916 in tolls was paid by 1,185,216 vehicles. An official report released by the county commission

254

revealed that 1,374,380 vehicles were expected to cross the causeway in 1979, paying $2,048,100.

The new city expected numerous lawsuits and they came—thirty in its four years of existence. Fourteen were unresolved in July 1979. Most charged a violation of vested rights but some challenged the validity of the land use plan itself. Although the city had been very successful, pursuing them through the courts was very expensive with about 18 percent of the operating budget used for this purpose. This became a matter of concern. Even before the plan was finalized some residents began to do something about it. Sometimes in envelopes shoved toward the mayor before a public meeting, sometimes mailed to the city treasurer, large and small amounts of money, even stock certificates, were given to the city. Through the efforts of resident Charlotte Heimann, a special bank account, Sanibel Environmental Defense Fund, was set up at Bank of the Islands. By June, 1978, $36,217.74 has been contributed, plus stock certificates worth more than nine thousand dollars. The money had come not only from residents but also from friends of Sanibel everywhere.

Although Sanibel issued far fewer building permits in 1977 (516 for housing) than Cape Coral or Fort Myers, the total evaluation was high—$26,428,300 or 20 percent of the county's total. Compared to other Florida cities with a population of 2,500 to five thousand. Sanibel ranked second in assessed value. Its exact population would be determined by the 1980 census but it was believed to be close to three thousand in 1979.

In fact, it was building and growth which most concerned Sanibel's voters, according to a Committee of the Islands poll lin 1978. Although 63 percent felt that Sanibel was better off incorporated than unincorporated, 55 percent believed that growth had been too fast. Sixty-three percent favored an ordinance which would limit the number of dwelling units built each year. Particularly unpopular were the huge condominium complexes, especially those with interval ownership.

In response to the tally, COTI circulated a petition requesting that the city council consider a rate of growth ordinance which would limit new construction to 108 units per year. Public meetings were held to discuss the subject and COTI brought in experts from Petaluma, California and Boulder, Colorado to explain how such laws worked in their towns. The idea gained supporters and the city council decided to place the issue on the November 21 ballot.

Other things would also be decided at that time. The city was interested in buying two strategically located tracts of land, the twenty-eight acre causeway property at the entrance to the island for $1.75 million, and the thirty-acre Brown or Algiers property, with one-thousand feet of Gulf beach, for $1.3 million. It was argued that the entrance to Sanibel should be noncommercial with a park, a public building, perhaps, and possibly a screened parking area should Sanibel have to go to public transit.

The Brown property had a remodeled ferryboat on it with an interesting history. In 1958, a very wealthy New York couple, Lathrop and Helen Brown, bought the land from Dr. Louise Perry and decided to put a winter home on it. When she was in New Orleans in 1958, Mrs. Brown had taken a fancy to the *S.S. Algiers,* a one hundred fifty foot ferryboat with two decks and a pilot house. When it was put up for auction, she bought it and had it towed to Fort Myers. Architect William Frizzel was commissioned to turn it into a palatial home. As instructed, he remodeled it completely, adding ornate stacks and a paddle wheel to make it look like an authentic Mississippi river boat.

Handsome outside, elegant within, the waif-turned-lady was towed to Sanibel where a crew of men labored mightily to beach her on the property. The plan was simple enough: build a dike at the back of the site, cut a channel through the beach, "ease 'er up," then pump in ten feet of sand "to kept 'er there." But the fates were not cooperative. A Sanibel style nor'wester closed the first channel and getting through the second was not easy. The pumps on hand were inadequate so the fire department's pumper was sent for. As everyone's attention was riveted on the rising water level, the pumper caught fire and completely burned up. Finally the *Algiers* was in place with the Browns in it. They soon replaced the lost pumper with a brand new one

Sadly enough, they did not have long to enjoy their unusual home. Lathrop died two months after they moved in and his widow did not remain long on Sanibel. She never returned and died in 1977. She was remembered as "rather standoffish" by local women, but to those who worked for them both of the Browns were down to earth and very generous. The property was on and off the market for several years before the city became interested in it.

November 21, 1978, would loom large in island history. On that day 72 percent of those voting approved the rate of growth ordinance, making Sanibel the only city east of the Rocky Mountains to have a growth control law. The purchase of the causeway property was approved by 68.9 percent and 58.1 approved buying the Brown tract. Both would be financed through a five percent, forty-year Farmers Home Administration loan. On the same ballot, Zelda Butler and Duane White were reelected to the city council. White would succeed Mrs. Butler as mayor.

Sanibel distinguished itself again in April, 1979, when the city council approved an amendment to the Comprehensive Land Use Plan which put certain restrictions on time-sharing resort housing. A similar state law was forthcoming but Sanibel was apparently

257

first in the nation to implement one.

By the end of the decade, it had become obvious that there were some very undesirable changes on Sanibel. These were the battles lost. But there had been some astonishing victories, too, which must be credited to the islanders themselves. Somehow, there seemed to be a thin, rather tenuous thread between them and islanders of a much earlier time. The Spaniards had described the Calusa as proud, intelligent and energetic. Also, they were turbulent, fractious and intractable. Still, Father Rogel found them more sinned against than sinning.

Considered in the context of the times, perhaps there was not too much wrong in 1979. The seers had predicted five more years of struggle for the City of Sanibel but no one seemed to fear for its future. Despite disagreements, it remained a loyal, cohesive society with pride in its accomplishments, expecially in the fields of growth control and environmental protection. While others had plodded along the same old well-worn paths, Sanibel people had been bold and innovative. They had dared to fly.

> "All it takes is faith and trust—and—
> Oh—something I forgot!
> A little bit of pixie dust."*

* Walt Disney's Happiest Songs. "We Can Fly," Golden Records, DL3509.

EPILOGUE

By 1987 Sanibel and Captiva were feeling the pressure of people. From October 1, 1985 to September 30, 1986 almost 2.5 million vehicles crossed Sanibel Causeway. In 1986 about 500,000 visitors and 171,400 cars drove through J.N. "Ding" Darling Sanctuary. For the whole refuge system, which included the Sanctuary, the Louise Perry tract and the Bailey tract, there were about 800,000 visitors.

Often, during the peak seasons, double lines of cars more than a mile long waiting to cross the causeway were confronted with a sign reading "Beach Access Parking Areas Full." Besides more visitors, Sanibel had acquired more residents. In 1987 about 7,000 dwelling units had been built there. The Comprehensive Land Use Plan, CLUP, allowed about 8,900. There were about 4,400 permanent residents. No longer could city government operate out of a few offices as it grew to meet the demands put upon it.

The city acquired twenty-two acres of secluded but accessible land in 1981 on which it would build the city hall. The building, dedicated November 19, 1983, was old Sanibel style, influenced by the lighthouse keepers quarters, in harmony with its natural surroundings and history. Beyond the courtyard was a lagoon with a short dock reminiscent of an earlier one at the lighthouse. The grounds were landscaped with native vegetation and there was a simulated Indian mound suggesting the island's prehistory. Designed by Stewart Corporation of Tampa, it received the Governor's Design Award "Given in recognition of outstanding achievement in the development of public facilities" in 1986. It was built by Stinson-Head, Inc.

In 1978, the city bought property at the entrance to the causeway and the Brown property which became Gulfside Park. An extensive recreational complex was built next to Sanibel Elementary School in 1981. When Clarence Rutland, Sanibel pioneer, died in 1982, the Muench family bought his property on Periwinkle Way and donated the house to the city. It was moved to city hall property and restored. November 10, 1984 it was dedicated as Island Historical museum. Another building, donated to the city by Barrier Islands Group for the Arts (BIG Arts) was moved to land next to it in 1987. It would become a center for the performing arts.

As required by state law, Sanibel's land use plan provided for low cost housing although land on Sanibel was expensive. A group of concerned residents, headed by Peter Valtin, formed a non-profit organization which incorporated in 1979 as Community Housing and Resources Foundation, its aim to help low and medium income families find housing. In 1983, the city council passed a below market rate housing (to be known as BMRH) ordinance which permitted it to subsidize this program and act as contractor and landlord. To encourage developers and allow them a satisfactory return on their investment, it relaxed its density and land use standards on a case by case basis. To be eligible for this housing, tenants were required to be employed residents of Sanibel with low or moderate incomes. The size of the unit available to them depended on the size of their families. Four units were completed in 1986 and it was expected that five more would be ready for occupancy by the end of 1987.

Looking back, most islanders believed that incorporation had been a good move. The Land Development Code adopted in 1985 replaced development regulations previously a part of CLUP. Another ordinance, 86-25, established regulations for commercial development. The Rate of Growth ordinance was repealed in 1987. The city was operating in the black as required by state law. Its budget for the fiscal year 1987-1988 was $6.1

million with a carry over from the previous year of $1.7 million.

Preservation of natural resources remained the primary concern. There was .25 mills added to the budget for buying up wetlands so they would not be built upon. The city already had $246,000 willed to it for that purpose by Mario Hutton, who died in 1982. It seemed certain that the Florida cabinet would approve the recommendation of Florida Marine Fisheries that a restriction be placed on live shelling on Sanibel within 300 feet of mean sea level. A sheller taking more than two live shells a day could face a fine up to $500. Born out of the Conservation Foundation's concern for the survivial of the island's finest resource, it would be the first law of its kind anywhere.

In all of Florida, only Sanibel had state licensed alligator handlers. Mark Westall and ten volunteer policemen and firemen were trained to remove pesky alligators from human haunts and release them in wild areas. With the help of a volunteer organization, Program for Animal Welfare on Sanibel, PAWS, the city administered a program for dealing with homeless animals. The Reverend Thomas Madden, who died in 1985, willed money for their care. As yet unresolved was the plight of the endangered gopher tortoise whose upland burrows were incompatible with sodded lawns.

Inevitably, growth and rising real estate values were changing Sanibel. There was much more opulence and elegance than ever before. There were pockets of resistance, too, the oases of old timers who still lived simply in rustic settings. Fortunately, there also were idealists who were determined that it should remain a different kind of place.

BIBLIOGRAPHY

List of Works Consulted

Chap. I

Cooley, George R. "The Vegetation of Sanibel Island, Lee Co., Florida," *Rhodora,* Journal of the New England Botanical Club, Vol. 57, No. 682, Oct. 1955.

Hale, H. Stephen. "A Predictive Model of Settlement and Subsistance Patterns for the Charlotte Harbor/Pine Island Sound Estuaries, Southwest Florida, Based on Sea Level Fluctuation." Southeastern Archaeological Converence, Birmingham, Alabama, November 7, 1985.

Chap. II

Beriauit, John. "Frank Cushing and His Key Marco Discoveries." *The Timepiece* Vol. III, No's 1, 2, 3, 1975. Collier Co. Historical Society.

Beta Analytic Inc. Lab. No. Beta-19961. Coral Gables, Florida. 1987.

Bullen, Ripley P. "Florida's Prehistory," *Florida From Indian Trail to Space Age.* Tebeau, Carson, *et al.* Delray Beach. 1985.

Bullen, Ripley P. "Southern Limit of Timacua Territory," *The Florida Historical Quarterly,* Vol. XLVII. No. 4, Apr. 1969.

Clausen, C.J. "Little Salt Spring, Florida: A Unique Underwater Site", *Science,* Vol. 203, No. 4381, Feb. 16, 1979.

Collins, Henry B. "The 'Lost' Calusa Indians of Southwestern Florida", *Explorations and Fieldwork of the Smithsonian Insstitution in 1928,* Washington, D.C.

Covington, James W. *The Story of Southwestern Florida,* New York: Lewis Historical Publ. Co., 1957.

Cushing, Frank H. "Explorations of Ancient Key Dwellers' Remains on the Gulf Coast of Florida," *Proceedings of the American Philosophical Society,* XXXV, Aug. 10, 1897.

Fradkin, Arlene. "The Wightman Site: A Study of Prehistoric Culture and Environment on Sanibel Island. Lee County, Florida". A Thesis. U. of Florida, 1976.

Larson, Peter. "Florida's Time Capsule", *Island Reporter,* Mar. 16, 1979.

Marquardt, William H. "The Development of Cultural Complexity in Southwest Florida." Southeastern Archaeological Conference, Pensacola, Florida, November 9, 1984.

Milanich, Jerald T. "A Proposal to Isotopes Foundation for a Preliminary Study of the Prehistoric and Historic Calusa Aborigines of Southwest Florida." Gainesville, Fla. Jan. 1975.

"Spring Artifact Find Suggests Florida Man Hunted Big Game," Ft. Myers News-Press, Oct. 28, 1973.

Squires, Karl. "Pre-Columbian Man in South Florida," *Tequesta*, Vol. I, No. 1.
"Underwater Find Places Man at 8,000 B.C.," Ft. Myers News-Press, Sept. 23, 1973.
"Uncovered Skull Dated 10,000 Years Old," Ft. Myers News-Press, June 14, 1973.
Willey, Gordon R. *Archaeology of the Florida Gulf Coast.* Wash., The Smithsonian Institute, Dec. 29, 1949.

Chap. III

Celi, Don Francisco Maria. "De Havana al Puerto de Tampa, Ano de 1957, Diario de Reconocimientos Ocean Atlantico Septentrional." Trans. by John D. Ware, 1971.
Connor, Jeanette T. *Translation of the Memorial of Pedro Menendez de Ariles by Solis de Meras.* Deland, 1923.
Covington, James. *op. cit.*
Davis T. Frederick. "History of Ponce de Leon Voyages to Florida," *Florida Historical Quarterly,* July 1935.
Degado, Paulino Castaneda, et al. Alonso de Chaves, *Quatri Partitu en Cosmografia Practica, y por Otro Nombre Espejo de Navegantes.* Instituto de Historia y Cultura Naval. Madrid. 1983.
Doherty, Hubert J. "Did Amerigo Vespucci Discover Florida?" Unpubl. paper. P.K. Yonge Library of Florida History, Gainesville.
Dupont, Benjamin B. "The Letters of Menendex," a manuscript. P.K. Yonge Library of Florida History. Gainesville.
Fontaneda, Hernando Escalante. *Memoir.* Trans. by Buckingham Smith, 1945.
Grismer, Karl. *The Story of Ft. Myers.* St. Petersburg: 1949.
Harrisse, Henry. "The Discovery of North American," Chap. II, *The Discovery of Florida and Its Discoverer, Juan Ponce de Leon.* Lawson, Edward W., St. Augustine, 1946.
Lewis, Theodore, "The Narrative of the Expedition of Hernando de Soto by the Gentleman of Elvas," *Spanish Explorers in the Southern United States* 1528-1543. Barnes and Noble. 1946.
Lowery, Woodbury. *The Spanish Settlements Within the Present Limits of the United States I.* New York: 1901.
Phillips, P. Lee. *Life and Works of Bernard Romans.* 1924.
Romans, Bernard. *A concise Natural History of East and West Florida, Vol. I.* New York: 1775.
Schell, Rolfe. *1000 Years on Mound Key.* Ft. Myers Beach, Fla.: The Island Press, 1968.
Schuck, J.P. "Ten Florida Sites Added to the National Register of Historic Places," *Archives and History News,* Vol. I, No. 4. Tallahassee. (Nov.-Dec. 1970).
True, David, "Some Early Maps Relating to Florida," *Imago Mundi, Review of Early Cartography.* Stockholm: Brill-Leiden, 1954.
Varner, John and Varner, Jeanette. *The Florida of the Inca.* U. of Texas Press, 1951.
Velasco, Juan Lopez de. *Geografia y Descripeion Universal de Las Indies, 1571-1574.* Madrid: 1894.
William, John Lee. *The Territory of Florida.* 1837.

Also: Maps from the P.K. Yonge Library of Florida History. The Rare Books Div. of the Library of the University of North Carolina. The Karpinski Collection of Copies of Early Maps of America. (Wm. Clements Library of Americana) U. of Michigan. The Library of Congress.

Chap. IV

Bullen, Ripley P. "Southern Limit of Timacua Territory." *op. cit.*
Covington, James W. *op. cit.*
Davis, T. Frederick. *op. cit.*
Fontaneda, Hernando Escalante. *op. cit.*
Harrissee, Henry. *op. cit.*
Kerrigan, Anthony, Trans. *Barcia's Chronological History of the Continent of Florida,* Gainesville, 1951.
Lawson, Edward W. *The Discovery of Florida and Its Discoverer, Juan Ponce de Leon. St. Augustine: 1946*
Varner, John and Varner, Jeanette. *op. cit.*
Velasco, Juan Lopez. *op. cit.*

Chaps. V, VI, VII:

Bullen, Adelaide K. "Why the Seminoles Survived." Florida Indians of Past and Present. Gainesville: U. of Fla. Press. 1965.
Connor, Jeanette, T. *Colonial Records of Spanish Florida,* Vol. I, *1570-1577.* Florida Historical Soc., Vol. I, No. 5, Deland, 1925.
Connor, Jeanette T. *op. cit.*
Covington, James W. "Migrations of the Seminoles into Florida. 1700-1820." *Florida Historical Quarterly.* Apr. 1968.
Fontaneda, Hernando Escalente. *op. cit.*
Gannon, Michael T. *The Cross in the Sand.* Gainesville: U. of Fla. Press, 1965.
Gibbons, Euell. *Stalking the Blue-Eyed Scallop.* David McKay Co., New York.
Grismer, *op. cit.*
Goggin, John M. *op. cit.*
Goodenough, Ward T. "The Calusa: A Stratified, Non-Agricultural Society (With Notes on Sibling Marriage), *Explorations in Cultural Anthropology* New York: McGraw-Hill. 1964.
Kenny, Michael. *The Life and Deeds of Pedro Menendez de Ariles by Bartoleme Barrientos.* Gainesville: U. of Fla. Press. 1965.
Lowery, Woodbury. *The Spanish Settlements Within the Present Limits of the United States II, 1562-1574.* New York: 1901.
Lyon, Eugene. "The Captives of Florida,"*Florida Historical Quarterly* July, 1971.
Neill, Wilfred T. "The Identity of Florida's Spanish Indians," *Florida Anthropologist,* June, 1955.
Phillips, P. Lee. *op. cit.*
Schell, Rolf. *op. cit.*
Sturtevant, William C. "Chakaika and the Spanish Indians," *Tequesta,* XIII. U. of Miami Press, Coral Gables, Fla.
Swanton, John R. "Early History of the Creek Indians and Their Neighbors," Smithsonian Institute, Bur. of Amer. Ethnology, Bull. 73.

Ugarte, Ruben Vargas. "First Jesuit Mission in Florida." *U. S. Catholic Historical Society Studies,* XXV (1935).
Velasco, Juan Lopez. *op. cit.*
Wenhold, Lucy. "A 17th Century Letter of Gabriel Dias Vara," *Smithsonian Collection,* XC, No. 16.
Zubillaga. Felix. *Monumenta antiguae Floridae, 1566-1572.* Rome: 1946.
Zubillaga, Felix. *Monuments Historica, La Florida, la mision jesuitica, 1566-1572 y la colonization espanola.* Rome: 1941.

PART II

Chaps. VIII, IX, X:

Allen, Gardner W. *Our Nary and the West Indian Pirates.* Salem: Essex Inst., 1929.
Bradlee, Francis B.C. *Piracy in the West Indies and Its Suppression.* Salem: Essex Inst. 1923.
Browne, Jefferson B. *Key West The Old and The New.* U. of Florida Press, 1973.
Buker, George E. "Lt. Levin M. Powell, U.S.N., Pioneer of Riverine Warfare," *Florida Historical Quarterly,* Jan. 1969.
Calkins, C. G. "Repression of Piracy in the West Indies, *1814-1825,"* United States Naval Proceedings, Dec. 1911.
Covington, James W. *op. cit.*
Covington, James W. "A Petition from Some Latin-American Fishermen: *1838,"* *Tequesta,* XIV (1954).
Gatewood, George W. *On Florida's Coconut Coasts.* The Punta Gorda Herald, 1944.
Gosse, Phillip. *The Pirates Who's Who.* Boston: Chas. Lauriat Co. 1924.
Grismer, Karl. *op. cit.*
Hammond, E.A. "Sanibel Island and Its Vicinity, 1833, A Document," *Florida Historical Quarterly,* Apr. 1970.
Hammond, E.A. "The Spanish Fisheries of Charlotte Harbor," *Florida Historical Quarterly,* Apr. 1973.
"Let That Old Sanibel Light Shine," *Ft. Myers News-Press,* Nov. 2, 1972.
Melsek, Lee. "Seamen's Homing Beam May Soon Flicker Out," *Ft. Myers News-Press,* Oct. 20, 1972.
Monroe County Deed Book A, 1833.
Peters, Thelma. "William Adee Whitehead's Reminiscences of Key West," *Tequesta,* XXV, U. of Miami.
Record Group 26, Lighthouse Site File, Florida No. 44. The National Archives, Washington, D.C. 1968.
Robbins, Peggy. "The Story of Lafitte the Pirate," *The American Legion Magazine,* Nov. 1971.
Tebeau, Charlton W. *Florida's Last Frontier.* U. of Miami Press, 1957.
William, John Lee. *op. cit.*

Chaps. XI, XII, XIII, XIV:

Ammann, Pat. "The Caloosahatchee," Ft. Myers News. Press, Dec. 19, 1971-Jan. 16, 1972.

Dickey, Julia. Unpublished notes on the history of Captiva. 1943.
Dunn, Gordon. *Florida Hurricanes.* Technical Memorandum WBTM Sr-38. Ft.
  Worth, Texas, Nov. 1967.
Feirich, Charles. "Hurricane Donna", *Island Reporter,* Mar. 28, 1975 *Ft. Myers
  News-Press,* 1959-1973.
Givens, Lawrence. "Federal and State Roles in the Establishment of the J.N.
  "Ding" Darling National Wildlife Refuge", A Speach. Feb. 4, 1978.
Grismer, Karl. *op. cit.*
Hawkins, Betty. "Capt. Johnson: Portrait of Seafarer of Bygone Days." Fort
  Myers News-Press. Undated.
Hawkins, Betty. "Twice Upon A Time," Ft. Myers News-Press, 1969-72.
Hosmer, George L. *An Historical Sketch of the Town of Deer Isle, Maine.* Boston:
  1886.
Hutchinson, Vernal. *A Maine Town in the Civil War.* Freeport, Maine: 1957.
Island Reporter, Nov. 1973-Aug. 1979.
LeBuff, Charles R., Jr. *The Marine Turtles of Sanibel and Captira Islands,
  Florida,* Sanibel-Captiva Conservation Foundation. 1969.
"Letters of George O. Barnes," Louisville Courier-Journal. 1883.
Loveland, Ned. "Notes on Lee County Schools," (1889-1937). Southwest Florida
  Historical Society. 1971.
Monroe, Loretta. *Old Bottles Found Along the Florida Keys.* Wake-Brook House,
  Coral Gables, Fla. 1967.
"Our 'Ding' Darling Dies; Pulitzer Prize Cartoonist," *New York Herald Tribune,*
  Feb. 13, 1962.
Pearse, Eleanor Dean. *Florida's Vanishing Ear.* 1954.
"The Mountain Evangelist," *Louisville Evening Post,* Apr. 10, 1911.
Island's Newsletter, Jan.-May, 1961.
The Sanibel Islander, Dec. 1934-Mar. 1937.
The Sanibel-Captiva Islander. Nov. 1961-1978.

Chap. XV:

Clark, John. *The Sanibel Report.* The Conservation Foundatin of Washington,
  D.C. 1974.
Ft. Myers News-Press, 1973-1979.
Islanders Reporter, 1973-1979.
S-C Islander, 1973-1979.

INDEX

269